RACE AND RACISM IN INTERNATIONAL RELATIONS

International Relations, as a discipline, does not grant race and racism explanatory agency in its conventional analyses, despite such issues being integral to the birth of the discipline. *Race and Racism in International Relations* seeks to remedy this oversight by acting as a catalyst for remembering, exposing and critically re-articulating the central importance of race and racism in international relations.

Departing from the theoretical and political legacy of W. E. B. Du Bois's concept of the 'colour line', the cutting-edge contributions in this text provide an accessible entry point for both international relations students and scholars into the literature and debates on race and racism by borrowing insights from disciplines such as history, anthropology and sociology where race and race theory figure more prominently; yet they also suggest that the field of International Relations is itself an intellectual and strategic field through which to further confront the global colour line.

Drawing together a wide range of contributors, this much-needed text will be essential reading for students and scholars in a range of areas including postcolonial studies, race/racism in world politics and international relations theory.

Alexander Anievas is a Leverhulme Early Career Research Fellow at the Department of Politics and International Studies, University of Cambridge.

Nivi Manchanda is a PhD candidate at the Department of Politics and International Studies at the University of Cambridge.

Robbie Shilliam is Reader in International Relations at Queen Mary, University of London.

Interventions

Edited by:
Jenny Edkins, Aberystwyth University and Nick Vaughan-Williams,
University of Warwick

'As Michel Foucault has famously stated, "knowledge is not made for understanding; it is made for cutting." In this spirit the Edkins–Vaughan-Williams Interventions series solicits cutting edge, critical works that challenge mainstream understandings in international relations. It is the best place to contribute post disciplinary works that think rather than merely recognize and affirm the world recycled in IR's traditional geopolitical imaginary.'

Michael J. Shapiro, University of Hawai'i at Mãnoa, USA

The series aims to advance understanding of the key areas in which scholars working within broad critical post-structural and post-colonial traditions have chosen to make their interventions, and to present innovative analyses of important topics.

Titles in the series engage with critical thinkers in philosophy, sociology, politics and other disciplines and provide situated historical, empirical and textual studies in international politics.

Critical Theorists and International Relations
Edited by Jenny Edkins and Nick Vaughan-Williams

Ethics as Foreign Policy
Britain, the EU and the other
Dan Bulley

Universality, Ethics and International Relations
A grammatical reading
Véronique Pin-Fat

The Time of the City
Politics, philosophy, and genre
Michael J. Shapiro

Governing Sustainable Development
Partnership, protest and power at the world summit
Carl Death

Insuring Security
Biopolitics, security and risk
Luis Lobo-Guerrero

Foucault and International Relations
New critical engagements
Edited by Nicholas J. Kiersey and Doug Stokes

International Relations and Non-Western Thought
Imperialism, colonialism and investigations of global modernity
Edited by Robbie Shilliam

Autobiographical International Relations
I, IR
Edited by Naeem Inayatullah

War and Rape
Law, memory and justice
Nicola Henry

Madness in International Relations
Psychology, security and the global governance of mental health
Alison Howell

RACE AND RACISM IN INTERNATIONAL RELATIONS

Confronting the global colour line

*Alexander Anievas, Nivi Manchanda
and Robbie Shilliam*

Routledge
Taylor & Francis Group

LONDON AND NEW YORK

First published 2015
by Routledge
2 Park Square, Milton Park, Abingdon, Oxon OX14 4RN

And by Routledge
711 Third Avenue, New York, NY 10017

Routledge is an imprint of the Taylor & Francis Group, an informa business

British Library Cataloguing in Publication Data
A catalogue record for this book is available from the British Library

Library of Congress Cataloging in Publication Data
Race and racism in international relations : confronting the global colour line / edited by Alexander Anievas, Nivi Manchanda and Robbie Shilliam.
pages cm. -- (Interventions)
Includes bibliographical references and index.
1. International relations--Social aspects. 2. Racism--Political aspects. 3. Race--Political aspects. I. Anievas, Alexander, editor of compilation. II. Manchanda, Nivi, editor of compilation. III. Shilliam, Robbie, 1969- editor of compilation.
JZ1251.R34 2015
327.1089--dc23
2014017962

ISBN: 978-0-415-72434-0 (hbk)
ISBN: 978-0-415-72435-7 (pbk)
ISBN: 978-1-315-85729-9 (ebk)

Typeset in Bembo
by Taylor & Francis Books

Printed and bound by CPI Group (UK) Ltd, Croydon, CR0 4YY

CONTENTS

ACKNOWLEDGEMENTS

The editors would like to acknowledge the support of series editors Jenny Edkins and Nick Vaughan-Williams, and Peter Harris and Craig Fowlie at Routledge. The editors also thank the anonymous reviewers for their kind and constructive comments. The editorial team at the *Cambridge Review of International Affairs* worked hard to make possible the special issue on 'Confronting the Global Colour Line', wherein earlier versions of some of the chapters in this book first appeared. Finally, the editors would like to extend their heartfelt thanks to the contributors to this book for their intellectual and personal generosity.

1

CONFRONTING THE GLOBAL COLOUR LINE

An introduction

Alexander Anievas, Nivi Manchanda and Robbie Shilliam

Race, racism and international relations

Kenneth Waltz may have surprised many of his contemporaries when, in the influential 1979 publication *Theory of International Relations*, he chose V. I. Lenin to be his key interlocutor.[1] Rather than consign Lenin's significance to moral or ideological realms, Waltz claimed that the Bolshevik had provided one of the first theories of international relations in the twentieth century with his considerations on imperialism. Waltz could also have looked closer to home. There, an African American sociologist called W. E. B. Du Bois had published a thesis (1915) on the imperial determinants of the First World War one year before Lenin. Waltz might have also consulted more closely the pages of *Foreign Affairs*, the pre-eminent US journal on the science of foreign policy. In its pages, in 1925, Du Bois also published an article entitled "Worlds of color" that revisited a statement he had made over twenty years earlier:

> The problem of the twentieth century is the problem of the color-line – the relation of the darker to the lighter races of men in Asia and Africa, in America and the islands of the sea (Du Bois 1961, 23).

In "Worlds of color", Du Bois (1925, 423) proposed that the "present Problem of Problems", namely, the global structure of the exploitation of labour, needed to be re-envisioned with respect to the "dark colonial shadow" cast by European empires. Undertaking a comparative analysis of these empires, Du Bois (1925, 423) noted that modern imperialism wore a "democratic face" at home and a "stern and unyielding autocracy" in the colonies. Du Bois argued that the denial of democracy in the colonies hindered its complete realisation in Europe. "It is this", he suggested to Western foreign policy makers, "that makes the colour problem and the labor problem to so great an extent two sides of the same human tangle" (Du Bois 1925, 442). Ten years later, Du Bois (1935) wrote again for *Foreign Affairs* and delivered a prognosis that the Italian/Ethiopian war would further inflame the global colour line. In these ways and more, Du Bois illuminated the crucial significance of race and racism as fundamental organising principles of international politics; axes of hierarchy and oppression structuring the logics of world politics as we know it.

Though questions of race and racism have been often side-lined to the margins of contemporary IR, such issues were in fact integral to the birth of the discipline. IR was founded, in large part, as a policy science designed to solve the dilemmas posed by empire-building and colonial administration facing the white Western powers expanding into and occupying the so-called 'waste places of the earth', as the Global South was commonly referred to by contemporaries (see Schmidt 1998; Long and Schmidt 2005; Vitalis 2005; Bell 2013). Thus, within the Anglo-Saxon nations, and particularly the US and UK, the field of IR took flight around such issues as empire, imperialism and inter-racial relations (Barkawi 2010). The discipline's 'founding' journal, *Foreign Affairs,* first published in 1922 by the highly influential Council on Foreign Relations, had previously gone under the title *Journal of Race Development* (Vitalis 2010). Additionally, South African scholar Charles Manning, Montague Burton Professor of International Relations at LSE between 1930 and 1962, was also a jurisprudential advocate of race administration both in terms of the mandates system of the League of Nations and, later, South African apartheid (Suganami 2001, Manning 1964). However, aside from Du Bois, a cadre of black academics in the United States including Ralph Bunch also engaged with these imperial discourses on race in this early period of the discipline's history (Vitalis *forthcoming*; Henry 1995). Outside of academic halls, of course, many anti-colonial writers from across the globe were publishing cognate tracts critical of empire and race administration (see, for example, Polsgrove 2009).

Post-World War II IR scholars occasionally discussed the importance of race and racism, especially in reaction to – or in the context of – liberation movements and Third World challenges to the West (see Isaacs 1969; Bull 1979; Vincent 1984; Mazrui 1968, Shepherd and LeMelle 1970; Rosenau 1970). But race and racism seem to have receded in the subsequent years, especially with regard to the many re-narrations of the discipline's foundation and history that took place during the post-Cold War period. According to James Mittleman (2009, 100), a search of paper titles presented at the annual meetings of the International Studies Association (ISA) shows that the words 'race', 'racism', 'racialised' and 'racist' appear in only 0.37 per cent of these titles (80 of 21,688 titles). Further, a search for the same words in article titles appearing in ISA's premier journal, *International Studies Quarterly,* between January 2000 and December 2007 reveal a finding of 0 per cent (0 of 260 titles). Indeed, one might presently speak of IR's 'racial aphasia' – a 'calculated forgetting' obstructing 'discourse, language and speech' (Krishna 2001; Thompson 2013).

Nevertheless, a number of scholars have seriously challenged the systematic 'silence and evasion' (Vitalis 2000, 333) over their own imperial-racial origins of IR so as to more adequately confront issues related to race and racism in world politics (see, for example, Vitalis, 2005, 2010; Schmidt 1998; Long and Schmidt 2005; Hobson 2012). These recent works have been part of a wider resurgence of studies that elucidate the many ways in which 'prevalent constructions of race have shaped visions and practices of international politics, thus helping to sustain and reproduce a deeply unjust stratified global order' (Bell 2013, 2). Thus, scholars of IR have begun to once again confront the problem of the global colour line identified by Du Bois but curiously dispatched from the centre of the discipline. The ground re-covered in a relatively short time has been impressive: for example, scholars have questioned the complicity of mainstream IR's key theoretical resources, moral calculus, and categories to racialised or racist assumptions to examining past and contemporary practices of 'racialisation' and racial identity formation to analysing the deep historical interconnections between imperial practices and the production of racialised categories; they have drawn attention to the notions of 'backward/ inferior' and 'advanced/superior' races as well as geopolitical identities such as the 'Anglo-Saxon powers'; and they have traced the myriad ways that race, gender and class intertwine in the making of world order (see, respectively, Persuad and Walker 2001; Grovogui 1996; Malik 2000; Hobson 2012; Watson 2001; Persuad 2001; Shilliam 2006, 2009; Suzuki 2009; Doty 1996; Vucetic 2011; Bell 2012; Persuad and Walker 2001; Chowdhry and Nair 2004; Agathangelou and Ling 2004).

Though explicitly racial tropes and conceptualisations of world order have been largely (though not entirely) eliminated from mainstream discourses in the post-World War II era, questions concerning the extent to which race and racism continue to subliminally structure contemporary world politics, in both material and ideological ways, remain as significant as ever. For example, inspirations from postcolonial theory have enabled scholars to elucidate the intimate interconnections between orientalist/racial frameworks of analysis and processes of grand strategy making, interstate conflict and war (Barkawi and Stanski 2012; Barkawi and Brighton 2013). This work complements, and brings into the present, efforts in American History to explicate the influence of domestic racism on US foreign policy (for example, LeMelle 1972; Anderson 2003). Additionally, as Branwen Gruffydd Jones has argued (2008), despite the formal transcendence of racism in modern institutions of world order, global inequalities in power and wealth retain a fundamentally racialised character produced through centuries of colonial dispossession. Examining and explaining such racialised structures of global power, inequality, oppression and violence in the contemporary world is indeed a topic in need of further research.

Our intention in putting together this edited volume is that it should act as a further catalyst for remembering, exposing and critically re-articulating the central importance of race and racism in the field of IR. In what follows we lay out in a little more detail the legacy of Du Bois and what we wish to take from it, focusing especially on the theoretical and political content of his concept – the "colour line". We will then use this discussion as a heuristic device with which to clarify the contemporary disciplinary challenges of IR when confronted with a research agenda of race and racism. Finally, we will position the various chapters vis-à-vis this confrontation with the global colour line.

The global colour line as a research agenda

As suggested above, Du Bois' response to the causes of World War I and the prospects of world peace were systematically framed through a consideration of the political effects of race-thinking and race-ordering. For Du Bois (1925, 502), the war was no aberration of European civilisation but its clearest expression, and the main causes of European greatness – overseas expansion and colonial aggrandise- ment – were also the very causes of the war. "It is the duty of white Europe", opined Du Bois (1925, 503) sardonically, "to divide up the darker world and administer it for Europe's good". So long as these practices remained the mainstay of post-war European global governance, prospects for peace were dim. "Above all", Du Bois (1925, 512) pleaded, "industry must minister to the wants of the many and not to the few, and the Negro, the Indian, the Mongolian and the South Sea Islander must be among the many as well as Germans, Frenchmen and Englishmen".

Du Bois' argument resonated with Marxist theory. But it was the thoughts and experiences of enslaved Africans in North America and the impact of their struggle for liberation that formed the key inspiration for his "international theory" of the colour line. Indeed, Du Bois had not only spent long periods teaching but also living with and learning from the black peoples of the South (see Holt 2013). Indeed, the term "colour line" was not Du Bois' invention but already part of the grammar of debate over the reconstruction of the US South after the emancipation proclamation. Before Du Bois, Frederick Douglass (1881) was arguing for the elimination of the colour line, while his opponents predicted the end of civilisation if that were to happen. A fuller reproduction of his famous statement in the 1903 publication, *The Souls of Black Folk*, testifies to these influences:

> The problem of the twentieth century is the problem of the color-line – the relation of the darker to the lighter races of men in Asia and Africa, in America and the islands of the sea. It was a phase of this problem that caused the Civil War; and however much they who marched South and North in 1861 may have fixed on the technical points, of union and local autonomy as a shibboleth, all nevertheless knew, as we know, that the question of Negro slavery was the real cause of the conflict (Du Bois 1961, 23).

Du Bois (1961, 123) was convinced that, with regard to the phenomenon of "race contact", the US South was "as fine a field for such a study as the world affords" and he saw nothing provincial in its recent history. After all, the Haitian Revolution had fundamentally shaken the worldwide "trade in men", putting the Southern system under notice; Native Americans were being driven from their lands as the plantation system pushed ever westwards; and after the civil war a new breed of capitalist was sweeping down from the North to "woo this coy dark soil", accompanied by Russian Jews and other migrants of the Old World hoping to claim a stake in the old plantation lands (see, for example, Du Bois 1961, 89, 95, 103). Mingling in the South, all these peoples and struggles had their fate entwined through the attempt to answer one question: after emancipation, "what shall be done with the Negroes?" (Du Bois 1961, 23).

Du Bois was adamant that it was black peoples who, by deserting and undermining the plantation economy during the civil war, had forced this question onto the agenda (for example, Du Bois 1961, 29; and in general, Du Bois 1995). The Freedmen's Bureau, a "government of millions of men" erected "at the stroke of a pen", sought to substantiate the new freedom by providing education, law courts and property for Southern blacks on an equitable footing with past slaveholders and privileged whites. But, Du Bois recounted, the Bureau was scuppered by entrenched Southern interests, to be replaced by a purely formal assurance in the fifteenth amendment of the Constitution that no one could be denied the right to vote based on race, colour or previous state of servitude (Du Bois 1961, 40). In this climate Du Bois argued that freed blacks could not accept administration by Southern patriarchs. And he directed the same argument towards the prospects of "the darker races of the world", who would also have to be meaningfully included in global governance of the post-World War I era (Du Bois 1996a, 556).

Crucially, Du Bois did not only comment upon or mount a political campaign against the global colour line; he also built a research agenda around it. Specifically, his theoretical explorations of the colour line were founded on the precept that "lived experience" – to use a Fanonian trope (Fanon 1986, ch. 5) – was productive of knowledge claims. In his address before the American Negro Academy in 1897, Du Bois (1996b, 43) posed an existential question: "What … am I? Am I an American or am I a Negro? Can I be both?" Reminiscing on his childhood, Du Bois recounted that at some point he realised that he was "different from the others … shut out from their world by a vast veil" (Du Bois 1996c, 16). This is the problem pursued in Du Bois' *Souls of Black Folk*. Even in the post-emancipation era, the legal, material and psychological constitutions of the American polity still forbid the Negro from becoming an inhabitant of its protective and enabling skein. Unable to inhabit the American world in "true self-consciousness" as an American, the Negro had to see him- or herself through "the revelation of the other world". The double – rather than self – consciousness that the Negro inhabited was traumatic, giving rise to "two unreconciled strivings" (Du Bois 1961, 17).

Hence, Du Bois' episteme of the global colour line was built around the heuristic of the "veil", which he had garnered from African spiritual retentions and Biblical grammar as well as other more mainstream sources (for a discussion of the term see Schrager 1996). The veil seems to perform a double function in Du Bois' writings: it symbolises the lived experience of racism and also is responsible for generating thought about this experience. In being Black, the veil was something that was always worn. Covered in the veil, descendants of enslaved Africans were marked as existential problems for a coherent polity and a common humanity

(Du Bois 1961, 15; Du Bois 1996a, 539). Being black, one could not rise above the veil except in death, in moments of spiritual ecstasy, in psychological withdrawal, or perhaps in artistic abstraction.[2] Yet second, in a quotidian sense, being black was to *have* to sense life *through* the veil. In this respect, the veil was also a "thought-thing", "intangible, tenuous, but true and terrible" (Du Bois 1996a, 607). And those born with it were paradoxically "gifted with second-sight in this American world" (Du Bois 1961, 16).

By invoking the veil, Du Bois was explicating what might nowadays be called "border-thinking" (Dussel 1985; Mignolo 2000). Du Bois' episteme would have to make relational sense of the colour line – we are this because you are that, and vice versa – whereas a white episteme had the privilege of methodological individualism – we are this, while you are that.[3] In this respect, apprehended from behind the veil, one of the most grievous effects of the colour line was the erasure of any relational apprehension of power, hierarchy and division and a denial of the agency of those living behind the veil:

> Lions have no historians, and therefore lion hunts are thrilling and satisfactory human reading. Negroes had no bards, and therefore it has been widely told how American philanthropy freed the slave (Du Bois 1996a, 551).

What is more, Du Bois was adamant that the lion's story would reveal not just the agency of the enslaved and the wretched within their own liberation, but how the colour line was constituted through multiple dimensions – geographical, political, economic, psychological, spiritual and social – and that its dismantling would have to match this multi-dimensionality.[4]

As with all other aspects of his writings, these considerations connect to Dubois' musings on global governance in the aftermath of World War I and the wider question of the "darker races of men", which we have engaged with above. However, sometimes Du Bois travelled the colour line to its foreign coordinates and his experiences there also influenced its theorisation. Before he wrote the *Souls of Black Folk* Dubois had undertaken two formative years of graduate study at the University of Berlin (see Barkin 2000). Du Bois' later musings on the Warsaw Ghetto in 1952 are especially instructive. Returning to the destroyed city after the Second World War, he suggested that a clearer understanding of the "Jewish problem" had afforded him a "real and more complete understanding of the Negro problem" and that he no longer conceived of slavery and caste as separate conditions (Du Bois 1996d, 472). Du Bois publically challenged himself, despite his North American experiences, to apprehend race as "no longer even solely a matter of color and physical characteristics" but one that "cut across lines of color and physique and belief and status". As a matter of "cultural patterns and perverted teachings", the problem of race "reached all sorts of people" (Du Bois 1996d, 472; see also Rothberg 2001).

Nevertheless, it remains an open question as to whether Du Bois' episteme holds a more universal applicability; i.e. whether it could be directly related to the lived experience of caste in India, or Japanese imperialism in Manchuria (see, for example, Slate 2011; Mullen and Watson 2005). And while Du Bois politics were certainly not narrowly North American – he remained throughout his life a Pan-Africanist and an informal internationalist socialist – nevertheless, the core of his praxis was cultivated specifically to address the colour line created through slavery in the United States. Moreover, although Du Bois consistently argued that the struggle of women's suffrage was integral to the struggle against the colour line (see Yellin 1973), his object of inquiry remained primarily the antagonism between the black and white man.

We propose, then, that the utility of revisiting Du Bois' work lies less in the claim that it provides an off-the-shelf theory of international relations and more in the fact that it signals a rich and venerable research agenda for the interrogation of international relations through an episteme that focuses upon the operations of race and racism. This episteme rests upon three key propositions. First, world order is constitutively – and not derivatively – structured, re-structured and contested along lines of race. Second, when world order is conceived in this way, the sites of analysis – geographical, social, economic and intellectual – shift; some sites might be unfamiliar to IR and common sites might be rendered unfamiliar. And third, as suggested by Du Bois, the proposition that the power that is exercised through the global colour line has woven through it modalities other than race, strictly speaking, especially those of capitalism, patriarchy and (inter-)state development and (neo-)imperial rule.

The global colour line as a research agenda for IR

As we have noted above, there presently exists a relatively small but very active community of scholars in IR whose work, although not necessarily using an episteme of the "veil", still resonates with key theoretical and substantive issues identified by Du Bois in his explication of the global colour line. We would like to contextualise this scholarly community – to which we claim affiliation – within the critical and politically focused research agenda signalled by Du Bois in opposition to the still dominant race-science/race-thinking of imperial global governance (with all its derivatives and iterations) that he decried. What is more, retrieving, deepening and extending this research agenda in IR impel us to garner insights and inspirations from other disciplines that have been relatively more sensitive and responsive to the multiple ways in which race-thinking is deeply imbricated in all modern social formations.

For this purpose, the lessons provided by anthropology may be germane to IR. As an academic field of enquiry long dedicated to the study of the Other, anthropology has for some time now confronted its Eurocentric past and made an about-turn in its dealings with the racialised logics of knowledge production and its hitherto largely unproblematised – albeit highly problematic – ontological assumptions. Historically, anthropology played a key role in the creation and promulgation of the centrifugal "racial worldview" (Smedley 1993) that developed in

Europe and had spread around the world by the late nineteenth century. This racial worldview, based as it was on biological determinism, sought to distinguish the civilised from the savage and barbaric, thus creating a racial hierarchy on an ostensibly scientific foundation. Such a worldview was conjoined to the practices of slavery, colonialism and discrimination on the basis of skin colour and pheno-type (Asad 1973). But as Moses and Mukhopadyay (1997) argue, anthropology grew as a discipline and also 'participated actively in subsequent challenges to the racial worldview, collaborating to dismantle the very ideological edifice [it] helped create'.

This critical reorientation has important antecedents. It was Franz Boas, a con-temporary of Du Bois, who in the early twentieth century pioneered the critique of the typological rendering of race common to anthropological studies. Boas (1938) opposed the ideational holism at the root of "culture" and also "scrupulously severed the connections of race from culture" (Wolf 1992). Previously "race" had been the accepted organising principle of human difference, one that hierarchically compartmentalised humanity into five or six "types" on the basis of skin tone. The introduction of "culture" as an analytic category distinct from, and more mean-ingful than "race", heralded a new era of anthropological scholarship, led to a wholesale refashioning of the discipline, and was key in debunking the then popular ideologies of scientific racism and social Darwinism.

Boas's intellectual influence is evident in the UNESCO Statement on Race (1950/51). Announcing a new era in human understanding after the terrors of war and irrationalities of genocide, the main purpose of the statements was to separate the "biological fact" of race from its "social myth" (Montagu 1972, 10). More recently the insightful work of Lee Baker (1998), Johannes Fabian (2002), James Ferguson (1990, 2006, 2010) and Faye Harrison (1995), among others, on the "crisis of representation", the imperial and racial constructs of time and space, the emergence of "international development" as a racist enterprise, and the persistent forms of social inequalities structured along racial lines, have furthered Boas' legacy. Clearly, anthropology has been able to undertake a fundamental – if contested – review of its own disciplinary reliance upon – and involvement in crafting – a racial worldview. And in principle there is no reason why IR cannot embark on the same fundamental reassessment.

Yet it is not merely anthropology that can teach us. Scholars in history, philo-sophy, sociology, cultural studies, comparative literature, media studies, feminist theory and even linguistics (for the latter see Searle 1983 and Pennycook 1998) have all taken the question of race more seriously than IR and have generated an immense body of work – often multidisciplinary and interdisciplinary – that tackles the construct and problematique of race in diverse and exciting ways. For example, scholars have undertaken genealogies of racism (Lattas 1987; McWhorter 2009) highlighting the workings of white supremacy as a cohesive political system of thought conceptually on par with other "isms" like liberalism and fascism (Mills 1994; Taylor 2013) as well as in the formation of class consciousness (Roediger 1999). Others have theorised the race–power nexus by presenting the notion of "racial projects" that assign meaning to human bodies and distribute social goods based on "racial formation", that is "the sociohistorical process by which racial categories are created, inhabited, transformed, and destroyed" (Omi and Winant 1994, 55; see also Winant 2001; Wing 2000; Ferreira Da Silva 2007; Dikotter 2008). These sensibilities are also evident in critiques of the global "development project" (Duffield 1996; White 2002). Feminists, meanwhile, have explicated in great detail the seminal relationship of gender and sex to race (see, for example, Moraga and Anzaldúa 1983; Andersen and Collins 1998; and in IR, Chowdhry and Nair 2004). Crucially, scholars have brought to the fore the ironic predicament of knowledge generation, which in Rey Chow's words is that "theoretically sophisticated studies of the wretched of the earth tend to be undertaken by those in the most wealthy and prestigious institutes" (2006, 11). What these studies all have in common is an acute cognisance of the explanatory agency – and substantive complicity – of race and racism in all spheres of human activity, including academic knowledge production.

Nevertheless, fundamental issues remain with regard to the analysis of race. For example, more recently, anthropology's default position has perhaps become one of "race avoidance" (Mullings 2005, 670), embracing a no race policy and focusing instead on questions of ethnicity. Some might say that anthropology has lulled itself into a complacent belief that the "post-modern" era is also a "post-racial one". Ironically, the very severance of race from culture that Boas had so painstakingly undertaken might have simply led to the reification of the latter. Certainly, the defeat of the biological argument at UNESCO did not necessarily arrest the transfer of race determinism into the realm of culture and ethnicity (see, for example, Lentin 2005; Gilroy 2000, 32–9). While initially introduced as a non-hierarchical means of conceptualising human diversity, culture and ethnicity are now essentia-lised and racialised in less obvious but more insidious ways (Ansell 1997; Balibar 1991; Bonilla-Silva 2003). Furthermore, by exposing racism as "a misconstrued attitude based on misleading, pseudoscientific information" (Lentin 2005, 388) new scholarship could be in danger of relegating questions of race to the individualised domain of ignorance and irrational prejudice.

It is in this conjuncture that we place the contribution of this edited volume. We support the voices that have already demanded that IR take its legacies of race and racism seriously. Moreover, given that IR's disciplinary straitjacket is weakening – with the rigid demarcations and stark dichotomies between "inside" and "outside", "politics" and "economics" and the "personal" and "political" collapsing – the imperative to think about the relevance of race to world politics both historically and contemporaneously has become all the stronger. Additionally, we contend that IR could occupy a strategically distinct position in academia through which to facilitate examination of the link between race as a structuring principle and the transnational processes of accumulation, dispossession, violence and struggle that emerge in its wake. For example, we would suggest that not only is the emergence of the nation-state, and capitalist modernity as a project more generally, inex-tricably linked to racial logics, the very persistence of these logics is evident in contemporary liberal humanitarian intervention, nation-building and modern forms of slavery and trafficking. Thus, rather than talk of a post-racial world of theory or practice, we prefer to strategically reengage with the argument made by Du Bois that the problem of the twenty-first century is equally the problem of the colour line, albeit in shifting social constellations and physical geographies.

Although many of IR's concepts and concerns are increasingly being called into question, the new terms and vocabulary often remain embedded within the same racialised logics that they claim to displace or, at the very least, dispense with. Once the world-historical significance of race is recognised it becomes easy to see how ideas that are now ubiquitous in IR discourse, such as the notions of "rogue" or "failed" states and "small" or "new" wars, spring out of the familiar ontological assumptions that gave us the democratic peace theory, balance of power, and anarchy. This recognition also places focus upon the unambiguously racist implications of new technologies of war, of which drones and counterinsurgency campaigns are perhaps the most prominent examples. Finally, a confrontation with the global colour line sheds light on those global practices of boundary-making and border controls that mimic in explicit detail practices of colonial cartography, based as they were on white supremacist ideals. Arbitrary visa regimes, immigration controls and liberal modes of transnational incarceration are all testament to the institutionalisation of racism on a global scale. Indeed, the enshrining and reification of such exclusionary practices is the *modus operandi* of international relations.

As a final word of caution, it is undeniable that self-reflexivity often comes with the danger of falling into the trap of self-referentiality, a problem particularly palpable for IR, which remains caught up in its rather restricted grid of intelligibility. And scholars have, in point of fact, warned and been warned of invoking the "race, class, sex" mantra uncritically. One way to deal with such concerns is to recognise the need for the "destabilization of epistemic ground" (Chow 2006), away from what Charles Mills (1997) has called an "epistemology of ignorance" to an episteme that centres race and its interlocking modalities of especially patriarchy and capitalism across multiple dimensions – political, economic, cultural, psychological, etc. Confronting the global colour line requires us to both incorporate and move beyond the identity/difference nexus and to thereby no longer ride roughshod over the enduring concerns of Du Bois and other cognate thinkers.

Organisation of the book

We finish this introduction by situating the contributions to this book as part of the confrontation with the global colour line that we have argued defines our research agenda. And we organise the book around two key disciplinary challenges that this confrontation prompts.

The first is to support and extend a reflective exercise akin to that undertaken by anthropology. That is, we must excavate and assess the extent to which received themes, concepts and theories commonly used in IR are indebted to the racial constitution of world order. To address this challenge we must avoid, as we have already suggested, rhetoric and overly simplified charges of complicity, and instead unfold and reveal the warp and weft of the discipline, including its theoretical/ conceptual stock. In this respect we must also provide some alternative theoretical/ conceptual tools that are more adequate for our stated research agenda. The chapters in the first section of the book all contribute to this reflective exercise.

In Chapter 2, Errol Henderson directs his critique at the very heart of IR theory: realism and liberalism, two of the most prominent paradigms of the discipline. He examines the extent to which these major paradigms of world politics, despite their ostensible oppositionality, are in fact orientated by racist – primarily, white supremacist – precepts that inhere within their foundational construct, that of anarchy. Henderson maintains that due to the centrality of anarchy and other racially infused constructs within these prominent theories, white supremacist precepts are not only associated with the origins of the field, but have an enduring impact on IR theory, and continue to influence contemporary theses ranging from neorealist conceptions of the international system, liberal democratic peace claims, and even constructivist debates. Henderson's chapter therefore exposes the deep complicity of IR at a theoretical level in the maintenance of the global colour line.

Debra Thompson moves this reflection on IR's constitutive categories and concepts from "anarchy" to the "transnational". In Chapter 3, she argues that, though race is most commonly associated with domestic politics, the concept itself was born in the transnational realm. Thompson analytically sharpens Du Bois' poetic ascription of the formatively global nature of the colour line. She conceptualises race as a system of global power relations that has changed over time, manifests differently across space, and exists on multiple analytical levels. Drawing from the insights of IR, comparative politics and critical race theory, Thompson argues that race is a transnational norm or idea that can independently affect both domestic policy outcomes and relations among nation-states. Thompson then explores several promising avenues of research in the exploration of the varied manifestations of race in international and domestic realms and identifies continuing challenges and future research agendas in the comparative and international study of race.

In Chapter 4, Branwen Grufydd Jones directs attention to a key category deployed in IR theory and policy-making – the "failed state". Jones tackles the way in which current international policy discourse routinely characterises the condition of African states in terms of either "good governance", on the one hand, or fragility and failure, on the other. This conceptual vocabulary and analytical approach has become entrenched within the public imagination more broadly, and is reproduced in academic analysis, largely without serious questioning or critique. Jones argues that although ostensibly free from explicitly racialised tropes, the failed state discourse employs a conceptual vocabulary that is rooted in racialised international thought. Carrying forward the early twentieth-century critiques that we have mentioned above of IR as a science of race administration, Jones testifies to the importance of questioning "common sense" concepts deployed in IR by contextualising them within a much longer genealogy of imperial discourse about Africa and other non-European societies.

John Hobson's chapter extends an argument that he makes in his recent book, *The Eurocentric Conception of World Politics,* that seeks to conceptually differentiate Eurocentrism – or what he calls "Eurocentric institutionalism" – from scientific racism. In this respect, Hobson picks up on Boas' problematique that we have noted above – that is, the post-World War II movement of racial determinism from the language of biology to that of culture. Hobson's chapter demonstrates how this movement was implicated in disciplinary IR as well. In contrast to claims by liberal scholars in IR who see a benign discourse of racial tolerance and cultural pluralism following the defeat of scientific racism, Hobson excavates an alternative discourse at work – that of "subliminal Eurocentric-institutional intolerance". The chapter therefore demonstrates the importance of carefully sifting through the various registers and sources of argumentation in IR in order to better understand the multi-valiant influence of "race thinking" on the discipline.

Similar to Hobson, Srdjan Vucetic takes a step into philosophies of race in order to undertake a careful reading of the use and deployment of concepts that might help scholars in IR cultivate an episteme sensitive to race and racism. In Chapter 6, Vucetic brings focus to bear on the "race taboo" that ironically undermines the lived experience of racism everywhere. He argues that the allegedly compelling and increasingly popular argument of eliminating "race" as a category of thought suffers from one major shortfall: it erases the theoretical and philosophical basis for anti-racist politics that is supposed to have motivated scholarship in the first place. Vucetic reflects on the continuities and changes in the ways the category of race has been deployed via three debates in the philosophy of race: the semantic, the ontological and the normative. Ultimately making a case for the use of categories of racialisation and racialised identity over the category of race, Vucetic suggests that IR theorists would do well to mine tools from the burgeoning literatures on racial habits and racial cognition.

The second challenge prompted by a confrontation of the global colour line is to re-affirm and critically extend the example set by Du Bois; that is, to demonstrate the explanatory potential of substantive analyses of the global colour line. Here the challenge is to contribute alternative insights into the constitution, contestation and re-constitution of a racialised world order. In this respect, some of the work undertaken would have to revisit theoretical and empirical terrain that is familiar to the IR discipline in order to make it unfamiliar; yet other work would dwell on sites and issues that have never been familiar to IR. By undertaking both sets of work it would be possible to more adequately address – but not be constrained by – the existing epistemic frames of IR. The chapters in the second section of this edited volume all demonstrate such potential.

In Chapter 7, Randolph Persaud introduces an unfamiliar site to IR – the plantations of British Guiana – and unfamiliar peoples – indentured women who were widely abused, maimed and murdered there. Persaud is keen to examine the routine forms of colonial governance and the quotidian nature of violence that accompanied them. To this end, Persaud turns to the post-abolition sugar economies and argues that the social and political relations governing accumulation were restructured so as to maintain violent control over the new indentured labour force. Crucially, Persaud demonstrates the implication of gender in the colour line, as well as the ways in which this line is demarcated violently. This violence structured not only the relationship between the plantocracy and the indentured but also the relationship between indentured women and men.

Sankaran Krishna works with a reasonably familiar figure in IR – Mohandas Gandhi – but places him in a rather unfamiliar geo-cultural constellation – South Africa/India. In Chapter 8, Krishna argues that in his early years in South Africa, Gandhi completely internalised certain racist ideas and assumptions regarding the inferiority of Africans. Gandhi subsequently deployed this postcolonial rendition of racial and spatial order in his encounters with the Dalit leader Bhim Rao Ambedkar in the 1930s. Krishna exposes how this racial/spatial order was evident at the UN World Conference Against Racism held in 2001, when the Indian government successfully deflected efforts by India's Dalits to have casteism equated with racism or untouchability discussed as part of the proceedings. Krishna's chapter suggests that Du Bois's colour line cannot only be painted in the primary tones of black and white.

In Chapter 9, Richard Seymour returns us to a familiar historical site in IR: the Cold War. Nevertheless, Seymour makes this site unfamiliar by arguing that the impact of race in the Cold War has been largely neglected. In this respect, Seymour historically extends Du Bois's analysis of the colour line to make better sense of the signal global confrontation of the later twentieth century. Seymour examines the extent to which anticommunism can be understood as a form of racial practice, involved in helping to organise global racial orders as part of hegemonic strategies on the part of imperialist states, above all the United States. The chapter thereby illustrates the many crises and equivocations produced in US foreign policies by the impact of rival, incompatible racial projects on its commitment to the institutions of white supremacy in the global South and in the Deep South, culminating in a crest of defeats for white supremacy and reversals for the US globally.

In Chapter 10, Robert Knox brings our attention to a popular current issue in IR scholarship: military intervention. Recently, questions of empire and imperialism have caused the racialised nature of military interventions to come to the fore. But what is perhaps less well known is the role of international law in these debates. The self-described Third World Approaches to International Law (TWAIL) movement has become increasingly concerned with mapping these connections between empire, race, war and law. Knox provides a sympathetic critique of these approaches by exploring the changing nature of the legal justifications advanced for the use of force. Similarly to Hobson, Knox elides an easy rhetoric of race and racism and captures the dynamic and shifting nature of the global colour line by arguing that, contrary to a reified causal notion of "race", current interventions are embedded in the broader dynamics of international capitalism and the rivalries it throws up.

The book finishes with reflective chapters from two eminent non-IR scholars. David Roediger comments on the book project from the perspective of a historian of labour struggles who has been a seminal force in cultivating the concept of "whiteness" through his drawing out of the racial dimensions of labour struggles. And Charles Mills provides reflections from the perspective of a philosopher who has challenged his all-too-abstract discipline to engage seriously with the "racial contract" and the structures of white supremacy. These commentaries signal the fact that IR scholars have much to learn from cognate work in other fields; yet they also suggest that the field of IR is itself an intellectually and strategic field through which to further confront the global colour line.

Notes

1 Our thanks to Errol Henderson, Srdjan Vucetic and Sankaran Krishna for their very helpful critical comments.
2 See, for example, Dubois' autobiographical comments in Du Bois (1996a, 489; 1961, 156).
3 "He hears so little that there almost seems to be a conspiracy of silence" (Du Bois 1961, 135).
4 Du Bois investigates the relationality of all these dimensions in Chapter 9 (Du Bois 1961, 114–32).

Bibliography

Agathangelou, Anna M. and Ling, L. H. M. (2004) The House of IR: From Family Power Politics to the *Poisies* of Worldism. *International Studies Review*, 6 (4), 21–49.
Anderson, Carol (2003) *Eyes Off the Prize: The United Nations and the African American Struggle for Human Rights, 1944–1955*. Cambridge: Cambridge University Press.
Andersen, Margaret L. and Collins, Patricia Hill (eds) (1998) *Race, Class and Gender: An Anthology*. London: Wadsworth.
Ansell, Amy Elizabeth (1997) *New Right, New Racism: Race and Reaction in the United States and Britain*. Washington Square, NY: New York University Press.
Asad, Talal (1973) *Anthropology and the Colonial Encounter*. New York, NY: Humanities Press.
Balibar, Étienne (1991) Is There a 'Neo-Racism'? In Balibar, É. and Wallerstein, I. (eds) *Race, Nation, Class: Ambiguous Identities*. London: Verso, 17–28.
Barkin, Kenneth D. (2000) "Berlin Days" 1892–94: W. E. B. Du Bois and German Political Economy. *Boundary 2*, 27 (3), 79–101.
Boas, Franz (1938) *The Mind of Primitive Man*. New York, NY: Macmillan.
Bonilla-Silva, Eduardo (2003) *Racism without Racists: Color-blind Racism and the Persistence of Racial Inequality in the United States*. Lanham, MD: Rowman & Littlefield.
Chowdhry, Geeta and Nair, Sheila (2002) *Power, Postcolonialism and International Relations: Reading Race, Gender and Class*. London: Routledge.
Douglass, Frederick (1881) The Color Line. In Lowell, J. R. (ed.) *North American Review*, 132. Available at: http://etext.lib.virginia.edu/toc/modeng/public/DouColo.html.
Du Bois, W. E. B. (1915) African Roots of War. The Atlantic *Monthly*, 115 (5), 707–14.
——(1925) Worlds of Color. *Foreign Affairs*, 3 (3), 423–44.
——(1935) Inter-Racial Implications of the Ethiopian Crisis: A Negro View. *Foreign Affairs*, 14 (1), 82–92.
——(1961) *The Souls of Black Folk*. New York, NY: Crest Books.
——(1995) *Black Reconstruction in America*. New York, NY: Simon & Schuster.

——(1996a [1920]) Darkwater: Voices from Within the Veil. In Sundquist, E. J. (ed.) *The Oxford W. E. B. Du Bois Reader*. New York, NY: Oxford University Press, 483–623.

——(1996b [1897]) The Conservation of the Races. In Sundquist, E. J. (ed.) *The Oxford W. E. B. Du Bois Reader*. New York, NY: Oxford University Press, 37–8.

——(1996c [1900]) To the Nations of the World. In Sundquist, E. J. (ed.) *The Oxford W. E. B. Du Bois Reader*. New York, NY: Oxford University Press, 625–7.

——(1996d [1952]) 'The Negro and the Warsaw Ghetto'. In Sundquist, E. J. (ed.) *The Oxford W. E. B. Du Bois Reader*. New York, NY: Oxford University Press, 469–73.

Dussel, Enrique (1985) *Philosophy of Liberation*. Translated by A. Martinez and C. Morkovsky. New York, NY: Orbis Books.

Fanon, Frantz (1986) *Black Skin, White Masks*. London: Pluto Press.

Gilroy, Paul (2000) *Against Race: Imagining Political Culture Beyond the Color Line*. Cambridge, MA: Harvard University Press.

Henry, Charles P. (1995) Abram Harris, E. Franklin Frazier, and Ralph Bunche: The Howard School of Thought on the Problem of Race. *National Political Science Review*, 5, 36–56.

Holt, Thomas C. (2013) 'A Story of Ordinary Human Beings': The Sources of Du Bois's Historical Imagination in Black Reconstruction. *South Atlantic Quarterly*, 112 (3), 419–35.

Manning, Charles A. W. (1964) In Defense of Apartheid. *Foreign Affairs*, 43 (1), 135–49.

Mignolo, Walter (2000) *Local Histories/Global Designs: Coloniality, Subaltern Knowledges, and Border Thinking*. Princeton, NJ: Princeton University Press.

Montagu, Ashley (1972) *Statement on Race*. 3rd ed. Oxford: Oxford University Press.

Mullen, Bill V. and Watson, Cathryn (2005) 'Introduction: Crossing the World Color Line. In Mullen, Bill V. and Watson, Cathryn (eds) *W. E. B. Du Bois on Asia: Crossing the World Color Line*. Jackson, MS: University Press of Mississippi, vii–xxvii.

Persaud, Randolph and Walker, R. B. J. (2001) Apertura: Race in International Relations. *Alternatives*, 26 (4), 373–6.

Polsgrove, Carol (2009) *Ending British Rule in Africa: Writers in a Common Cause*. Manchester: Manchester University Press.

Rothberg, Michael (2001) 'W. E. B. Du Bois in Warsaw: Holocaust Memory and the Color Line, 1949–52. *The Yale Journal of Criticism*, 14 (1), 169–89.

Rosenau, James N. (1970) *Race in International Politics: A Dialogue in Five Parts*. Denver, CO: University of Denver Press.

Schrager, Cynthia D. (1996) Both Sides of the Veil: Race, Science, and Mysticism in W. E. B. Du Bois. *American Quarterly*, 48 (4), 551–86.

Shepherd, G. W. and LeMelle, T. J. (1970) *Race among Nations: A Conceptual Approach*. Lexington, MA: Heath Lexington Books.

Slate, Nico (2011) Translating Race and Caste. *Journal of Historical Sociology*. 24 (1), 62–79.

Suganami, Hidemi (2001) C. A. W. Manning and the Study of International Relations. *Review of International Studies*, 27 (1), 91–107

Vitalis, Robert (forthcoming). *The End of Empire in International Relations*.

Yellin, Jean Fagan (1973) Dubois' Crisis and Woman's Suffrage. *The Massachusetts Review* 14 (2), 365–75.

Watson, Hilbourne (2001) Theorizing the Racialization of Global Politics and the Caribbean Experience. *Alternatives*, 26 (4), 449–83.

White, Sarah (2002) Thinking Race, Thinking Development. *Third World Quarterly*, 23 (3), 407–19.

Winant, Howard (2001) *The World is a Ghetto: Race and Democracy since World War II*. New York, NY: Basic Books.

Wing, A. Katherine (2000) *Global Critical Race Feminism: An International Reader*. New York, NY: New York University Press.

PART I

Conceptualising the international relations of race and racism

2

HIDDEN IN PLAIN SIGHT

Racism in international relations theory

Errol A. Henderson

Introduction

This chapter addresses the centrality of racism in international relations (IR) theory; specifically, in realism and liberalism, two of the most prominent paradigms of IR. It examines the extent to which these major paradigms of world politics are oriented by racist – primarily, white supremacist – precepts that inhere within their foundational construct, namely, anarchy. I maintain that due to the centrality of anarchy – and other racially infused constructs – within these prominent paradigms, white supremacist precepts are not only nominally associated with the origins of the field but have an enduring impact on IR theory, influencing contemporary theses ranging from neorealist conceptions of the global system, liberal democratic peace claims, and constructivist theses as well. The essay proceeds in several sections. First, I briefly review the centrality of white supremacism in the origins of IR as an academic field of study. Second, I discuss the role of white supremacism in the foundational constructs of IR theory; namely, the social contract theses that inform our conception of anarchy, which is the starting point for most paradigms of world politics. I maintain that social contract theses that are often cast as "race-neutral" actually suggest one type of relations for white people, their institutions, and states, and another for nonwhite people, their institutions, and states. This discourse provided the point of departure for subsequent IR theorising among realists, liberals, and constructivists on the relations among states in the global system. Therefore, third, I discuss how realism, liberalism, and constructivism derive their notions of anarchy from social contract theses which are based in a racist dualism that dichotomises humanity and the relations of states comprised of different peoples. Before turning to this broader discussion, let us consider the manner in which racism influences IR in general.

The study of race and racism in international relations

Racism is the belief, practice, and policy of domination based on the specious concept of race (Henderson 2007). It is not simply bigotry or prejudice, but beliefs, practices, and policies reflective of and supported by institutional power, primarily state power. For more than a century, social scientists have maintained, in general, that race and racism are among the most important factors in world politics. As discussed to a greater extent in the introduction to this volume, prominent anti-racist scholars such as W. E. B. Du Bois (1903, 23) had acknowledged at the outset of the last century that "the problem of the twentieth century is the problem of the colour line – the relation of the darker to the lighter races of men in Asia and Africa in America and the islands of the sea". Less appreciated today is the centrality of race and racism to the core theorists of the incipient academic field of international relations. Their early works were firmly situated in the prominent social Darwinist evolutionary theses of the day that assumed a hierarchy of races dominated by white Europeans and their major diasporic offshoots in the Americas, Australia, and South Africa, with nonwhites occupying subordinate positions and none lower than blacks. A white supremacist evolutionary teleology informed the domestic and international policies of major Western states and rationalised their policies of white racial domination epitomised in slavery, imperial conquest, colonisation, and genocide. In this conception, whites were assumed to be favored by God and biologically distinct from nonwhites. Uniquely among the races, whites were assumed to possess civilization, while nonwhites were assumed to occupy a lower stage of development characterised by either barbarism or savagery. Further, it assumed that in order to traverse the evolutionary ladder to achieve civilisation and its attendant culture, nonwhites would have to be tutored by whites who would – often magnanimously – assume this "white man's burden" so that the lesser races might rise above their barbarism and savagery. The lesser races were assumed to be not only biologically inferior to whites but also in a state of almost perpetual conflict; therefore, the "civilising mission" of those who would take up the "white man's burden" could be imposed by force. This orientation not only rationalised enslavement, imperial conquest, colonisation, and genocide but also provided an intellectual rationale to justify these pursuits. To the extent that the racial hierarchy guided the international politics of the predominantly white states in their interaction with other polities, then the international relations of the time were more accurately "interracial relations" (Du Bois 1915; Lauren 1996). Thus, it is not surprising that the early works that gave rise to the modern academic field of IR focused squarely on race as its main axis of inquiry.

For example, in *An Introduction to the Study of International Relations*, Kerr (1916) argued that "one of the most fundamental facts in human history" is that "[m]ankind is divided into a graduated scale" (1916, 142) ranging from the civilised to the barbarian, which necessitated colonisation of the latter by the former (1916, 163). Giddings (1898) viewed the "governing" of "the inferior races of mankind" as the duty of the civilised and drew on Kidd's *The Control of the Tropics*

(1898, 15), which admonished superior races to assume their responsibility to cultivate the riches of the "tropics". The competition for these resources could lead to major wars among "civilised" states, as Hobson, Angell, and Lenin would famously argue. In fact, Du Bois (1915) had argued in "The African roots of the war", prior to publication of Lenin's more famous tract, *Imperialism: The Highest Stage of Capitalism*, that World War I was largely the result of disputes over imperial acquisitions that fused the interests of bourgeoisie and proletariat in European states in a mutually reinforcing pursuit of racist and economic domination of African and Asian nations. One brief aside: although Du Bois had published this argument prior to Lenin's more famous pamphlet, it is rarely anthologised or even mentioned in contemporary IR textbooks, readers, or in the discussion of imperialism – much less on the origins of World War I. The present volume contributes to filling such voids in contemporary IR literature.

Earlier Reinsch (1900, 9), whom Schmidt (1998, 75) maintains "must be considered one of the founding figures of the field of international relations", noted in what may be considered the first monograph in the field of IR, *World Politics at the End of the Nineteenth Century* (1900), that "national imperialism" was transforming the landscape of international relations as states attempted "to increase the resources of the national state through the absorption or exploitation of undeveloped regions and inferior races", without "impos[ing] political control upon highly civilized nations" (1900, 14). Olson and Groom (1991, 47) note that Reinsch's work "suggests that the discipline of international relations had its real beginnings in studies of imperialism"; and studies of imperialism at the time were firmly grounded in racist assumptions of white supremacy. Moreover, Reinsch's (1905a, 154–5) "The Negro race and European civilization" concurred with prominent anthropometric arguments that there were physiological differences between the brains of blacks and those of whites, such that for the former, "organic development of the faculties seem to cease at puberty"; however, he also opined that the development capacity of blacks could be facilitated under white tutelage, which "amounted to an American variant of what British colonial reformers would come to call the policy of 'indirect rule'" (Vitalis 2010, 932). In fact, Reinsch's *Colonial Government* (1902) and *Colonial Administration* (1905b) placed him among the leading experts on colonial administration, as well. In the 1920s, Buell's (1929) *International Relations*, which Vitalis (2000, 353) describes as "the most important US textbook" of the decade, "opens with the classic trope of the discipline, a man on the moon looking down upon an earth divided 'into different hues'".

The centrality of race to the incipient field of IR is evident in the genealogy of one of the most popular journals in international affairs, *Foreign Affairs*. *Foreign Affairs* became the house organ of the Council on Foreign Relations in 1922 after changing its name from the *Journal of International Relations*, which it had since 1919; but from 1910 to 1919 the publication was known as the *Journal of Race Development* (Iriye 1997, 67). Reeves (2004, 26) notes that "the move from race to international relations would seem to represent both a qualitative and quantitative change in subjects matter, yet, to the journal editors, the change was, obviously, less dramatic" given that "Volume 10, the *Journal of International Relations*, simply followed on from where Volume 9, the *Journal of Race Development*, left off". For her, "the choices of the journal's title tells us something of what early IR scholars considered the subject of international relations to be about" (2004, 26). Following Vitalis, Blatt (2004, 707) views the *Journal of Race Development* as central to a corpus of scholarship at the turn of the twentieth century that placed race at the centre of the study of world politics through its association with a "racialized and biological understanding of 'development'".

Subsequent scholarship in the incipient field of IR retained a focus on race and white racial supremacy; and in the interwar era it often projected, rationalised, and echoed alarmist sentiments that augured a race war that would result from the teeming masses of nonwhite peoples who were becomingly increasingly assertive (i.e. "race conscious"). Figures on demographic growth in the colonial world were brought to bear to justify the growing fear of "race war" during the interwar period and focused attention away from the genocidal schemes of the emerging fascist regimes in Europe. For example, Spengler's *Decline of the West* and Stoddard's *The Rising Tide of Color against White World Supremacy* heightened the sense of impending inter-racial warfare between the white West and its colonised darker minions – but actually, any of the "lesser races" that were assumed to have a "natural" place in the hierarchy of races below white Europeans and their racial kin. One result was that "every Western setback" from the defeat of Russia by the Japanese in 1905 to the Turkish defeat of the Greeks in 1923 "was a direct boost to anti-white conscious-ness" and augured greater conflicts to come (Furedi 1998, 58). For example, one of the most influential British IR scholars, Alfred Zimmern, noted at the time that the defeat of Russia by Japan in 1905 was "the most important historical event which has happened or is likely to happen, in our lifetime; the victory of a non-white people over a white people" (1926, 82). Nevertheless, given a concern with fomenting "race war", a view emerged that "public displays of white racial super-iority had become dangerous since they invited an explosion of racial resentment" (Furedi 1998, 79). For the most part, "this was an approach that self-consciously ignored the fundamental question of racial oppression and focused its concern on the etiquette of race relations" (Furedi 1998, 79). In effect, it was the intellectual rationalisation of the separate but equal doctrine of apartheid, or Jim Crow, as "[t]he new racial pragmatism presented itself as an alternative to racial supremacist philosophy" (Furedi 1998, 93) and even promoted, at times, notions of cultural relativism. Actually, cultural relativism was quite compatible with white suprema-cist tenets[1], and its ascendance in academia and policy circles simply represented the most recent morphing of white supremacist discourse.[2]

The justification for white racism had progressed through several distinct but often overlapping and at times mutually reinforcing rationalisations rooted initially in theology, then biology, and subsequently in anthropology. The religious and biological justifications of white supremacy are well known. Boas is credited with evolving the academic discourse of race away from biology and towards anthro-pology and in so doing ushering in an era of cultural relativism and modern anthropological analyses of race. Boas (1911) challenged anthropometric "evidence" of correspondence between cranial capacity of peoples of different races and intelligence, and prevailing genetic arguments of racial heredity. For example, he noted that immigrants to the US who had undergone years of American socialisation evinced cultural characteristics approximating those of other Americans. Arguing against social Darwinism, he rejected the notion of a hierarchy of culture and argued instead that all peoples have cultures that reflect their own beliefs, values, and practices that are internally valid and should be evaluated on their own terms and not in relation to some cultural hierarchy. This perspective undermined the assumed scientific legitimacy of white supremacism based on notions of white cultural superiority and ushered in the discourse of cultural relativism in social science. Less well known is the contribution to racial discourse of the first African American Rhodes Scholar, Alain Locke, who accepted much of the Boasian perspective on culture – thus he rejected the view that culture was determined by race – but argued against the anthropological view of race and aspects of Boas's cultural relativism as well, suggesting instead that race was mainly a sociological construct.

In the first of his series of five lectures at Howard University in 1916 entitled, "The Theoretical and Scientific Conceptions of Race", he argued that anthropology had not isolated any permanent or static features of race. For Locke (1992, 11), "when the modern man talks about race[,] he is not talking about the anthropological or biological idea at all. [He is really talking about the historical record of success or failure of] an ethnic group", but "these groups, from the point of view of anthropology, are ethnic fictions". Interestingly, he notes that "This does not mean that they do not exist[,] but it can be shown [that these groups do] not have as [permanent] designations those very factors upon which they pride themselves". That is, "[t]hey have neither purity of [blood] nor purity of type"; instead, "[t]hey are the products of countless interminglings of types[,] and they are the results of infinite crossings of types" and "maintain in name only this fetish of biological [purity]" (Locke 1992, 11).

On the face of it, Locke's contention seems to be that of Boas; however, while Boas rejected biological renderings of race in favor of anthropological ones, he nonetheless opined that some elements of race may be rooted in heredity. This understanding led Boas to propose racial intermarriage as a prescription for the eradication of US racism. Locke disagreed. He insisted that there was neither a biological nor an anthropological basis for race; and in this way transcended Boas's conceptualisation of cultural relativism and laid the basis for his "critical relativism". That is, even as the scientific understanding of race progressed under Boas's influence from biological definitions to anthropological ones, Locke (1992, 10) went further and argued that "[e]ven the anthropological factors are variable, and pseudo-scientific, except for purposes of descriptive classification"; therefore, "there are no static factors of race at all" (Locke 1992, 10). As Stewart (1992, xxiv) notes, for Locke, race was sociological. It "was simply another word for a social or national group that shared a common history or culture and occupied a geographical region"; but "as applied to social and ethnic groups" race "has no meaning at all beyond that sense of kind, that sense of kith and kin"; it is "an ethnic fiction". For Locke, to the extent that a person has a race, "he has inherited either a favorable or an unfavorable social heredity, which unfortunately is [typically] ascribed to factors which have not produced [it,] factors which will in no way determine either the period of those inequalities or their eradication" (Locke 1992, 12). Through this conceptualisation, Locke "was standing racialist theories of culture on their heads: rather than particular races creating Culture, it was culture – social, political, and economic processes – that produced racial character" (Locke 1992, xxv). Locke had removed race from its biological *and* anthropological moorings and placed it "squarely on a cultural foundation"; fundamentally, race was sociological – or in today's verbiage, a "social construct". Locke's contributions are as prescient and profound as they are ignored in contemporary scholarship on racism in IR or political science in general – or sociology, anthropology, and philosophy.

To be sure, Locke's arguments from his Howard University lectures of 1914–16 went unpublished in his lifetime; therefore the inattention of scholars to his sociological thesis of race is to some extent understandable. However, even within the ostensible mainstream of IR scholarship in the interwar era, there was the little appreciated – and rarely cited – analysis of race in domestic and international affairs of political scientist and future Nobel Laureate, Ralph Bunche (1936). In his *A World View of Race* he eschewed the alarmist tendencies of the day and – informed in part by Locke's earlier arguments – offered a sober analysis of racism in world politics that focused on the non-scientific basis of race and the often greater salience of class in ostensibly "racial" conflicts; and in so doing anticipated much of the postwar scholarship – including post-Cold War scholarship – on racism in world politics.

Engagement against the Nazi regime in World War II compelled Western elites to disassociate themselves at least superficially from the doctrine of the regime that had just been defeated. Nevertheless, Du Bois (1946 [1987], 23) raised the hypocrisy of Western condemnation of Nazi atrocities in light of Western practices in its colonies and asserted that "there was no Nazi atrocity – concentration camps, wholesale maiming and murder, defilement of women or ghastly blasphemy of childhood – which the Christian civilisation of Europe had not long been practicing against colored folk in all parts of the world in the name of and for the defense of a Superior Race born to rule the world". Subsequently, the international order would not substantively alter the racial status quo even as it promoted racial equality in its major international institutions such as the UN – continuing to countenance the subjugation of billions of nonwhite people by the imperialist powers who were victors of World War II. The anti-colonial struggle in the third world would challenge this status quo and issues of race and racism were increasingly examined in the postwar era to address the decline of empires. Nevertheless, the postwar rise of "area studies" situated many such analyses of race within the context of comparative politics (or in the study of domestic politics of individual states) and outside of IR, such that even in prominent IR texts such as *Politics*

Among Nations, Hans Morgenthau (1985, 369), one of the most influential IR scholars of the twentieth century, could refer to "the politically empty spaces of Africa and Asia".

To be sure, race and racism are not only foundational to the field of IR, but were seminal to the development of the field given their centrality in the conduct of international affairs. For example, near the end of the Cold War, Lauren (1996, 4) acknowledged that:

> The first global attempt to speak of equality focused upon race. The first human rights provisions in the United Nations Charter were placed there because of race. The first international challenge to a country's claim of domestic jurisdiction and exclusive treatment of its own citizens centred upon race. The international convention with the greatest number of signatories is that on race. Within the United Nations, more resolutions deal with race than any other subject. And certainly one of the most long-standing and frustrating problems in the United Nations is that of race. Nearly one hundred eighty governments, for example, recently went as far as to conclude that racial discrimination and racism still represent the most serious problems for the world today.

Persaud and Walker (2001, 374) add that "the significance of race [in IR] goes much beyond various multilateral and other diplomatic achievements" because "race has been a fundamental force in the very *making* of the modern world system and in the representations and explanations of how that system emerged and how it works". For Persaud (2001, 116) "race … has been at the center of gravity for a substantial part of the modern world system".

The centrality of race and racism in the foundations of IR and their enduring impact on world affairs towards the end of the millennium are contrasted to the relative dearth of mainstream scholarship on the subject in IR. For example, Doty's (1998, 136) survey of mainstream journals in IR for the period of 1945–93 (i.e. *World Politics, International Studies Quarterly, International Organization, Journal of Conflict Resolution, Review of International Studies*) "revealed only one article with the word race in the title, four with the term minorities and 13 with the term ethnicity". Given that at its inception IR focused heavily on issues of race and racism, then the marginalisation of race and racism in mainstream IR journals (and texts) begs the question of what accounts for the apparent disparity? Doty (1998, 145) argues that "the dominant understandings of theory and explanation in International Relations" preclude conceptualisations of "complex issues/concepts such as race" and results in their marginalisation or forces them "into constraining modes of conceptualization and explanation". For Krishna (2001, 401), the complexity is related less to the issue of racism than with the methodological orientations that often privilege abstract theorising over historical analyses, which allows IR theorists to whitewash the historical content of global affairs, especially "the violence, genocide, and theft that marked the encounter between the rest and the West in the post-Columbian era". Ignoring the role of racism facilitates this whitewash. He adds that

> abstraction, usually presented as the desire of the discipline to engage in theory-building rather than in descriptive or historical analysis, is a screen that simultaneously rationalises and elides the details of these encounters. By encouraging students to display their virtuosity in abstraction the discipline brackets questions of theft of land, violence, and slavery – the three processes that have historically underlain the unequal global order we now find ourselves in.
>
> *(Krishna 2001, 401–2)*

Further, "overattention" on the part of scholars or graduate students to issues related to racism in IR "is disciplined by professional practices that work as taboo" and may label such orientations as "too historical or descriptive" and label such students "not adequately theoretical" and "lacking in intellectual rigor" (Krishna 2001, 402). Moreover, where the impact of race and racism is analysed, insufficient attention is paid to the relevance of struggles related to race and racism on our basic conceptions of fundamental issues in world politics such as power, war, freedom, or democracy. For example, Persaud (2001, 116) maintains that "what needs to be underlined is that the struggle for racial equality has been fundamental to the emergence of *democracy as a whole*, not just for the colored world".

Persaud and Walker (2001, 374) claim that race has not been ignored in IR as much as it "has been given the epistemological status of silence". This silence is linked by Maclean (1981, 110) to "invisibility", which "refers to the removal (not necessarily through conscious action) from a field of enquiry, either concrete aspects of social relations or of certain forms of thought about them". Vitalis (2000) also acknowledges a "norm against noticing" white racism throughout mainstream IR discourse (see also Depelchin 2005). Each of these processes perpetuates the racist assumptions embedded in the foundations of IR theory where they serve as the "priors" of the main propositions. These assumptions may be exposed by tracing the racist claims that inform IR theory. This approach is different from that undertaken in most studies of racism in IR, which usually focus on one of four approaches: (1) *examinations of the impact of non-racial factors on racial outcomes*, such as the geographical studies of Linneaus and the physical anthropological works of Blumenbach and Kant, which attempted to determine the extent to which environmental and climatic factors led to the creation of different races;[3] (2) *examinations of the impact of racial outcomes on non-racial factors*, such as studies of the effects of racial stratification on domestic outcomes (e.g. development or democracy) or the impact of racial differences on the likelihood of violence within or between states (e.g. Deutsch 1970; Shepherd and Lemelle 1970); (3) *examinations of the impact of racist practices on the international relations of states and non-state actors*, such as studies of diplomatic historians on racist practices such as international slavery, imperial conquest, colonialism, genocide, apartheid, occupation, or racial discrimination, among single states, several states, or international organisations (e.g. Elkins 2004; Hochschild 1998; Tinker 1977; Vincent 1982; Winant 2001); and (4) *examinations of the impact of racist ideology on the international relations of states and non-state actors*, such as studies on the impact of racism on foreign policy (e.g. Hunt 1987; Lauren 1996; Anderson 2003), imperialism (e.g. Rodney 1974), state-making (e.g. Cell 1982; Fredrickson 1982; Mamdani 1996; Marx 1998), diasporisation (Harris 1982; Walters 1993), or international war (Dower 1986).

While studies utilising each of these approaches have contributed to our understanding of the role of racism in world politics, they have largely ignored the issue of primary concern to us here: how racism informs the major paradigms of IR theory such as realism and liberalism.[4] Racism informs IR theory mainly through its influence on the empirical, ethical, and epistemological assumptions that undergird its paradigms. These assumptions operate individually and in combination. For example, racist empirical assumptions bifurcate humanity on the basis of race and determine our view of what/whom we study and how we study it/ them – privileging the experiences of "superior" peoples, their societies and institutions. These assumptions also lead us to privilege ethical orientations of the "superior" peoples that justify their privileged status. In such a context, epistemological assumptions that reflect and reinforce the racist dualism are more likely to become ascendant, and "knowledge" that supports the racist dichotomy – both the privileged position of the racial hegemon and the underprivileged position of the racial subaltern – are more likely to be viewed as valid. Such knowledge drawn from the empirical domain becomes legitimised through ethical justifications that "naturalise" the racial hierarchy. In this way, the separate dimensions often reinforce each other.

Whether or not the empirical, ethical and epistemological assumptions operate singly or in combination, it is important to demonstrate the role of these assumptions in IR theory today, especially given that mainstream IR also provides prominent critiques of racism. Ignoring these critiques would misrepresent the degree of racism in the field and disregard the challenge to racist discourse within IR by IR theorists, themselves. For example, few IR scholars openly embrace a racist ontology that assumes for whites a higher order of being than for nonwhites.[5] Moreover, racist ethical assumptions usually receive the opprobrium they deserve in present IR discourse. Racist epistemological assumptions are largely challenged by the prevalence in IR theory of the view that our "knowledge" of world politics usually requires us to have something approximating evidence to determine the accuracy of rival truth claims. Finally, racist empirical assumptions are checked by the dominant view in IR that our theses should be broadly applicable across states and societies and should be substantiated by cross-national and cross-temporal tests. But the sanguine view of the propensity of IR literature to check racist assumptions or to generate a non-racist theoretical discourse for the field, begs a fuller exploration of how ethical, epistemological, and empirical assumptions underlie prominent theses in IR. The main sources of these racist assumptions that inform our present IR discourse are the primary theoretical constructs for most IR theory:

the state of nature, the social contract, and the conception of anarchy that derives from them.

The racial contract as the basis of the social contract

IR theory takes as its point of departure the state of nature and the social contract given that these constructs reflect and inform our conceptions of anarchy, which is widely perceived as the key variable that differentiates international politics from domestic politics. Anarchy is "the Rosetta Stone of International Relations" (Lipson 1984, 22) and provides the conceptual linchpin upon which the major paradigms of IR rests. Our conceptualisation of anarchy in IR theory derives from the insights of social contract theorists such as Hobbes, Locke, Rousseau, and Kant, whose characterisation of the state of nature, which is the hypothetical condition characterised by human interaction prior to the establishment of society, was adopted by IR theorists to conceptualise the global system. But Charles Mills (1997) insists that the social contract that is the focus of each of these theorists is embedded in a broader "racial contract". Unlike the social contract, which presumably proposes a singular homogeneous humanity from which civil society would emerge, the racial contract established a heterogeneous humanity hierarchically arranged and reflecting a fundamental dualism demarcated by race. This racial dualism inherent in social contract theses was passed on to the IR theory that drew from them; and it persists today in the paradigms that rest on their assumptions.

For example, realism, the dominant paradigm in IR, roots its conception of anarchy in the Hobbesian view of the state of nature. Hobbes' state of nature is depicted famously as a "warre of all against all" wherein life is "nasty, brutish, and short". Mills argues that on one level Hobbes' depiction may seem "non-racist" and "equally applicable to everybody"; however, he asks us to consider Hobbes' view that "there was never such a time, nor condition of warre as this', nor was this condition ever the general state of humankind throughout the world" (Mills 1997, 64–5). Nevertheless, Hobbes asserts that "there are many places, where they live so now,'" for example "'the savage people in many places of *America*'" (Mills 1997, 64–5). Mills finds Hobbes assertion ironic insofar as "a nonwhite people, indeed the very nonwhite people upon whose land his fellow Europeans were then encroaching, is his only real-life example of people in a state of nature" (Mills 1997, 65). Hobbes continues that "'though there had never been any time, wherein particular men were in a condition of warre one against another,' there is 'in all times' a state of 'continuall jealousies' between kings and persons of sovereign authority". Mills challenges (1997, 65): "How could it simultaneously be the case that 'there had never been' any such literal state-of-nature war, when in the previous paragraph he had just said that some *were* living like that now?".

Mills states (1997, 65–6) that "this minor mystery can be cleared up once we recognise that there is a tacit racial logic in the text: the *literal* state of nature is reserved for nonwhites; for whites the state of nature is *hypothetical*". Herein lays the dualism that Mills argues inheres in social contract theses: there is one set of assumptions for whites and another for nonwhites. Mills asserts that for Hobbes

> the conflict between whites is the conflict between those with *sovereigns*, that is, those who are already (and have always been) in society. From this conflict, one can extrapolate … to what might happen in the absence of a ruling sovereign. But really we know that whites are too rational to allow this to happen to *them*. So the most notorious state of nature in the contractarian literature—the bestial war of all against all—is really a *nonwhite figure*, a racial object lesson for the more rational whites, whose superior grasp of natural law (here in its prudential rather than altruistic version) will enable them to take the necessary steps to avoid it and not to behave as 'savages'.
>
> *Mills (1997, 66)*

Mills views Hobbes as a transitional figure "caught between feudal absolutism and the rise of parliamentarianism, who uses the contract now classically associated with the emergence of liberalism to defend absolutism"; but he contends that Hobbes is transitional in another way given that "in mid-seventeenth century Britain the imperial project was not yet so fully developed that the intellectual apparatus of racial subordination had been completely elaborated" (Mills 1997, 66). In such a context, "Hobbes remains enough of a racial egalitarian that, while singling out Native Americans for his real-life example, he suggests that without a sovereign *even Europeans* could descend to their state, and that the absolutist government appropriate for nonwhites could also be appropriate for whites" (Mills 1997, 66). For Mills,

> the uproar that greeted his work can be seen as attributable at least in part to this moral/political suggestion. The spread of colonialism would consolidate an intellectual world in which this bestial state of nature would be reserved for nonwhite savages, to be despotically governed, while civil Europeans would enjoy the benefits of liberal parliamentarianism. *The Racial Contract began to rewrite the social contract.*
>
> *Mills (1997, 66–7)*

Such an orientation would be more clearly articulated in the work of John Locke, which envisions a state of nature that stands in contrast to that of Hobbes and is, in fact, quite civil.

For Mills (1997, 67), Locke's state of nature is "moralised" and "normatively regulated by traditional (altruistic, nonprudential) natural law" and is one in which both private property and money exist. He notes that "Locke famously argues that God gave the world 'to the use of the Industrious and Rational', which qualities were indicated by labour. So while industrious and rational Englishmen were toiling away at home, in America, by contrast, one found 'wild woods and uncultivated wast[e] ... left to Nature' by the idle Indians" (Mills 1997, 67). Failing to add value to the land through "industrious and rational" production, Native Americans secure only non-property rights to the land, "thereby rendering their territories normatively open for seizure once those who have long since *left* the state of nature (Europeans) encounter them" (Mills 1997, 67). In this way, Locke provided a normative rationalisation for "white civilization's conquest of America" as well as "other white settler states" (Mills 1997, 67).

Locke's dualism is applicable to slavery as well. Mills notes that, "in the *Second Treatise*, Locke defends slavery resulting from a just war, for example, a defensive war against aggression", but while "Locke explicitly opposes hereditary slavery and the enslavement of wives and children", he "had investments in the slave-trading Royal Africa Company and earlier assisted in writing the slave constitution of Carolina". Mills concludes that

> one could argue that the Racial Contract manifests itself here in an astonishing inconsistency, which could be resolved by the supposition that Locke saw blacks as not fully human and thus as subject to a different set of normative rules. Or perhaps the same Lockean moral logic that covered Native Americans can be extended to blacks also. They weren't appropriating their home continent of Africa; they're not rational; they can be enslaved.
>
> *(Mills 1997, 67–8)*

Turning to Rousseau, Mills asserts that his conceptualisation seems even less racialised than Hobbes' or Locke's given that it is peopled by the "noble savage". In Rousseau's *Discourse on Inequality* it seems clear that everyone regardless of race had been in the state of nature (and therefore 'savage'); nevertheless, Mills points out that "a careful reading of the text reveals, once again, crucial racial distinctions". His main point is that "the only natural savages cited are nonwhite savages, examples of European savages being restricted to reports of feral children raised by wolves and bears, child-rearing practices (we are told) comparable to those of Hottentots and Caribs. (Europeans are so intrinsically civilized that it takes upbringing by animals to turn them into savages)" (Mills 1997, 68). He adds that, "for Europe, savagery is in the dim distant past", since Europe had long since developed expertise in metallurgy and agriculture, which Rousseau argues are among the harbingers of civilisation, which he speculated gave rise to the advanced civilisation of Europe over other regions. "But Rousseau", Mills adds,

> was writing more than two hundred years after the European encounter with the great Aztec and Inca empires; wasn't there at least a little metallurgy and agriculture in evidence there? Apparently not: 'Both metallurgy and agriculture were unknown to the savages of America, who have always therefore remained savages'. So even what might initially seem to be a more open environmental determinism, which would open the door to racial egalitarianism rather than racial hierarchy, degenerates into massive historical

amnesia and factual misrepresentation, driven by the presupposition of the Racial Contract.

(Mills 1997, 69)

Mills' major point is that

> even if some of Rousseau's nonwhite savages are 'noble', physically and psychologically healthier than the Europeans of the degraded and corrupt society produced by the real-life bogus contract, they are still *savages*. So they are primitive beings who are not actually part of civil society, barely raised above animals, without language.

(Mills 1997, 60)

It is necessary to leave the state of nature in order to become "fully human moral agents, beings capable of justice" (Mills 1997, 69). Therefore, Rousseau's

> praise for nonwhite savages is a limited paternalistic praise, tantamount to admiration for healthy animals, in no way to be taken to imply their equality, let alone superiority, to the civilised European of the ideal polity. The underlying racial dichotomisation and hierarchy of civilised and savage remains quite clear.

(Mills 1997, 69)

The racist dualism of the theses of the social contract theorists informed IR discourse on anarchy, which drew on their conceptions of the state of nature. Mills contends that Kant's conceptualisation of the social contract is in some ways the best illustration of the racial contract and its centrality to social contract theses as they inform IR theory. Drawing on the work of Emmanuel Eze, which traces the racist claims that are both implicit and explicit in Kant's writings, he argues that the orthodox view of Kant as the faithful father of ethical philosophy is "radically misleading", such that "the nature of Kantian 'persons' and the Kantian 'contract' must really be rethought". This conceptualisation subsumes his major theoretical arguments from his notions of the state of nature to his conception of "republican peace", which is viewed widely as prefiguring the democratic peace thesis (Mills 1997, 70). For example, according to Kant, blacks are inferior to whites. He is clear that "so fundamental is the difference between these two races of man (whites and Negroes), and it appears to be as great in regard to mental capacities as in color" (Kant 1960, 111). For Kant, "talent" was an "'essential', natural ingredient for aptitude in higher rational and moral achievement" that was unequally distributed across races, with whites possessing the greatest "gift" of talent and blacks largely lacking it (Eze 1995, 227). In his *Anthropology from a Pragmatic Point of View*, Kant argues that whites occupy the highest position in his "racial rational and moral order", "'followed by the 'yellow', the 'black', and then the 'red'" and this rank reflected their relative "capacity to realize reason and rational-moral perfectibility through education" (Eze 1995, 218). Therefore, "it cannot ... be argued that skin color for Kant was merely a physical characteristic" but "evidence of an unchanging and unchangeable moral quality" (Eze 1995, 218–19). Mills (1997, 71) agrees that, "in complete opposition to the image of his work that has come down to us and is standardly taught in introductory ethics courses, full personhood for Kant is actually dependent on race".

In Kant's (1960, 113) *Observations of the Feeling of the Beautiful and Sublime*, he affirms that "this fellow was quite black from head to foot, a clear proof that what he said was stupid". He adds that "the Negroes of Africa have by nature no feeling that rises above the trifling" (Kant 1960, 110). For Kant they are incapable of achieving the level of rationality required of moral agents. Negroes "can be educated but only as servants (slaves); that is they allow themselves to be trained" (Eze 1995, 215). Such training does not require reason but only repetition. Cognitive inabilities of blacks require of their masters a stern disposition and informed instruction in their catechism that Kant does not hesitate to supply in providing guidance on the proper method of punishment for blacks:

> Kant "advises us to use a split bamboo cane instead of a whip, so that the 'negro' will suffer a great deal of pains (because of the 'negro's' thick skin, he would not be racked with sufficient agonies through a whip) but without dying'. To beat 'the Negro' efficiently therefore requires 'a cane but it has to be split one, so that the cane will cause wounds large enough that prevent suppuration underneath the 'negro's' thick skin'".
>
> *(Eze 1995, 215)*

Neugebauer (1990, 264) points out that Kant's advice to use a split bamboo cane instead of a whip was intended to ensure that the slave suffered – "because of the 'negro's' thick skin, he would not be racked with sufficient agonies through a whip" – without actually dying. Only if the black person is not fully human can one reconcile this instruction with Kant's imperative that we always treat humanity, whether in our own person or that of any other, never simply as a means but always as an end, as well. Blacks do not meet the minimal requirements for moral agency and thus of personhood for Kant; personhood, for Kant, is circumscribed by his white supremacism.

Nevertheless, prominent democratic peace advocates such as Ray (1995, 3) insist that Kant provides "an important symbolic as well as substantive source of inspiration for advocates of the democratic peace proposition". For Doyle (1997, 302), Kant's thesis "lays a special claim to what world politics is and can be: a state of peace", and it "claims a special property right in what shapes the politics of Liberal states – liberty and democracy". Russett (1993, 4) is even more adoring of Kant's "republican constitutionalism", which he asserts is "compatible with basic contemporary understandings of democracy". But Kant's ethical and political theory is unequivocally racist: it excises whole swathes of humanity from its processes. The republicanism Kant espouses – in contrast to Russett's claims – is quite a distance from democracy popularly conceived: it is a Herrenvolk democracy for whites that provides for "perpetual peace". Mills (1997, 72) explains that

> the embarrassing fact for the white West (which doubtless explains its concealment) is that their most important moral theorist of the past three hundred years is also the foundational theorist in the modern period of the division between Herrenvolk and Untermenschen, persons and subpersons, upon which Nazi theory would later draw. Modern moral theory and modern racial theory have the same father [emphasis in original].

Mainstream IR theory in general and the democratic peace literature in particular are silent on this aspect of Kant's writing and its implications for his "perpetual peace". Similarly, constructivist arguments such as proffered by Wendt ignore this aspect of Kantian thought that should inform their understanding of a "Kantian" state of nature that they insist is orientated toward amicable relations among states and peoples. Even realist counterarguments to the Kantian claims of liberal and constructivist neo-Kantians rarely evoke Kant's racism as a factor undermining his thesis.

What should be clear is that the social contract theses that underlie prominent conceptions of the global anarchy in which world politics is situated for many realists, idealists/liberals, constructivists, and some Marxists as well, suggest a racist dualism that rests on a fundamental dichotomy with respect to the emergence of society and, thus, the conduct of social affairs for whites, who are constructed as developmentally superior, and blacks, who are constructed as developmentally inferior. Having discussed briefly the racist dualism in prominent conceptions of the state of nature derived from Hobbes, Locke, Rousseau and Kant, in the next section we discuss how the racism that inheres in the social contract theses became central to the theses of IR theorists who drew on them to devise the paradigms that continue to orientate the field.

Anarchy and world politics: the tropical roots of IR theory

A racist conceptualisation of anarchy became the centerpiece of the major paradigms of world politics: realism and liberalism/idealism, and their recent offshoot, constructivism. Today, realism is the dominant paradigm in world politics; or, specifically, neorealism, which rests on Waltz's revision of the traditional realism of Schuman and Morgenthau. Neorealism asserts that the international system is anarchic and that states are the dominant actors. The anarchic structure of the system mandates a self-help orientation among the states because without an authority above them, individual states must ensure their own security. In such a system, security is the basic objective of states and power is essential to achieving state aims and resisting those of others. Realists argue that states seek to maximise their power to ensure their security; but, the security dilemma ensures that, ironically, each state's pursuit of its own security leads ultimately to its greater insecurity. Balance of power practices become essential in this conflict-laden global system in which power – especially military power – is the ultimate arbiter of conflicts of interest. Liberalism (or idealism) – the paradigmatic counterpoise of realism – is similarly grounded in a preoccupation with anarchy. Idealists accept the view that the global system is anarchic and that anarchy could lead to security dilemmas, balance of power politics, and interstate war, but unlike realists, they do not accept that these are the inevitable outcomes of international interactions. Grounded in the Enlightenment belief in the perfectibility of the individual, they transferred their view of domestic politics to the international realm and argued that conflict and wars were largely a result of "bad" institutions such as autocratic regimes, and that by democratising regimes, facilitating international commerce, and encouraging international institutions then international cooperation would ensue. In this view, states are not destined to predation borne of anarchy, the persistent pursuit of power and the security dilemma, as realists maintain. Instead, the spread of democracy, liberal international trade policies, and international law would allow states to overcome the security dilemma and cooperate with each other. Foreign policy is assumed to reflect domestic policy such that states that are peaceful domestically (e.g. democracies) are more likely to be peaceful abroad and those that are more violent domestically (e.g. autocracies) are more likely to be violent abroad.

One of the key idealists of the twentieth century, who is also viewed as one of the progenitors of the field of IR, was Woodrow Wilson (Ray 1995, 7). But the view that Wilson – especially Wilson of the post-World War I period – established IR is more received wisdom than actual fact, obfuscating less salutary but more significant factors leading to the field's emergence. As noted above, at its birth, IR was concerned with issues of anarchy and power; however, this anarchy was largely assumed to inhere in the "primitive" polities of the "inferior" races – primarily in the tropical domains of what we would now consider the "third world". At the same time, the relevant power was that wielded by the "civilised" white race through their "modern" states. The mechanism of "efficient" and "rational" colonial administration, many early IR theorists maintained, could ensure that "anarchy" did not spread to the "modern" world and lead to violence among the major (white) powers. So the concerns among realists and idealists with anarchy are grounded in a racist discourse that is concerned with the obligations of superior peoples to impose order on the anarchic domains of inferior peoples in order to prevent the chaos presumed to be endemic in the latter from spilling over into the former's territories or self-proclaimed spheres of interest. Similarly, the realist and idealist concern with power was grounded in a racist discourse concerned largely with the power of whites to control the tropics, subjugate its people, steal its resources, and superimpose themselves through colonial administration. Therefore, the roots of realism – the dominant paradigm in world politics, are grounded in a rationalisation for the construction of a hierarchical racial order to be imposed upon the anarchy allegedly arising from the "tropics", which begs for rational colonial administration from whites. It is little more than an intellectual justification for colonialism and imperialism in the guise of the "white man's burden". Also, the roots of idealism are found less in idealised versions of classical liberal precepts regarding the perfectibility of humanity, the primacy of "God-given" individual rights, and the spread of democracy, free trade, and the rule of law, than with the imposition of a white racist order on indigenous peoples throughout Africa, Asia, Latin America, and the Caribbean.

Given the imperative for "progress" and "development" and the view that the unspoiled lands were not being sufficiently exploited by the indigenous peoples, realists and idealists agreed that the incentive for imperialist conquest could lead to conflict among whites; therefore, a rational distribution of territory and its appropriate administration by colonial agencies was necessary. Realists and idealists disagreed on the implications of the global system for the interaction of white peoples and their states and political institutions, but often they accepted or justified the subjugation of non-whites by whites. In this way they found congruence in their policy recommendations for the domestic and international spheres at least in this regard: they supported white racial domination through racial discrimination of non-white minorities at home and white imperialism through racial domination of non-white polities abroad. Nowhere were these racist policies more evident than in Africa – and in the treatment of the racial minorities of the African diaspora in Western Europe and the Americas.

While realism and idealism converge on a white supremacist logic that has been evident since the establishment of the field of IR, I maintain that this racism was not only present at the creation of the field but continues to inform the major paradigms, primarily – though not uniquely – through their conceptions of anarchy. For example, Sampson (2002, 429) argues that "the discourse of international politics employs a particular conception of anarchy – tropical anarchy – that portrays the international system as 'primitive'". This "tropical anarchy", the social contract theorists assumed, was the primeval condition of non-white peoples, which Kidd (1898), among many others, rationalised as a basis for Western colonialism. The anarchical world – the state of nature – was the preserve of non-Europeans, primitive peoples. Sampson views anarchy as a "trope" more than a "natural state of affairs"; but he is clear that, "while scholars may define anarchy variously, the primitive images that *anarchy* evokes remain constant". Not only are the paradigmatic roots of IR theory saturated by the racist stream of tropical anarchy, Sampson is even more explicit that "the foundation upon which much of the discipline rests is not anarchy but rather an image of primitive society popularised by British social anthropologists during the 1930s and 1940s" (Sampson 2002, 429). For example, Sampson argues that Waltz's thesis on system structure derives from the obsolete, anarchic, and in many ways racist conceptualisation of African primitive society of anthropologist S. F. Nadel. Sampson (2002, 444) does not argue that Waltz's definition of system structure – so crucial to his rendering of "structural realism –borrows from Nadel, "but the structure Waltz employs *is Nadel's*" (emphasis in original). Waltz analogises Nadel's view of the structure of African primitive societies to the global structure in which international politics takes place. He adds that Waltz "derived all three components of his theory of international politics (ordering principles, functional differentiation, and the distribution of material capabilities) form a theory of primitive society published by Nadel in 1957" (Sampson 2002, 430); and he documents Waltz's allusions to Nadel in his *Theory of International Politics* as well as in prior and subsequent works.

Sampson notes (2002, 431) that "[p]rimitive societies have long intrigued theorists of international politics" but "[n]one of these theorists, however, challenge the categorisation of systems, societies, or peoples as primitive". While since the 1960s anthropologists have "questioned the 'ambiguous and inconsistent' notion of primitive society", the field of IR "continues to recycle definitions constructed nearly a century before" (Sampson 2002: 431). He explains:

> In early anthropology and social theory, primitive *systems* are portrayed as decentralised, disorganised, and anarchic; modern ones are centralised, well organised, and hierarchic. Primitive *societies* are simple, traditional, uncivilised, premodern, and functionally undifferentiated; they resemble nonvertebrates like 'polyps' or; if they are slightly segmented, 'earthworms.' Modern societies, on the other hand, are complex, advanced, civilised, and functionally differentiated; they have skeletons, central nervous systems, discrete organs, and heads with the capacity to think and act rationally (unlike primitive societies, where actions are products of passionate reflexes). Primitive *peoples* are described as devoid of individuality, remarkable only through their homogeneity.
>
> *(Sampson 2002, 431)*

For Sampson, there are several "dangers of employing claims about a supposedly primitive society to the foundation for analysis" (Sampson 2002, 429). First, "primitive systems and societies are inventions that no longer serve as valid categories of classification" (Sampson 2002, 429). Second, in taking an explicit focus of social anthropology, the characteristics of "primitive African" social systems, and transposing them "into an implicit theoretical assumption" about the structure of the global system, "we prejudge the nature of international politics" (Sampson 2002, 429). Third, "using primitive society as the starting point for scholarship creates an inescapable logic that reduces possible policy responses to a simple choice: either maintain the primitive's status quo or civilise the world" (Sampson 2002, 429). For Sampson (2002, 429), Waltz's neorealism "selects the first option", and Wendt's social constructivism "chooses the second". He notes that "[a]t first glance, one might find it ironic that a theory 'necessarily based on the great powers' and 'states that make the most difference' owes its existence to anthropological fieldwork in Africa" (Sampson 2002, 430). Beyond irony, "Waltz's appropriation of a theory originally intended to help colonial administrators control primitive African societies produces an image of international politics that privileges power over progress, equilibrium over change, and preventative measures over curative ones" (Sampson 2002, 430).

The neorealist conception of system structure is generally accepted by liberal theorists, who mainly differentiate among states – particularly democratic states, which they argue have assembled a separate peace among themselves, thus overcoming the Hobbesian anarchy and replacing it with a Kantian one. It also converges with the view of neoliberal institutionalists, who largely accept the realist version of homo politicus as an egoistic, rational, expected utility maximiser while retaining the liberal focus on interstate cooperation; however, in this conceptualisation cooperation is not contingent on democracy but the actions of state and non-state actors attempting to address recurring problems of market failure (Henderson 1999; 2002). International anarchy, sovereignty, and self-help regularise the behavior of states throughout the system, with interstate cooperation emerging from a homogenisation process, ironically, similar to that proposed by Waltz (1979, 73–7); but, in the liberal view, cooperation ensues from a reduction in transaction costs, decreased uncertainty, and the formation of institutions to reward cooperation and punish non-cooperation – international regimes. Importantly, (neo)realist and (neo)liberal arguments have as their point of departure the global anarchy of Waltz, which is the tropical anarchy of primitive African social systems.

For social constructivists the convergence with Waltz's system structure is even more apparent. The differentiation that Waltz fails to observe in world politics is captured in Wendt's distinction between Hobbesian, Lockean, and Kantian international systems. Wendt views the essential relationships among sovereigns in a Hobbesian anarchy as one of enemies, while in a Lockean anarchy it is one of rivals, and lastly, in a Kantian anarchy it is one of friends. His most culturally evolved system, the Kantian, is one shared primarily by the Western powers, while others exist within Lockean and Hobbesian contexts. This meant that only the Western states could be entrusted to transfer to the third world the requisites for a higher level of social evolution to elevate them out of their lower condition.[6] Therefore, "the 'burden" of structural transformation, the responsibility of 'teaching' the rest of the world how to evolve, falls squarely on the shoulders of great powers. Less powerful states have little or no hope of transforming the international system on their own" (Waltz 1979, 449). Sampson characterises Wendt's "social theory of international relations" as "remarkably un-international". He states that while Wendt chastises Waltz's study for lacking a reference to "role" in its index, Sampson counters that "discounting Montezuma and the Aztecs, one might say the same of Wendt's social theory for the entire 'Third World'" (Sampson 2002, 448–9). He adds that

> Wendt's text is largely an attempt to explain how Europe and the United States pulled themselves out of 'nature's realm'. It tells us how NATO and Europe evolved into complex social kinds through a process dubbed 'cultural selection'. There is no mention of non-Western social kinds. It is not even clear whether African or Asian states could 'evolve' without the help of bigger, more powerful benefactors.
>
> *(Sampson 2002, 449)*

Sampson notes that counter to the title of Wendt's most popular article, "anarchy is only what *some* states make of it". In fact it is as constrained by the logic of tropical anarchy as is Waltz's; only that where Waltz rationalises the stasis of the status quo equilibrium (i.e. the balance of power, or, by analogy, the maintenance of Western power in the colonies), Wendt rationalises the transformation of the status quo within limits governed by the status quo powers (i.e. Kantian social evolution, or, by analogy, the establishment of colonial administration in the colonies as a function of the "white man's burden" or mission civilatrice). He concludes that,

> by arguing that 'anarchy is what states make of it', Wendt suggests that powerful, civilised states have the capacity to lift weaker, primitive states out of the heart of darkness and into the light of democratic peace. Thus super-powers like the United States should shoulder the global burden of civilising international society. This reverses Waltz's conclusions. Waltz seeks system maintenance and equilibrium. Wendt seeks transformation. Waltz privileges power over progress. Wendt suggests the opposite.
>
> *(Sampson 2002, 450)*

Waltz's framework resurrects anthropology's misrepresentation of African political systems of the 1950s and Wendt reproduces anthropological debates of the 1930s and 1940s (Sampson 2002, 451). Both paradigms converge on a notion of tropical anarchy, which reinforces a racist dualism in world politics that is manifest, in turn, in prominent theses that derive from these paradigms.

Summary

Thus, it is not difficult to trace the historical and contemporary role and impact of racism in IR theory. Racism has not only informed the paradigms of world politics, it was fundamental to the conceptualisation of its key theoretical touchstone: anarchy. The social contract theorists rooted their conceptualisations of the state of nature in a broader "racial contract" that dichotomised humanity racially and established a white supremacist hierarchy in their foundational conceptions of society. Late nineteenth and early twentieth-century IR theorists built on this racist dualism as they constructed their conception of a global anarchy and the role of "civilised" whites to provide, maintain, and ensure order within it by a system of international power relations among whites – or at minimum, dominated by whites, and a system of colonial subjugation for non-whites – or those nonwhites who failed to successfully resist their domination militarily. The impact and role of racism is manifest through the major paradigms operative today – realism, neorealism, liberalism/idealism, and constructivism – mainly through their continued reliance on a racist conception of anarchy; in the case of neorealism through its grounding in African primitivism, while for Marxism, its reliance on and "normalising" of a Eurocentric teleology of economic development for the world.

To be sure, the dualism at the broad theoretical level of paradigms underscores, guides, and informs the more specific dichotomies at the level of theories, models, and theses that are derived from these paradigms – especially those that are applied to Africa's political processes, and those of other regions as well. In the case of African international relations, they both contextualise and rationalise a black African primitivism juxtaposed to a white Western progressivism, a black African peculiaristic savagery and a white Western universalist humanity, resulting in an enduring African tribal/ethnic warfare frame of reference contrasted to an evolved Western democratic peace; in each case a static ossified ahistorical permanence contrasted to a dynamic evolving transcendence. One result is that one must endure what are considered to be "meaningful" or "appropriate" or even "incisive" or "cutting-edge" discussions of Africa's domestic and international politics that have as their point of departure loose and often obtuse references to "hearts of darkness", "greed versus grievance", "tribal warfare", "warlordism", "frontiersmen", or a litany of other metaphors that would not pass the editor's desk at most top-tier academic journals as legitimate contexts through which to observe and examine contemporary armed conflicts in the Western world[7]. Notably, rarely do those same journals publish work on the historical and enduring racism embedded in the major paradigms of world politics or discuss the implications of such a condition if it were shown to obtain.

In fact, the "norm against noticing" white racism is so intense that it engenders a "silencing" of those who would raise it; or it ensures against publication in mainstream outlets for such work except that it provides appropriate euphemisms for the atrocities associated with white racism – especially against blacks – or the requisite "balance" to emphasise the role of non-whites in their own subjugation – as if white supremacism and the imperialism, colonialism, neocolonialism and internal colonialism that it employed against Africans, Asians, and Native Americans are somehow the responsibility of groups other than the whites who created it, maintained it, and continue to profit from it. Thus, the racist dualism in world politics creates, in turn, a dual quandary for IR scholars and many Africanists seeking to publish in Western journals – and many non-Western ones, too – wherein white racist expectations of the appropriateness of certain lines of inquiry often limits the discourse of African politics to hollow phraseology and meaningless metaphors, while they simultaneously check informed challenges to historical and contemporary expressions, practices, and institutions of white racism in academia by ensuring that such racism is rarely confronted in the major publications in IR/world politics in clear and direct terms.

Another result is that it leaves IR scholars teaching a history of the development of international relations that ignores the salience of colonialism as the centerpiece in the origins of the field. That is, in continuing to teach the fiction that the field emerged following the devastation of World War I, as "idealists" led by Wilson and others such as Lowes Dickinson, Zimmern, Giddings, and Kerr sought to provide the institutional checks on realpolitik that was implicated in the "war to end all wars", we belie the reality of the centrality of colonialism, race development, and white racial supremacy to the development of the academic field of IR. Thus, our narrative creates an academic fiction that hovers outside of its own history. The presence of this narrative is as much a testament to the white supremacism that is a centrepiece of the field given that its role is to ensure a "norm against noticing" the centrality of white racism in world politics while simultaneously "silencing" or making marginal those who would focus on the importance of white racism in the development of the field of IR/world politics, or those who would raise this as a legitimate research focus for the most sensible of reasons: it happens to be true.

Conclusion

In this chapter I have attempted to address the centrality of racism in international relations (IR) theory. It examines the extent to which realism, liberalism, and constructivism are orientated by racist precepts grounded in the intellectual foundation of IR. Specifically, a racist dualism inheres within the assumptions informing the foundational construct of IR: namely, anarchy; and due to the centrality of this construct within prominent theses that draw on it, racist precepts have an enduring impact on IR theory today. In sum, a racist latticework undergirds major theoretical frameworks that inform research and policy in IR. Theses that rest on racist claims are not simply odious, but are untethered to the reality (i.e. world politics itself) that they purport to explain. Vitalis (2000) is correct that there is a "norm against noticing" white supremacism in mainstream IR discourse. The failure to address it leaves IR analysts ill-equipped to address its intellectual history, its theoretical development, and its prospects for theory building that will generate meaningful research and policy for the vast majority of the world's people.

Notes

1 These sentiments were echoed in the arguments of prominent cultural relativists such as Bronislaw Malinowski, and they also resonated in the arguments of such prominent political scientists as Burgess and such sociologists as Parks. For example, Furedi (1998, 93) points out that 'Malinowski was as scathing of Nordic supremacist theories as he was of ideas of race equality'. Malinowski rationalized support for the 'colour bar' in his 'A plea for an effective colour bar' in 1931. Burgess proffered a white supremacist hierarchy of races in his *The foundations of political science*. Park's social contact thesis portended racial conflict as a result of contact between races.

2 On racial formation and re-formation, see Omi and Winant (1996). For a critique of the mystification of white supremacism in racial formation theses, see Henderson (2007, 340–343).

3 Research on the social construction of racial identity also falls within this category although its focus is on the role of the social rather than the physical environment in the construction of racial categories (for example, Winant 2001).

4 Exceptions include Vitalis (2000) and Henderson (1995; 2007).

5 There are exceptions: *The Helsinki Sanomat* international edition (12 August 2004) reports that Tatu Vanhanen, former professor of political science at the University of Tampere in Finland (and father of Finnish Prime Minister Matti Vanhanen), who studies the role of democratization among African states, caused a stir when he insinuated that evolution has made Europeans and North Americans more intelligent than Africans. He

argued that African poverty is largely a result of the low IQ of Africans as compared with Europeans. Similar racist arguments are found in the strain of sociobiology and biopolitics that focuses on international affairs.

6 See Vitalis (2000) for a critique of racist conceptions in popular liberal academic arguments on the evolution of Western 'humanitarian' norms.

7 For an examination of these issues with respect to Africa's international conflicts, see Henderson (2015).

Bibliography

Anderson, Carole (2003) *Eyes Off the Prize: The United Nations and the African American Struggle for Human Rights, 1944–1955*. Cambridge: Cambridge University Press.

Blatt, Jessica (2004) 'To Bring out the Best that is in Their Blood': Race, Reform, and Civilization in the Journal of Race Development (1910–19). *Ethnic and Racial Studies*, 27 (5), 691–709.

Boas, Franz (1911) *The Mind of Primitive Man*. New York, NY: Macmillan.

Buell, Raymond Leslie (1929) *International Relations*. Rev. ed. New York, NY: Henry Holt.

Bunche, Ralph (1936) *A World View of Race*. Albany, NY: J. B. Lyons.

Cell, John (1982) *The Highest Stage of White Supremacy*. Cambridge: Cambridge University Press.

Depelchin, Jacques (2005) *Silences in African History*. Dar es Salaam: Mkuki na Nyoyta.

Deutsch, Karl (1970) Research Problems on Race in Intranational and International Relations. In Shepperd, G. W. Jr. and LeMelle, T. J. (eds) *Race Among Nations*. Lexington, MA: DC Heath.

Doty, Roxanne (1998) The Bounds of 'Race' in International Relations. In Jacquin-Berdal, Dominique, Oros, Andrew and Verweij, Marco (eds) *Culture in World Politics*. New York, NY: St Martin's Press, 134–55.

Dower, John (1986) *War Without Mercy: Race and Power in the Pacific War*. New York, NY: Random House.

Doyle, Michael (1997) *Ways of War and Peace*. New York, NY: W. W. Norton.

Du Bois, W. E. B. (1915) The African Roots of War. *Atlantic Monthly*, 115 (5), 707–14.

——(1961 [1903]) *The Souls of Black Folk*. New York, NY: Fawcett.

——(1987 [1946]) *The World and Africa*. New York, NY: International Publishers.

Elkins, Caroline (2004) *Imperial Reckoning: The Untold Story of Britain's Gulag in Kenya*. New York, NY: Henry Holt & Co.

Eze, Emmanuel (1995) The Color of Reason: The Idea of 'Race' in Kant's Anthropology. In Faull, Katherine (ed.) *Anthropology and the German Enlightenment*. Lewisburg, PA: Bucknell University, 200–41.

Fredrickson, George (1982) *White Supremacy: A Comparative Study of American and South African History*. New York, NY: Oxford University Press.

Furedi, Frank (1998) *The Silent War, Imperialism and the Changing Perception of Race*. New Brunswick, NJ: Rutgers University Press.

Giddings, Franklin (1898) Imperialism? *Political Science Quarterly*, 13 (4), 585–605.

Harris, Joseph (ed.) (1982) *Global Dimensions of the African Diaspora*. Washington, DC: Howard University Press.

Henderson, Errol (1995) *Afrocentrism and World Politics: Towards a New Paradigm*. Westport, CT: Praeger.

——(1999) Neoidealism and the Democratic Peace. *Journal of Peace Research*, 36 (2), 203–31.

——(2002) *Democracy and War: The End of an Illusion?* Boulder, CO: Lynne Rienner Press.

——(2007) Navigating the Muddy Waters of the Mainstream: Tracing the Mystification of Racism in International Relations. In Rich, Wilbur (ed.) *The State of the Political Science Discipline: An African-American Perspective*. Philadelphia, PA. Temple University Press, 325–63.

——(2015) *African Realism? International Relations Theory and Africa's Wars in the Post-colonial Era*. Lanham, MD: Rowman & Littlefield.

Hochschild, Adam (1998) *King Leopold's Ghost: A Story of Greed, Terror, and Heroism in Colonial Africa*. New York, NY: Houghton Mifflin.

Hunt, Michael (1987) *Ideology and US Foreign Policy*. New Haven, CT: Yale University Press.

Iriye, Akira (1997) *Cultural Internationalism and World Order*. Baltimore, MD: Johns Hopkins University Press.

Kant, Immanuel (1960) *Observations on the Feeling of the Beautiful and Sublime*, translated by John T. Goldthwait. Berkeley, CA: University of California.

——(1974) *Anthropology From a Pragmatic Point of View*, translated by Mary J. Gregor. The Hague: Nijhoff.

Kerr, P. H. (1916) Political Relations between Advanced and Backward Peoples. In Grant, A. J., Greenwood, Arthur, Hughes, J. D. I., Kerr, P. H. and Urquhart, F. F. (eds) *An Introduction to the Study of International Relations*. London: Macmillan and Co.

Kidd, Benjamin (1894) *Social Evolution*. New York, NY: Macmillan and Co.

——(1898) *The Control of the Tropics*. New York, NY: Macmillan and Co.

Krishna, Sankaran (2001) Race, Amnesia, and the Education of International Relations. *Alternatives*, 26 (4), 373–76.

Lauren, Paul (1996) *Power and Prejudice*. 2nd edn. Boulder, CO: Westview.

LeMelle, Tilden (1972) 'Race, International Relations, US Foreign Policy, and the African Liberation Struggle. *Journal of Black Studies*, 3 (1), 95–109.

Locke, Alain (1992 [1916] *Race Contacts and Interracial Relations: Lectures on the Theory and Practice of Race*. Jeffrey Stewart (ed.). Washington, DC: Howard University Press.

Long, David and Brian Schmidt (eds) (2005) *Imperialism and Internationalism in Tthe Discipline of International Relations*. Albany, NY: State University of New York Press.

Maclean, John (1981) Political Theory, International Theory, and Problems of Ideology. *Millennium*, 10 (2), 102–25.

Mamdani, Mahmood (1996) *Citizen and Subject*. Princeton, NJ: Princeton University Press.

Marx, Anthony (1998) *Making Race and Nation*. Cambridge: Cambridge University Press.

Mills, Charles (1997) *The Racial Contract*. Ithaca, NY: Cornell University.

Morgenthau, Hans (1948) *Politics among Nations*. New York, NY: Alfred A. Knopf.

Neugebauer, Christian (1990) 'The racism of Hegel and Kant'. In Oruka, Odera (ed.) *Sage Philosophy*. Leiden: E. J. Brill, 259–72.

Olson, William and Groom, A. J. R. (1991) *International Relations Then and Now*. London: HarperCollins.

Omi, William and Winant, Howard (1994) *Racial Formation in the United States*. 2nd edn. New York, NY: Routledge.

Persaud, Randolph and Walker, R. B. J. (2001) Apertura: Race in International Relations. *Alternatives*, 26 (4), 373–76.

Ray, James (1995) *Democracy and International Conflict*. Columbia, SC: University of South Carolina.

Reeves, Julie (2004) *Culture and International Relations: Narratives, Natives, and Tourists*. New York, NY: Routledge.

Reinsch, Paul (1900) *World Politics at the End of the Nineteenth Century*. New York, NY: Macmillan.

——(1902) *Colonial Government*. New York, NY: Macmillan.

——(1905a) The Negro Race and European Civilization. *American Journal of Sociology*, 11 (2), 145–67.

——(1905b) *Colonial Administration*. New York, NY: Macmillan.

Rodney, Walter (1974) *How Europe Underdeveloped Africa*. Washington, DC: Howard University Press.

Russett, Bruce (1993) *Grasping the Democratic Peace*. Princeton, NJ: Princeton University Press.

Sampson, Aaron (2002) Tropical Anarchy: Waltz, Wendt, and the Way We Imagine International Politics. *Alternatives*, 27 (4), 429–57.

Schmidt, Brian (1998) *The Political Discourse of Anarchy*. Albany, NY: SUNY Press.

Shepherd, G. W. (1970) *Racial Influences on American Foreign Policy*. New York, NY: Basic Books.

Shepherd, G. W. and LeMelle, T. J. (eds) (1970) *Race among Nations*. Lexington, MA: DC Heath.

Stewart, Jeffrey (1992) Introduction. In Stewart, Jeffrey (ed.) *Alain Locke: Race Contacts and Interracial Relations*. Washington, DC: Howard University Press, xix–lix.

Tinker, Hugh (1977) *Race, Conflict, and the International Order*. London: Macmillan.

Vincent, R. J. (1982) Race in International Relations. *International Affairs*, 58 (4), 658–70.

Vitalis, Robert (2000) The Graceful and Generous Liberal Gesture: Making Racism Invisible in American International Relations. *Millennium*. 29 (2), 331–56.

——(2010) The Noble American Science of Imperial Relations and Its Laws of Race Development. *Comparative Studies in Society and History*, 52 (4), 909–38.

Walters, Ronald (1993) *Pan-Africanism in the African Diaspora*. Detroit, MI: Wayne State University Press.

Waltz, Kenneth (1979) *Theory of International Politics*. Reading, MA: Addison-Wesley.

Winant, Howard (2001) *The World is a Ghetto*. New York, NY: Basic Books.

Zimmern, Alfred (1926) *The Third British Empire*. London: Oxford University Press.

3

THROUGH, AGAINST, AND BEYOND THE RACIAL STATE

The transnational stratum of race

Debra Thompson

When W. E. B. Du Bois predicted that the problem of the twentieth century would be the problem of the colour line, he was in fact referring to a *global* colour line, 'the relations of the darker to the lighter races of men in Asia and Africa, in America and the islands of the sea' (Du Bois 1903, 13). Over a century later Du Bois' words need only be pluralised: colour lines and hierarchies abound world-wide. Together, the chapters of this volume are but one attempt to examine the formidable research paradigms that emerge from a serious and sustained consideration of the dynamics, processes, and consequences of the global colour line.

As noted in the introduction to this volume, mainstream international relations (IR) scholarship has been surprisingly silent on race. Given the astounding shift in international law from protecting the sovereignty of racism at the beginning of the twentieth century to openly combatting it by the beginning of the new millennium (Jones 2008), the persistence of global racial inequality in spite of institutionalised international commitments to principles of non-discrimination (Chowdhry and Nair 2002), North–South relations (Doty 1993), and racial discourse in foreign policy, immigration and security (Doty 1996; Lauren 1996; Persaud 2002), this dearth is particularly curious. Similarly, the conceptual substance of race in compara-tive political science is often domesticated and depoliticised. Race is typically and uncritically perceived as an apolitical force and a wholly domestic issue; so domestic, in fact, that even comparison between countries is difficult. The politics of colo-nialism, slavery, race-based immigration exclusions, the racial regulation of public and private life, socio-economic stratification along racial lines, anti-discrimination laws, and contemporary debates about multiculturalism, integration, citizenship, are most commonly associated with domestic politics within sovereign states. Where comparison does occur, regional parochialisms and orthodoxies prevail.

As it turns out, both IR and comparative politics suffer from the same malady: racial aphasia. This is not the same as amnesia, which indicates some unfortunate series of events that led to an unintentional forgetting of how the modern world system was founded on, and continues as, a hierarchical racial order. Racial amnesia obscures the power involved in purposeful evasion, suggesting that, like a B-list movie plot, we must have accidentally fallen, hit our heads, and forgotten our racist past. Amnesia disavows intent. Aphasia, on the other hand, indicates a calculated forgetting, an obstruction of discourse, language and speech. Ann Laura Stoler argues that France's colonial aphasia is 'a dismembering, a difficulty speaking, a difficulty generating a vocabulary that associates appropriate words and concepts with appropriate things', as well as a difficulty – though not necessarily an inability – of comprehending what is spoken (2011, 125). Similarly, recognising the reality of racial aphasia links our racist pasts to the still racist present, perhaps connected by collective silences as much as by the persistence of oppression, domination and inequality.

In fields dominated by racial aphasia, critical race scholars of IR and comparative politics face similar challenges. Institutions are largely perceived as colour blind, though they are more likely colour-coded. International bodies and states alike profess normative and legal commitments to racial equality, while racial stratification persists both between the developed and developing worlds and within most, if not all, racially heterogeneous societies. White supremacy as a global institution and racism as a pervasive social structure are obscured by the positivist dominance and focus on empiricism in IR and need to establish causality in comparative politics; as a result, racism is instead reduced to abhorrent individualistic acts or attitudes. The promise of the post-racial society is realised not through reparations or substantive equality but in the imposition of race-free discourses that keep international and domestic racial orders firmly entrenched.

Given racial aphasia – our collective inability to speak about race – and these common constraints, the purpose of this chapter is to suggest a way forward through these disciplinary (and disciplining) silos. Put another way, what do studies of race and racism in comparative politics and international relations have to learn from one another? The point is not to integrate insights from these two subfields, but rather to open the potential for meaningful dialogue and interdisciplinary exchange. I suggest that one viable set of research agendas – surely, among many others – is through a focus on race and racism as objects of inquiry in and of themselves and their consequences for international and domestic politics. Both comparative politics and IR have made substantial, though fragmented, progress in this endeavour. In particular, I engage the constructivist literature on norms and the comparative politics literature on the causal influence of ideas, demonstrating the potential that both hold to broaden our understandings of race as a transnational phenomenon. The first and second sections of this chapter draw from recent work in IR, comparative politics, sociology, history and critical race theory to offer a definition of race as a global norm or idea that exists in excess of national boundaries, which nonetheless carries ontological and material consequences. The third section considers three promising avenues of research in the exploration of the varied manifestations of race in international and domestic realms. I end with a brief discussion of continuing challenges and future research agendas in the comparative and international study of race.

Conceptualising race

In their ground-breaking work on racial formation in the United States, Michael Omi and Howard Winant (1994, 55) define race as

> a concept that signifies and symbolizes socio-political conflicts and interests in reference to different types of human bodies. Although the concept of race appeals to biologically based human characteristics (so-called phenotypes), selection of these particular human features for the purpose of racial signification is always and necessarily a social and historical process).

In essence, the concept of race is neither objective nor neutral. It is a complex of social meanings under constant reconstruction through processes in which the selection of biologically based human characteristics is highly social and historical. Problematically, this definition hinges on the idea that there are, in fact, racial differences among different types of bodies. Barnor Hesse (2007; 2011) warns that this reliance on corporeality is insufficient; the bodily identification of race is a *privileged metonym* for a larger idea of the constructed differences between Europeans and non-Europeans, intimately tied to both modernity and colonial rule.

Not only are skin colour and other morphological characteristics inadequate to delineate between different races, but their invocation is fundamentally part of the construct itself. There is power involved in constructing race. This power is not monopolised by the state; race is both embedded in and created by numerous practices of the state and society, however defined, and is under constant renegotiation. The meaning of race is both discursive and instrumental, existing within, through and beyond the reach of the state and the influence of domestic politics. In essence, race is more than supposed biological differences or modes or institutional categories. Rather, it is encompassed in ideas and ideologies about how society should operate and social order be maintained and animated through the many and varied practices and relationships of power. Over the past five hundred years, it has been employed and abused as a central organising axiom of and among modern Western societies.

There are two implications of defining race in this way. First, rather than being a signifier of physiological differences, race is more like a powerful set of *ideas or norms* about the identity, difference and organisation of a society and its constituents. As will be explored further below, it is a cognitive product that nonetheless carries mutually constituted ontological meanings and material consequences. Slavery, for example, was an economic system founded upon international trade and capital investment in slaves-as-commodities and the super-exploitation of slave labour with global profits that spurred the industrial revolution. This system also produced social meanings that associated dark skin with slave status (Jordan 1968) at the same time that whiteness emerged, for the first time, as a homogenised legal identity in the first codified miscegenation law in 1691 (Smedley 2007, 118). In other words, the idea of race has material, substantive and structural dimensions.

Scholars of comparative politics and IR have recently given more attention to the causal role of ideational variables (Hall 1989; Finnemore and Sikkink 1998; Berman 2001; Lieberman 2002; Béland and Cox 2011). In their helpful review of the literature, Skogstad and Schmidt (2011) identify two (and a half) distinct strands. The ideational turn in comparative politics focuses on how ideas become embedded in institutions and policy paradigms, acting as cognitive locks that guide, though do not predetermine, particular courses of action. In comparative politics, norms are important as causal belief systems that connect people and things, providing normative guides for action (Béland and Cox 2011); according to constructivists in IR, norms also work to define or constitute identities as well as proscribe and regulate behaviour (Checkel 1998a). Constructivists have also focused considerably on sets of ideas or norms that have diffused spatially, often focusing on the role of transnational actors such as international organisations, non-governmental organisations, advocacy networks and epistemic communities (Haas 1992; Risse et al. 1999). A related literature from the Stanford school of sociology envisions how ideas help to constitute a world culture that diffused and homogenised political institutions and state apparatuses, even though their inefficiencies were well known (Meyer et al. 1997; Boli and Thomas 1999).

How do norms and ideas influence domestic politics? Though ideas and norms are more often the reasons for actions rather than direct causes in the positivist sense (Finnemore and Sikkink 1998, 890), a major concern of the literature has involved identifying the causal mechanisms involved in the transfer between international and domestic realms (Blyth 1997; Berman 2001). This is difficult to identify and measure, for ideas may influence outcomes directly, by affecting the political behaviour of actors, or indirectly, by shaping the incentive structures surrounding different courses of action. Regardless, most of the literature on the influence of norms, ideas and culture is premised on the notion that carriers or entrepreneurs capable of persuading others to reconsider the status quo must champion the new paradigm (Berman 2001, 235). For example, Hansen and King (2001) contend that the influence of ideas is more likely when there is a synergy between interests and ideas, but go on to argue that two further conditions are *actors* who possess requisite enthusiasm for the idea and have the institutional position to influence policy and *timing,* which contributes to a broad constellation of preferences that reinforces the idea, whether through political crisis or an undermining of previous policies (2001, 239). This emphasis on individual or group actors alleviates the problem of epiphenomenality, whereby ideas are considered a secondary rather than primary or singular cause.

Conceptualising race as an idea is not an easy task. Like other ideas, such as Keynesianism, human rights or environmentalism, the ideational content of race has changed over time and may not necessarily be internally consistent. The concept of race is also analytically and functionally distinct from two of its outgrowths:

racialism and racism. Racialism is the operationalisation of race; the idea that people are marked by physiological or morphological characteristics that are generalisable, inherited, and shared by members of the same population group. Appiah (1990) argues that the belief in racial groups may be mistaken, but if it is not followed by claims of inherent superiority or inferiority the concept of race is not necessarily dangerous or bigoted. For example, some racialist imperatives, such as census categories, human rights legislation and affirmative action policies, create, invoke or reproduce racial schema in order to remedy circumstances of racial inequality. Racism, on the other hand, is fundamentally about exclusion from protection, privilege, property or profit (Goldberg 2009, 5). If racialism concerns the fabrication of homogenous social groupings, racism hierarchically orders those so marked, polices the boundaries that separate racial groups for possible transgressions and keeps those on the bottom from moving surreptitiously upwards without payment or punishment.

Racialism enables, and racism creates, arrangements through which agents have differential access to and experiences within international and domestic political economies. For example, as Hilbourne Watson demonstrates, in the Caribbean experience, race and class strategies of exploitation can coincide, in part because 'racial privilege normalizes techniques of domination and rules for surplus extraction and solidifies bonds among beneficiaries to the detriment of victims' (Watson 2001, 452). On an international scale, Jones links the profoundly uneven global distribution of property to the historical legacies of coerced appropriation of land and labour in capitalist processes of accumulation. The imposition of racial ideas occurred alongside (material) conquest, theft and dispossession. Genocide, enslavement, land alienation, appropriation of private property and forced appropriation of labour power were 'achieved and regulated though forms of political domination and control which entailed the partial or total denial of the rights or even the humanity of non-European peoples' (Jones 2008, 920). The racial contract is invariably a capitalistic contract; though white privilege is not reducible to class privilege, material inequality stratified by race is a central component of white supremacy (Mills 1997).

Race is therefore far more than simply and solely an idea; it is also both constitutive of and created by material and structural social relations.[1] An emphasis on the idea of race must not ignore or minimise the stubborn endurance of racialised power, inequalities and oppression on national and global scales (Jones 2008, 911). If race was just ideational, then the prevalence and widespread acceptance of principles of racial equality would have become internationally embedded long ago and in such ways that they would have worked to change on-the-ground racial practices. And yet, inexplicably, racial injustice continues, built into the very fabric of the international economic order. The greatest challenge is to separate the idea of race from the operation of racial politics and the instrumental invocation of race therein. As scholars of international norms have demonstrated, there is much analytical leverage to be gained by differentiating a specific conceptualisation of an idea or norm (such as race) from the institutional or behavioural changes that occur because of it (Finnemore and Sikkink 1998). This is made all the more difficult because the sociality and materiality of race are mutually constituted by and through relations of power.

Racial transnationalism

The second implication of this orientation is that if race is an idea, it is a *global* one. It is no coincidence that the idea of race emerged at the same time as the age of empire and nation-building. Hesse argues that it was 'between the modern regulatory vectors of structural administration within colonies and discursive authorisations from the metropoles that the category of race becomes instituted and naturalised around the boundaries between colour-coded sameness and non-European other-ness' (2007, 652). Race was born in the transnational realm and bred to be central to discourses of modernity, empire and capitalism. Race is linked with and re-articulated by the major transnational movements of the modern era – the global slave trade, abolitionism, Social Darwinism, eugenics, suffrage, Keynesianism, human rights, the anti-apartheid movement, and the new politics of terrorism of the twenty-first century have all reproduced and changed the meaning of race. Racial impulses are simultaneously local and global, taking on a 'characteristic specificity in the context of local, national, and state conditions, globally influenced and textured' (Goldberg 2009, 15). The many manifestations of race along multiple geographic and temporal scales raises an important broader question for scholars of international and comparative politics: how might we think within, through, and beyond the nation-state and its relationship with race?

Methodological nationalism and the focus on the state as an actor in domestic politics and in the international arena of nation-states make this a difficult task, particularly given the positivist orientation in comparative politics for 'most similar' or 'most different' research designs. In IR, thinking outside the container of state or nation is more feasible; it has been successfully done through the prisms of (post-)colonialism, the Atlantic slave trade, and imperialism/empire (Füredi 1999; Grovogui 2001; Hobson 2007; Barkawi and Laffey 2006; Shilliam 2006, 2008; Chowdhry 2007; Sabaratnam 2011). For example, Vucetic (2010) suggests that global governance has historically been controlled by the 'Anglosphere' – an exclusive international community united by the common (dominant) language of English and historical ties to Britain. The continuing international authority of this conglomerate originated in the nineteenth-century racial belief in the superiority of Anglo-Saxon people and civilisations. Rather than reinforce national distinctions or make new, broader borders that simply replace the old, Vucetic suggests that racialised identities are constituted through different levels of social practice, some of which may be in the fabric of empires, networks and civilisations. Similarly, Shilliam (2009) argues that the Atlantic community, now most commonly understood as the bastions of European civilisation or remnants of Cold War alliances, were first, foremost, and fundamentally a community forged and bound by the trans-Atlantic slave trade.

The processes by which state-level actors and institutions filter the global idea of race is an empirical question that demands more sustained scholarly attention. Two bodies of literature provide solid theoretical ground on which to begin. First, by understanding the nation as fragile, constructed and imagined, scholars of transnational history treat nation-states as one among a range of phenomena to be studied. Aiwah Ong (1999, 4) writes that the *trans* in transnational denotes

> moving through space or across lines, as well as changing the nature of something. Besides suggesting new relations between nation-states and capital, transnationality also alludes to the *trans*versal, the *trans*actional, the *trans*lational, and the *trans*gressive aspects of contemporary behavior and imagination that are incited, enabled, and regulated by the changing logics of states and capitalism.

Transnational research zooms in on interactions, exchanges, constructions and translations across borders as well as the significance of different national experiences of the same global phenomenon (Thelen 1999, 972–3). Second, international historical sociology challenges the methodology of 'ideal types' used in its comparative counterpart, which disguises an inherently Eurocentric orientation and focus and relegates non-European contributions and connections as either invisible or a product of European modernity. Bhambra argues that a new narrative for global historical sociology must emphasise interconnections among people, places and ideas through a methodology of connected histories or international interconnectedness (2010, 139).

Three types of racial transnationalism along these lines are immediately apparent. In the footsteps of Robert Vitalis (2000), race scholars could theorise white supremacy as a global norm and racism as an international institution and their lasting influence on the constitution of the world order. Second, the emergence, diffusion and effects of the global norm of racial equality in the post-war era spur numerous empirical puzzles. Audie Klotz's (1995) research, for example, asks why a number of international organisations and states adopted sanctions against South Africa when there were material incentives not to do so and historic relations that had flourished for decades in spite of the regime's commitment to apartheid. In tracing how racial discrimination became increasingly delegitimised in domestic and international spheres, Klotz points to the causal power of the global norm of racial equality in terms of its ability to redefine state interests. Finally, race itself could be explored as a transnational phenomenon that exists in excess of national boundaries, as Lake and Reynolds do in their conceptualisation of whiteness. 'Transnational in its inspirations and identifications but nationalist in its methods and goals' (2008, 4), Lake and Reynolds argue that global whiteness was a racial project formed in international conversations that instigated a sudden change of consciousness in the early twentieth century and political investments in the idea of the 'white man's country' across the globe.

Two cautionary notes are in order. First, this conceptualisation of race as transnational is not necessarily code for race as a Western or Eurocentric phenomenon.

Unlike models that posit a world historical center (Europe) from which developments and innovations diffuse outwards, the definition of race as power relations realised on a variety of overlapping geographic scales is more akin to the 'multiple modernities' traditions in critical IR (Bhambra 2010; 2011). In other words, race was – and continues to be – formed through connections, interactions, and relationships of power. To say race was central to European modernity, as many theorists – Arendt, Foucault, Goldberg, Gilroy, Balibar, Hannaford, Winant – do, actually works to *decentre* Eurocentric modernity; just as multiple modernities emerged from encounters between the West and other civilisations and cultural traditions, so too did the concept of race.

Second, the emphasis on racial transnationalism is not a negation of the nation-state, but is instead the displacement of its assumed primacy. To argue that race is a global phenomenon is simply to highlight one set of practices of social signification (among many others) that have a particularly transnational origin, existence, activation and effect. It is also to put the actions of the state alongside other units of analysis both bigger and smaller than the nation-state and to examine the range of phenomena that spill over, seep through, defy, extend, challenge or negate national boundaries. Comparisons through, between and beyond racial states can be used 'as a window into specific exchanges, interactions, and connections that cut across national boundaries without ignoring what state actors do and what matters about what they say' (Stoler 2001, 847).

Mechanisms of racial diffusion

The state clearly matters. The more important question, however, is to ask how much states matter and in what ways by interrogating the distinctive work race-making processes do, what interactions they have, and how these complexities help constitute the changing idea of race as it manifests in domestic and international realms. How does race become institutionalised globally, nationally and locally? Through what mechanisms do global conceptions of race influence domestic arenas? Why is race operationalised differentially over time and space? Why do racial norms have such powerful effects in some places but not in others? Neither IR nor comparative politics offer definitive answers to these important questions, though there are a number of promising avenues of research in both, in terms of: (1) the relationship between the influence and level of specificity of the idea of race; (2) the extent that diffusion pathways are determined or constrained by domestic factors; and (3) the ways in which domestic factors may, in turn, influence the transnational realm.

First, the relative influence of racial ideas is likely tied to the idea's level of specificity. The narrowest forms are ideas as policy positions. That is, given a particular problem and set of objectives, ideas can provide the means for solving said problem and achieving the identified objectives (Mehta 2011). Sheri Berman calls ideas that operate at the meso-level programmatic beliefs, 'the ideational framework within which *programs* of action are formulated' (1998, emphasis in original). These are specific to a particular policy realm, and while programmatic beliefs are not necessarily always vitally important to all policy areas, they are sometimes able to take on a life of their own and exert influence on policy outcomes when taken up by members of a policy network (Kisby 2007, 83). At the broadest level are worldviews, zeitgeists, ideologies and public philosophies, which cut across a number of substantive areas. Race operates on all three levels of ideational influence, corresponding with a number of different mechanisms of ideational diffusion.

Take racial worldviews as an example. Changing global ideas about the nature of race set the conditions of possibility for state action and inaction towards race relations, creating a transnational cultural code that provides actors with a range of acceptable options to draw from when making decisions (Triadafilopoulos 2004). Most race scholars agree that the Second World War marked a break or disruption of the logic of race and its many manifestations (Winant 2001). There were numerous causes of this normative change. As with so many other examples, such as the Haitian revolution, colonialism, decolonisation, the American civil rights movement and the anti-apartheid struggle, the causal role of war, force, struggle and conflict were crucial in the remaking of race and racial discourses. In this instance, the Holocaust and the demise of Nazi Germany seriously undermined the already crumbling foundations of biological racialism (Stepan 1982; Barkan 1992). The global anti-colonial movement and decolonisation were also violent struggles of and for freedom. In addition, naturalised racial hierarchies were under attack in the academy, as Franz Boas and his students worked to redefine understandings of race and racial difference in anthropology and beyond. International organisations institutionalised the emerging discourse against racism through the UN's Universal Declaration of Human Rights and UNESCO's statement, 'The Race Question', which condemned the human and social damage done by the myth of race (UNESCO 1950). Other international developments, such as the demands of newly sovereign nations in Asia and Africa that international organisations tackle issues of racial discrimination and the emerging foreign policy debates of the Cold War era, in which democracies claimed a superior system of governance based on principles of liberalism and equality and were forced to confront their hypocrisy (though at times only doing so in order to gain strategic leverage in Cold War politics) (Dudziak 2000; Klinkner and Smith 1999; Borstelmann 2002), contributed to the emerging transnational discourse of human rights. Domestic developments also contributed to the proliferation of these norms, the most obvious being the civil rights movement in the United States and the struggles of indigenous peoples in Canada, Australia, New Zealand and the United States for the right to self-determination (Cairns 1999).

By the end of this transnational moment the meaning of race had markedly changed. Rather than being perceived as a biological fact, race is now widely acknowledged as a product of social forces, part of a wider social fabric that includes gender and class relations. This rather ubiquitous manifestation of the global idea of race is made more finite through international organisations such as the UN, UNESCO and the European Union. These international organisations, however, did not bring this norm into being – they institutionalised norms that have already been incubated elsewhere. Similarly, the meaning of race does not simply solidify through institutional imperatives that encourage states to comply with various declarations. Rather, the more potent transnational mechanism is in the idea's ability to alter incentive structures for states to act or not act by changing perceptions of legitimacy among international and domestic-level citizenries. This shift did not occur quickly, automatically or without struggle and sacrifice; it was incremental, cumulative and in many ways remains incomplete. And yet, by the end of the twentieth century the normative context surrounding the meaning of race altered the terms of the debate in such a way that perceptions of democratic legitimacy in the Anglophone West depended in part on the state's acknowledgement and attempt to rectify circumstances of racial disadvantage.

Of course, the transnational does not affect the domestic realm without some modifications; an additional avenue of research could examine how diffusion pathways are determined or constrained by domestic factors. New ideas do not enter a normative vacuum; they instead emerge in an ideological space that is highly contested, filled with other norms and perceptions of interest (Finnemore and Sikkink 1998, 897). The diffusion of an isomorphic idea into different contexts is far more likely when the idea resonates with dominant paradigms already in place. Checkel (1998b) suggests that the 'cultural match' between an international norm and domestic structures is important, reflected in the congruence between discourse, the legal system, and the organisational ethos of bureaucratic agencies. Government officials and other social actors can also appeal to international norms to further their own interests, thereby incorporating the norm into domestic debates and at times influencing national-level policy choices (Cortell and Davis 1996). State-level institutions and actors also meditate, filter and translate global ideas of race to fit national and cultural repertoires. Acharya (2004) calls this 'localisation', a complex process and outcome through which 'norm-takers build congruence between transnational norms (including norms previously institutionalised in a region) and local beliefs and practices. In this process, foreign norms, which may not initially cohere with the latter, are incorporated into local norms' (2004, 241). In short, domestic factors can be important intervening variables in the process, extent, and outcome of norm diffusion.

Comparative research on the politics of race illustrates this point well. David Theo Goldberg (2002) makes the distinction between 'naturalist' and 'historicist' forms of racial rule and traditions of state formation. He argues that naturalist states in Europe and their satellites that tended to emphasise coercion in their emergence and national unification – Germany, apartheid South Africa, and presumably the United States – adopted doctrines of natural racial superiority and inferiority that necessitated state action in order to impose racial order and maintain racial control. In contrast, historicist states growing out of financial centres such as England and France emphasised racial inferiority and superiority as evidence of the 'fact' of historically produced progress and civilisation. While the former tended to use overt mechanisms of racial control (segregation, Black Codes, etc.) the latter were more likely to use informal or administrative mechanisms such as the unequal application of laws. Anthony Marx's (1998) comparison of the United States, Brazil and South Africa demonstrates that specific political, economic and social racial divisions emerged from each country's efforts to establish national unity and consolidate state power. Delving into more specific factors related to political economy, Patrick Wolfe (2001) suggests that broad types of race policies in settler societies actually depended on whether race was invoked for dispossession and theft of indigenous land (assimilationist policies) or the exploitation of black labour (segregationist policies). Each of these examples draws from a larger, implicitly global meaning of race that informs racialist schema and racist policies, though these are specific to national circumstances and the racial dynamics being analysed.

Finally, research on racial transnationalism must recognise that the causal arrow points in many directions. The incorporation of racial ideas into domestic policy is not the end of the story. Once norms have reached the point of internalisation and attained a taken-for-granted quality they are still susceptible to change through both domestic and transnational action. Simply put, *norms are not static.* There is an interaction between global and domestic spheres of influence and sometimes transnational racial norms morph precisely because of the ways in which they are adopted and institutionalised in national contexts. One of the most significant examples is the actions of the US civil rights movement, which gained legislative victories in America and simultaneously contributed to a reconceptualisation of the transnational norm surrounding the legitimacy of state action and inaction with regard to racial discrimination. During the 1960s racial politics in the United States made acute to other nations the need to avoid American-style racial tension, conflict and violence. Though the goal of avoiding conflict was replicated, the cause of racial tension was clearly interpreted differently in other contexts.

In this circumstance, the British state viewed the reality of racial discrimination and disadvantage as the spark for potential conflict similar to the United States (Solomos 2003, 81), as noted by Home Secretary Frank Soskice during the introduction of the 1965 Race Relations Act when he said, 'it is far better to put this Bill on the Statute Book now, before social stresses and ill-will have the change of corrupting and distorting our relationships'.[2] The American model did not of course perfectly transfer across the Atlantic; nor did elites desire to mimic it. Specific British concerns such as the protection of public order rather than the proclamation of individual rights and a deliberate aversion to explicit colour-consciousness and affirmative action have shaped policy outcomes. Unlike the United States, race relations and immigration policies in the United Kingdom are inextricably tied together. One strategy of the British government for avoiding racial conflict was to simultaneously restrict non-white immigration, assuming that the very presence of non-white people would be a source of conflict, and to link this external control to an internal policy of racial integration, since, in the words of Labour MP Roy Hattersley, 'Integration without control is impossible, but control without integration is indefensible' (Miles and Phizacklea 1984, 57). In short, racial politics in the United States worked to alter incentive structures elsewhere, demonstrating to watchful governments the potential for violence if circumstances of racial difference and discrimination went unaddressed.

The global idea of race is shaped by developments in domestic racial projects and formations, but not all events and all places have the same influence on transnational norms that define the meaning of race. Some circumstances have caught the world's attention – decolonisation, the American civil rights movement, the end of apartheid in South Africa – and worked to shape domestically specific racial projects elsewhere. The United States has been highly influential in shaping the transnational norm, more so than any other nation, but itself has often consumed racial information from South Africa (Klotz 1995). Incentives for action can thus be either positive, through social learning and lesson-drawing from developments in the politics of race in other places, or negative, as states make efforts to avoid racial practices gone awry. In sum, there is a circuitry of racial ideas that vary along temporal and spatial axes on scales both smaller and bigger than the nation-state; as they circumnavigate the globe, racial ideas morph in the course of their travels.

Conclusion

The global colour line is not only a means of maintaining the vestiges and reincarnations of imperial hierarchies but also a phenomenon that can itself be analysed. The assertion that race is a transnational idea that exists in excess of national boundaries is only a controversial claim at present. When we glance quickly over our shoulders at the not-so-distant past, the deeply entrenched coloniality and biological racialism of old were clearly transnational in origin and scope. The discourse of race was conceived in the encounters between European and non-European modernities. The proliferation of norms of race as a biological truism connected metropoles to colonies, enabled the enslavement and trade of human bodies in a global capitalist system and were debated among the international epistemic communities of the day. Yet, in the attempt to move away from the biological construction of race through rearticulation, emancipatory action, denial, negation and aphasia, the transnationalism of race has been obscured and concealed. It has been, in the words of David Theo Goldberg (2009), buried – but buried alive. This reframing of race is made possible in part because of the disassociation of race with biological determinism. If we no longer accept that race inheres in biology, if morphology does not dictate culture, temperament or morality and yet remains strongly correlated to quality of life, if skin colour cannot adequately describe who belongs in which racial designation, if individuals do not carry their races alongside them like swords in some cases and ploughs in others, then what explains the power and permanency of race?

I have argued that race is a set of powerful ideas under constant (re)articulation and (re)negotiation, often occurring through the excessive regulation of the state. But its origin lies in the transnational realm, and though its manifestations may most obviously and perhaps prominently be domestic in application, they are simultaneously globally textured. Future research along the lines of what Melissa

Weiner (2012) calls 'global critical race theory' is potentially endless. Alongside interrogations of historic and contemporary manifestations of race and processes of racialisation, Weiner suggests empirical analyses of the many and varied indicators of racialisation, including: citizenship laws; state control; external ascription and boundary permeability; criminalisation; geography and/or spatial segregation; socioeconomic status; popular and political discourse and images; daily interactions, experiences, and cognition; international racialised relationships; and anti-racist efforts.

My own work, for example, began as a comparative study of the political development of census questions on race in the United States, Canada, and Great Britain and the official racial schematics employed by states to make their national populations legible.[3] The census appears to be a wholly domestic enterprise, a quantitative container of the populace whose confines extend only so far as a nation's geographic boundaries permit. To echo Hochschild and Powell (2008), it is both the image of the nation and the mirror that governments and its citizens use to gaze at the national self-reflection, a state simplification that ultimately imagines a bound, finite community (Anderson 1991; Scott 1998). And yet, the limits of the national imagination have changed substantially over time, as have the purposes of racial enumeration over more than two hundred years of census-taking. Censuses were once used to institutionalise racial hierarchies and substantiate racial orders by protecting the shifting boundaries of whiteness from transgressions of the colour line. In more recent times, censuses are the primary source of statistical data for government and private sectors, essential to the formulation and monitoring of anti-discrimination policies in national, regional and global spheres. This broad shift from counting to manage and control racialised populations to counting by race for egalitarian ends in these three cases simultaneously occurs alongside more nuanced policy divergences in the rules of racial classification – that is, *who* counts as *what*.

This project of state simplification is neither simplistic nor bound by the state. Rather, change and continuity in the racial politics of the census reflect macro-level racial worldviews about the nature of race and racial difference and meso-level programmatic beliefs about whether racial statistics are a viable or problematic policy instrument. These transnational racial ideas were critical to international and domestic-level perceptions about the legitimate ends of race policies and the appropriate means of achieving those ends. During the era of biological racialism in the nineteenth and early twentieth centuries, for example, race was largely understood as a biological phenomenon superimposed by a natural human hierarchy. At the same time, international epistemic communities of statisticians saw the rise of statistical science as a justifiable instrument to solve pressing social problems – including the race problem. Democratic governments and colonial powers implemented temporally legitimate, though illiberal, exclusionary policies that segregated and disenfranchised non-white populations. The state's creation of racial census categories that reinforced the one-drop rule and use of census data to monitor, track and in some cases betray non-white citizens were appropriate means of adhering to the basic precepts of the racial worldview.

These transnational ideas are rarely accepted into domestic spheres without some modification. The state interactively mediates between transnational and domestic influences, translating worldviews and programmatic beliefs into localised cultural, legal, and political repertoires. Domestic-level racial projects – slavery, colonialism, immigration, civil rights, multiculturalism, post-racialism, and the like – operate alongside the census, creating incentives for governments to count or avoid counting by race and inflate state-endorsed racial taxonomies. Institutions such as the centralisation of decision-making authority, the autonomy of statistical agencies to operate free of partisan or societal influence, and nationally-specific protocols of census administration also constrain and enable the possibilities for policy change. For example, by the end of the twentieth century all three cases made efforts to count their mixed-race populations as never before. By the 1990s, multiraciality was becoming a viable and recognisable identity, at least in the Anglophone West. Led by a transnational worldview that positively valued properly managed diversity and ideational shift in the international epistemic community of statisticians about the necessity of self-identification, policymakers became uncomfortable with assigning identities and sought to give respondents the ability to identify as mixed race if they so desired. At the same time, each country's particular approach to multiracial enumeration was mediated by state institutions. Canada permitted multiple responses to its race question because of the path-dependent constraints that arose from its policy of encouraging respondents to 'mark all that apply' on its ethnic ancestry question. In Britain, the relatively closed structure of the policy network made its choice of stand-alone multiracial categories uncontroversial, while the open nature of the American federal review of racial classification in the 1990s necessitated that state and non-state actors form coalitions and bargain for their preferred outcome.

What began as a comparative story, therefore, is instead a study of the transnational movements of people and ideas, lessons drawn as models for action or avoidance, and the global connections among members of the statistical epistemic communities, the transnational networks of state actors involved in the design and execution of the census, and the ripples of diasporic consciousness that frame identities across and beyond the Black Atlantic.

What do critical race scholars in IR and comparative politics truly have to learn from one another? First, the eclecticism of the study of race translates into a wide array of methodological tools, theoretical traditions and disciplinary paradigms at our disposal. This article suggested a number of promising avenues of research along just one axiom: the cross-disciplinary interest in the causal role of ideas and norms. Combing insights from IR, comparative politics and especially critical race theory holds a great deal of potential for rectifying the paralysing racial aphasia that characterises so much of mainstream political science. Clearly, a number of challenges remain: the problematic methodological statism and the need to disaggregate, dehistoricise and denaturalise the state; the necessity of engaging with the vast theoretical literature on race, especially research that questions the definition of race and its intersection with other relations of power such as gender, class and sexuality; determining the role of history and colonial legacies in present-day politics; invoking transnationalism without decontextualising difference, or as Stoler (2001) puts it, without flattening complicated sets of racialised practices and representations; and exploring the varied and contradictory ways in which states construct the boundaries of race just as race constitutes the state itself.

Notes

1 Note, however, Jones' expansion of critical realism, which criticises 'the fallacy of sharp distinctions between "material" and "social" phenomena' (Jones 2008, 914).
2 *Hansard*, House of Commons, 3 May 1965, vol. 711, col. 942.
3 See Debra Thompson, *The Schematic State: Race, Transnationalism, and the Politics of the Census* (unpublished manuscript).

Bibliography

Acharya, Amitav (2004) 'How ideas spread: whose norms matter? Norm localization and institutional change in Asian regionalism', *International Organization* 58(2), 239–75.

Anderson, Benedict (1991) *Imagined Communities: Reflections on the Origins and Spread of Nationalism*, 2nd edition (London and New York: Verso).

Appiah, Kwame Anthony (1990) 'Racisms' in David Theo Goldberg (ed.) *Anatomy of Racism* (Minneapolis: University of Minnesota Press), 3–18.

Barkan, Elazar (1992) *The Retreat of Scientific Racism: Changing Concepts of Race in Britain and the United States between the World War* (Cambridge: Cambridge University Press).

Barkawi, Tarak and Laffey, Mark (2006) 'The postcolonial moment in security studies', *Review of International Studies* 32, 329–52.

Béland, Daniel and Cox, Robert Henry (2011) 'Introduction: Ideas and Politics' in Daniel Béland and Robert Henry Cox (eds) *Ideas and Politics in Social Science Research* (Oxford: Oxford University Press), 3–20.

Berman, Sheri (1998) *The Social Democratic Movement: Ideas and Politics in the Making of Interwar Europe* (Cambridge, MA: Harvard University Press).

——(2001) 'Review: ideas, norms, and culture in political analysis', *Comparative Politics* 33(2), 231–50.

Bhambra, Gurminder K. (2010) 'Historical sociology, international relations and connected histories', *Cambridge Review of International Affairs* 23(1), 127–43

——(2011) 'Talking among themselves? Weberian and Marxist historical sociologies as dialogues without "Others"', *Millennium – Journal of International Studies* 39(3), 667–81.

Blyth, Mark (1997) 'Any more bright ideas? The ideational turn of comparative political economy', *Comparative Politics* 29(2), 229–50.

Boli, John and Thomas, George M. (1999) *Constructing World Culture* (Stanford, CA: Stanford University Press).

Borstelmann, Thomas (2002) *The Cold War and the Color Line: American Race Relations in the Global Arena* (Cambridge, MA: Harvard University Press).

Cairns, Alan C (1999) 'Empire, globalization, and the fall and rise of diversity' in Alan C. Cairns et al. (eds) *Citizenship, Diversity and Pluralism: Canada and Comparative Perspective* (Montreal and Kingston: McGill-Queen's University Press), 23–57.

Checkel, Jeffrey (1998a) 'The constructivist turn in international relations theory', *World Politics* 50(2), 324–48.

——(1998b) 'Norms, Institutions and National Identity in Contemporary Europe', ARENA Working Paper 98/16 (Copenhagen: University of Oslo).

Chowdhry, Geeta (2007) 'Edward Said and contrapuntal reading: implications for critical interventions in international relations', *Millennium – Journal of International Studies* 36(1), 101–16.

Chowdhry, Geeta and Nair, Sheila (eds) (2002) *Power, Postcolonialism and International Relations: Reading Race, Gender and Class* (London: Routledge).

Cortell, Andrew and James Davis, Jr (1996) 'How do international institutions matter? The Ddomestic impact of international rules and norms', *International Studies Quarterly* 40(4), 451–78.

Doty, Roxanne (1993) 'The bounds of "race" in international relations', *Millennium – Journal of International Studies* 22(3), 443–61.

——(1996) *Imperial Encounter: The Politics of Representation in North-South Relations* (Minneapolis: University of Minnesota Press).

Du Bois, W. E. B. (1903) *The Souls of Black Folk* (Chicago: McClurg).

Dudziak, Mary L. (2000) *Cold War Civil Rights: Race and the Image of American Democracy* (Princeton: Princeton University Press)

Finnemore, Martha and Sikkink, Kathryn (1998) 'International norm dynamics and political change', *International Organization* 52(4), 887–917.

Füredi, Frank (1999) *The Silent War: Imperialism and the Changing Perception of Race* (New Brunswick: Rutgers University Press).

Goldberg, David Theo (2002) *The Racial State* (Malden, MA: Blackwell Publishing).

——(2009) *The Threat of Race: Reflections on Racial Neoliberalism* (Malden, MA: Blackwell Publishing).

Grovogui, Siba N. (2001) 'Come to Africa: a hermeneutics of race in international theory', *Alternatives* 26(4), 425–48.

Gruffydd Jones, Branwen (2008) 'Race in the ontology of international order', *Political Studies* 56, 907–27.

Haas, Peter (1992) 'Introduction: epistemic communities and international policy coordination', *International Organization* 46(1), 1–35.

Hall, Peter (1989) *The Political Power of Economic Ideas: Keynesianism Across Nations* (Princeton: Princeton University Press).

Hall, Stuart (1996) 'What is this "black" in black popular culture?' in David Morley and Juan-Hsing Chen (eds) *Stuart Hall: Critical Dialogues in Cultural Studies* (London and New York: Routledge), 465–75.

Hansen, Randall and King, Desmond (2001) 'Eugenic ideas, political interests, and policy variance: immigration and sterilization policy in Britain and the US', *World Politics* 53, 237–63.

Hesse, Barnor (2007) 'Racialized modernity: an analytics of white mythologies', *Ethnic and Racial Studies* 30(4), 643–63.

——(2011) 'Self-fulfilling prophecy: the postracial horizon', *South Atlantic Quarterly* 110(1), 155–78.

Hobson, John (2007) 'Is critical theory always for the white West and for Western imperialism? Beyond Westphilian towards a post-racial critical IR', *Review of International Studies* 33, 91–116.

Hochschild, Jennifer L. and Powell, Brenna Marea (2008) 'Racial reorganization and the United States census 1850–1930: mulattoes, half-breeds, mixed parentage, Hindoos and the Mexican race', *Studies in American Political Development* 22(2), 59–96.

Hylton, Kevin, Pilkington, Andrew. Warmington, Paul and Housee, Shirin (2011) *Atlantic Crossings: International Dialogues on Critical Race Theory* (Birmingham: University of Birmingham Higher Education Academic Network).

Jordan, Winthrop D. (1968) *White over Black: American Attitudes toward the Negro, 1550–1812* (Chapel Hill: University of North Carolina Press).

Kisby, Ben (2007) 'Analysing policy networks: towards an ideational approach', *Policy Studies* 28(1), 71–90.

Klinkner, Philip A. and Smith, Rogers M. (1999) *The Unsteady March: The Rise and Decline of Racial Equality in America* (Chicago: University of Chicago Press).

Klotz, Audie (1995) 'Norms reconstituting interests: global racial equality and US sanctions against South Africa', *International Organization* 49(3): 451–78.

Lake, Marilyn and Reynolds, Henry (2008) *Drawing the Global Colour Line: White Men's Countries and the International Challenge of Racial Equality* (Cambridge: Cambridge University Press).

Lauren, Paul G. (1996) *Power and Prejudice: the Politics and Diplomacy of Racial Discrimination*, 2nd edition (Boulder: Westview Press).

Lieberman, Robert C. (2002) 'Ideas, institutions, and political order: explaining political change', *American Political Science Review* 96(4), 697–712.

Marx, Anthony (1998) *Making Race and Nation: A Comparison of the United States, South Africa and Brazil* (New York: Cambridge University Press).

Mehta, Jal (2011) 'The varied roles of ideas in politics: from "whether" to "how"' in Daniel Béland and Robert Henry Cox (eds) *Ideas and Politics in Social Science Research* (Oxford: Oxford University Press), 23–46.

Meyer, John W., Boli, John., Thomas, George M. and Ramirez, Francisco O. (1997) 'World Society and the nation-state', *American Journal of Sociology* 103(1), 144–81.

Miles, Robert and Phizacklea, Annie (1984) *White Man's Country: Racism in British Politics* (London: Pluto Press).

Mills, Charles (1997) *The Racial Contract* (Ithaca: Cornell University Press).

Omi, Michael and Winant, Howard (1994) *Racial Formation in the United States: From the 1960s to the 1990s*, 2nd edition (New York and London: Routledge).

Ong, Aihwa (1999) *Flexible Citizenship: The Cultural Logics of Transnationality* (Durham, NC: Duke University Press).

Persaud, Randolph B. (2002) 'Situating race in international relations: the dialectics of civilizational security in American immigration,' in Geeta Chowdhry and Sheila Nair (eds) *Power, Postcolonialism and International Relations: Reading Race, Gender and Class* (London and New York: Routledge), 56–81.

Risse, Thomas, Ropp, Stephen C. and Sikkink, Kathryn (eds) (1999) *The Power of Human Rights, International Norms and Domestic Change* (New York: Cambridge University Press).

Sabaratnam, Meera (2011) 'IR in dialogue … but can we change the subjects? A typology of decolonising strategies for the study of world politics' *Millennium – Journal of International Studies* 39(3), 781–803.

Scott, James C (1998) *Seeing Like a State: How Certain Schemes to Improve the Human Condition Have Failed* (New Haven and London: Yale University Press).

Skogstad, Grace and Schmidt, Vivien (2011) 'Introduction' in Grace Skogstad (ed) *Policy Paradigms, Transnationalism and Domestic Politics* (Toronto: University of Toronto Press).

Shilliam, Robbie (2006) 'What about Marcus Garvey? Race and the transformation of sovereignty debate', *Review of International Studies* 32, 379–400.

——(2008) 'What the Haitian Revolution might tell us about development, security and the politics of race', *Comparative Studies in Society and History* 50(3), 778–808.

——(2009) 'The Atlantic as a vector of uneven and combined development', *Cambridge Review of International Affairs* 22(1), 69–88.

Smedley, Audrey (2007) *Race in North America: Origin and Evolution of a Worldview*, 3rd edition (Boulder: Westview Press).

Solomos, John (2003) *Race and Racism in Britain*, 3rd edition (New York: Palgrave Macmillan).

Stepan, Nancy (1982) *The Idea of Race in Science: Great Britain, 1800–1960* (Oxford: Macmillan).

Stoler, Ann Laura (2001) 'Tense and tender ties: the politics of comparison in North American history and (post)colonial studies', *The Journal of American History* 88(3), 829–65.

——(2011) 'Colonial aphasia: race and disabled histories in France' *Public Culture* 23(1), 121–56.

Thelen, David (1999) 'The nation and beyond: transnational perspectives on United States history', *Journal of American History* 86(3), 965–75.

Triadafilopoulos, Triadafilos (2004) 'Building walls, bounding nations: migration and exclusion in Canada and Germany, 1870–1939', *Journal of Historical Sociology* 17(4), 385–427.

UNESCO (1950) *The Race Question.* Available at http://unesdoc.unesco.org/images/0012/001282/128291eo.pdf.

Vitalis, Robert (2000) 'The graceful and generous liberal gesture: making racism invisible in American international relations', *Millennium – Journal of International Studies* 29(2), 331–56.

Vucetic, Srdjan (2010) 'Anglobal governance?' *Cambridge Review of International Affairs* 23(3), 455–74.

Watson, Hilbourne (2001) 'Theorizing the racialization of global politics and the Caribbean experience', *Alternatives* 26(4), 449–83.

Weiner, Melissa F. (2012) 'Towards a critical global race theory', *Sociology Compass* 6(4), 332–50.

Winant, Howard (2001) *The World is a Ghetto: Race and Democracy Since World War Two* (New York: Basic Books).

Wolfe, Patrick (2001) 'Land, labor, difference: elementary structures of race', *The American Historical Review* 106(3), 866–905.

4

'GOOD GOVERNANCE' AND 'STATE FAILURE'

The pseudo-science of statesmen in our times

Branwen Gruffydd Jones

[G]ood, earnest, even intelligent men have come by millions to believe almost religiously that white folk are a peculiar and chosen people whose one great accomplishment is civilisation and that civilisation must be protected from the rest of the world by cheating, stealing, lying, and murder. The propaganda, the terrible, ceaseless propaganda that buttresses this belief day by day – the propaganda of poet and novelist, the uncanny welter of romance, the half knowledge of scientists, the pseudo-science of statesmen – all these, united in the myth of mass inferiority of most men, have built a wall which many centuries will not break down.

Du Bois (1925, 442)

Introduction

In their opening critical survey of the neglect of race within the field of international relations, Anievas, Manchanda and Shilliam note that, "though explicitly racial tropes and conceptualisations of world order have been largely (though not entirely) eliminated from mainstream discourses in the post-World War II era, questions concerning the extent to which race and racism continue to subliminally structure contemporary world politics, in both material and ideological ways, remain as significant as ever". This chapter addresses a prominent strand of the mainstream academic and policy discourse about international order today which does indeed appear to be free from the language of race, free from explicitly racial tropes and conceptions of world order: the discourse of state failure.

The concepts of the failed or fragile state on the one hand and the need for good governance on the other are central to contemporary international policy discourse about the global south and, especially, Africa. The promotion of good governance has been an explicit component of World Bank policy in Africa since the late 1980s, and remains a common-place referent underpinning virtually all international policy initiatives and agendas, from the promotion of democracy to sustainable cities. The concept of state failure rose to prominence in the 1990s and was given additional emphasis following the events of 11 September 2001 and the ensuing war on terrorism. While encompassing all regions of the global south, Africa features especially prominently in this discourse (Di John 2010; Ndulo and Grieco 2010; Bates 2008; Kieh 2007).

These two strands of conceptual vocabulary are located firmly within the discourse of international development and security policy, elaborated by western states (especially the US and UK, also Australia and the EU), international institutions, bilateral and multilateral donor organisations and a host of think tanks and research institutions. These conceptual vocabularies have also been energetically promoted, elaborated and occasionally contested by academic scholars in development studies, international relations and comparative politics. The mutually reinforcing dynamics between the spheres of academic research and policy formulation have sustained an outpouring of publications, reports and analyses addressing problems of governance and the conditions of the failed or fragile state over the past decade. Understanding Africa's condition through the language of good governance and state failure is the commonsense of our time, a commonsense which helps to legitimise the spectrum of western intervention in Africa and other non-western societies, from military intervention to governance reform. For example, Liberia was long seen as an exemplar 'failed state' (International Crisis Group 2004; Levitt 2005; McGovern 2005). The official category of the 'fragile state' was part of the discursive legit-imation of the Governance and Economic Management Assistance Programme, the World Bank's extensive project of post-conflict reconstruction on liberal free market principles in Liberia. This programme forced extensive external control over national policy design and implementation – essentially, a contemporary mode of trusteeship (Bøås 2009; Andersen 2010; Hahn 2011).

The 'failed states' discourse, this 'ceaseless propaganda' of our times, has not gone without criticism. Many scholars question the reductive binarism of the core terms of this discourse, and object to the lack of definitional and analytical precision of the central categories of state failure, fragility and collapse. Such critics seek to refine or delimit the central categories, while accepting the validity and usefulness of the discourse more broadly (Bøås and Jennings 2005). Newman, for example, concludes that despite its many problems, the concept of state failure should not be abandoned; rather, "a more critical approach to defining and measuring failed states is necessary" (Newman 2009, 440). Call argues that the concept of 'failed state' in itself should be rejected, but that the search should continue for a more adequate conceptual language: he prefers the categories of weak state, collapsed state, war-torn state and authoritarian regime, but offers no significant alternative theoretical or historical approach to understanding the causes and characteristics of political and social crisis (Call 2008). These qualified objections are consistent with the increasing normalisation of the categories of failed and fragile state in academic analysis, which is manifest in the frequent inclusion of these themes in introductory textbooks (e.g. Mansbach and Taylor 2011, 157–63) and, especially in academic analyses of Africa, the widespread acceptance of this terminology as a valid conceptual vocabulary (e.g. Branch and Cheeseman 2009).

The majority of such criticisms fail, however, to move beyond the empiricism of the failed states discourse and thus remain oblivious to what Anievas, Manchanda and Shilliam, drawing on Du Bois's thought, term a 'relational apprehension of power, hierarchy and division' in world order. Others have elaborated stronger critiques of the failed states discourse which resonate with Du Bois's concerns in two regards. First is the rejection of 'state failure' discourse as an explanatory approach. The conceptual vocabulary and associated methodological vision is a flawed starting point for any attempt to understand the historical and global relations of current conditions and processes in Africa and elsewhere because, fundamentally, it is blind to what Du Bois termed the dark shadow of colonialism (Du Bois 1925, 423). Du Bois sought to delineate clearly the widely ignored articulations between imperialism and race in world order and to insist on the intimate connections between 'democracy' in the West and racial oppression for the rest (Du Bois 1966 [1946]). He urged an analysis which recognised and probed the historical relationships between the crisis of the west in the early twentieth century, manifesting in two world wars, and the global histories of imperialism. In perhaps a similar vein, critics of the state failure discourse have sought to elaborate an alternative, relational account of the historical production of conditions of socio-economic crisis and political violence in Africa and elsewhere – for example with respect to Congo (Grovogui 2002), Somalia (Gruffydd Jones 2008) and Sudan (Ayers 2010). Analyses of state failure take an ahistorical and eurocentric notion of the state as a point of departure and characteristically focus on processes and conditions within the state which are examined in isolation from their historical formation and global relations. The past of colonialism and the present of international intervention are sidelined in most analyses of state failure. These alternative accounts have demonstrated that state forms and conditions of social, political and economic crisis in contemporary Africa cannot be adequately understood or explained without seriously examining the character and legacy of colonialism and the effects and consequences of ongoing practices of international accumulation and intervention.

Second, critics have exposed and rejected the imperial and racialised conception of world order inherent in the failed states discourse. This mode of critique focuses on the content of the discourse and the ways in which it serves to legitimise specific imperial practices and broader imperial orders. For example, Jonathan Hill has drawn on the work of Said to expose the fundamentally orientalist structure of this discourse (Hill 2005), while Morton and Bilgin have located international concerns with the weakness of non-European states in the geopolitical knowledge formations of the Cold War (Morton and Bilgin 2002). This resonates with Du Bois' relentless critique of racial ideologies and colour prejudice, the "curious, most childish propaganda" (1925, 442) which legitimised European imperial rule over non-European peoples and lands. The present chapter contributes to this second form of critique by arguing that the discourse of good governance /state failure is irredeemably rooted in an imperial and racialised imagination. While the Cold War discourse of modernisation and state building is the immediate precursor to the failed states discourse, as Morton and Bilgin have rightly highlighted, we need to recognise that these current ideas are situated in a much longer genealogy of imperial discourse. In this regard, it is necessary to expand our focus beyond the form of 'race thinking' and 'race science' which prevailed in the late nineteenth and early twentieth centuries when Du Bois was developing his analysis of the colour line.

The discourse of state failure makes no reference to race. In what sense, then, does it embody a racialised imagination? While acknowledging the diversity of arguments tracing the origins of the idea of race to classical antiquity, the Renaissance or the Enlightenment, Vanita Seth foregrounds the epistemological transformations producing the body as an object of inquiry which underpinned nineteenth-century racial thought (Seth 2010, 173–232). However, the argument that the discourse of state failure is racialised requires a more expanded understanding of the historical constitution of racial thought in two senses. First, as Grovogui has argued, racialised thought is not reducible to ideas about race based on biology or skin colour. In his recent examination of European thought about race and blackness in the Age of Enlightenment, Andrew Curran explains that he uses the term 'racialising' in order to avoid disputes about whether specific thinkers of the eighteenth century should be judged 'racist'. Yet his conception of racialised thought remains restricted to a corporal or physiological understanding of race. Drawing on Hudson, Curran understands racialising thought as the arbitrary classification of populations based on "phenotypical or genetic differences" (Curran 2011, 21, 230; Hudson 1996). But the longer history of European expansion and imperialism which has produced racialised social orders requires that we consider a more expanded notion of racialised thought. Grovogui shares Curran's concern but articulates this broader scope and longer history: "By racialisation of international knowledge, I do not mean to impute racist motives to international theorists: I simply mean to stress the use of analytical methods that uphold ethnographic allusions associated with a hermeneutics of race and culture" (Grovogui 2001, 426). Grovogui identifies racialised international thought as producing an 'ontology of difference' which "emerged during the Renaissance, survived through the eighteenth-century Enlightenment debates on the nature of the moral order, and spanned nineteenth-century scientific racism to the present" (2001, 429).

Second, these changing ideas have been employed over centuries to *produce* race: to legitimise practices of conquest, enslavement, dispossession and domination which have produced racialised structures, social relations, practices and political orders. This is the burden of Hesse's insistence that the colonial articulation of race operated "in excess of the body" (Hesse 2007, 654). Hesse too underlines the 'multiple references of association' deployed in the historical articulation of race and emphasises that epistemological racialisation informed what he terms *governmental racialisation*: "the social routinisation and institutionalisation of regulatory, administrative power (e.g. laws, rules, policies, discipline, precepts)" exercised by European over non-European "as if this was a normal, inviolable or natural social arrangement" (2007, 653, 656).

The long history of racialised thought has been shaped by changing ideas about authoritative knowledge, situated in indirect ways within changing power relations and forms of political authority and rule. The changing relationships of epistemology and power within which racialised thought is situated have been international for centuries. This chapter charts the main contours of this longer history of racialised international thought in order to identify some of the varying ways in which underlying features of hierarchy and criteria of difference have been manifest and how these have informed specific imperial practices. The analysis traces the relationships between three realms: the specific *form and content* of racialised international thought; the broader and underlying *epistemological environment* – prevailing norms regulating what counts as authoritative knowledge; and the *historical and geopolitical context*. This approach is necessary in order to develop the two claims of this chapter: first, that the discourse of 'state failure' should be recognised as the latest variant in a long history of racialised international thought going much further back than the preoccupations of the Cold War; and second, that the state failure discourse constitutes a particular variant of this longer tradition whose form is shaped by the global conjuncture of the present.

The chapter examines three broad historical phases with distinct configurations of ideas, epistemologies and imperial politics. It was in the context of European expansion in the sixteenth century that racialised international thought first emerged, configured through the religious discourse which legitimised Portuguese and Spanish colonialism. In order to profile these relationships the first section examines the sixteenth-century debate over slavery in the Spanish colonial empire of the New World which culminated in Valladolid in 1550. These debates refined the hierarchy between European and non-European: the humanity of the African was established as less certain or significant than that of both European and Indian. The analysis then turns to examine the changing form, content, methods and epistemology of racialised international thought from the late seventeenth to the nineteenth century. As the transatlantic slave trade reached its peak and the religious basis of political and epistemological authority waned, the European Enlightenment heralded new systems of knowledge in which modified and novel ideas rationalised ongoing and new relations between European and non-European peoples. New ideas of a hierarchy of peoples rationalised on the basis of empirical scientific inquiry informed the colonial occupation of Africa at the end of the nineteenth century. The third section examines the contemporary failed states discourse in light of this longer history. This is the postcolonial era, the era of global finance, when the explicit vocabulary of race disappears from the content of racialised international thought.

Humanity in question? The Portuguese, the Spanish, the Indians and the Africans

During the first half of the sixteenth century the Spanish conquest of the islands of the Caribbean entailed increasingly violent treatment of Amerindians. Increasing numbers of Amerindians were brought forcibly from the mainland to the Spanish island colonies, where they were forced to work growing food and sugar for the colonial settlers (*encomenderos*) and panning for gold in rivers and streams. Similar labour regimes were later developed as the mainland was brought under Spanish colonial rule. But by mid-century the enslavement of Amerindians was outlawed and, instead, the Spanish turned to importing enslaved Africans to meet their demands for labour. This differential treatment of Indian and African by the Spanish was seen to hinge on questions of humanity.

The violence of colonial conquest generated criticism from Spanish clerics. Dominican friars Antonio de Montesinos, Bartolomé de Las Casas and others criticised the harsh exploitation of the Indians. They appealed to the Spanish crown, denouncing the brutality of the *encomenderos* on the island of Hispaniola and seeking protection for the Indians through legal reform. Their appeals had an effect: in 1542 the 'New Laws' were introduced by Cardinal Loaysa, president of the Council of the Indies, banning the enslavement of Indians in Spanish colonies of the New World (Huxley, 1980). Continuing criticisms of colonial practice led eventually to a formal debate in Valladolid in 1550, called by the Spanish King Charles V. Las Casas sought to protect the Indians from slavery on grounds of their humanity, against the arguments of Juan Ginés de Sepúlveda, a renowned Spanish scholar of Aristotle who drew on Aristotle's arguments about natural slavery to defend the forceful conquest and enslavement of Indians on the basis of their inferior civilisation (Huxley 1980; Hannaford 1996, 149–50).

Las Casas is widely seen as the father of humanism and human rights discourses (Hanke 1974; Carozza 2003; Clayton 2010). In 1992 Hayward Alker's presidential address to the International Studies Association presented Las Casas as inaugurating a moment of humanist commitment to universal human dignity which has survived into our own times (Alker 1992). Yet while appealing for protection of the Indians, Bartolomé de Las Casas and other Dominican clerics proposed that African people should be imported in increasing numbers, to work as slaves in place of the Indians. In 1510 Las Casas had recommended the importation of African slaves in place of Indians on the grounds that they 'had no souls' (Wilson 1957). Las Casas articulated this proposal on several occasions, in 1516, 1518, in a letter to the Council of the Indies in 1532, and again in 1542 (Rivera 1992).

Later in life Las Casas came to bitterly regret this position, denouncing the cruelty of African slavery and defending the humanity of Africans (Clayton 2009; Merediz and Salles-Reese 2008). The point here is neither to pin the blame for the African slave trade on the shoulders of Las Casas nor to absolve him given his subsequent change of views, but to highlight the structure of knowledge through which both the protection of Indians and the enslavement and trading of African people were legitimised and the broader framework of political authority and economic interest which underpinned that structure of knowledge. As scholars such as Patricia Seed and Luis Rivera have shown, the debate has to be understood in terms of the rival interests of the interlocutors, the prevailing meaning and significance of the core terms framing the arguments, and the broader political context of Spanish and Portuguese colonial expansion.

The question of the humanity of the Indians was central to the legitimacy of Spanish colonisation. The authority for Spanish colonisation of the New World rested on the goal of converting the native populations to Christianity. The relationship between the state, the monarch and the church in Europe was still fused in the fifteenth century. For several centuries the Pope, as representative of God, was recognised as the supreme seat of power on earth; in turn the Pope granted to monarchs the authority to rule in God's name in the terrestrial sphere. Through the issue of papal bulls the Pope granted to monarchs the authority to rule over all peoples and lands within the Holy Roman Empire and the duty to extend the rule of God over non-Christian lands and peoples. Although by the fifteenth century the power of the Catholic Pope within Europe was waning, it was this structure of power which, in the Alexandrian Bull *Inter Caetera* of 1493 and subsequently, extended legitimacy to the Spanish colonial conquests in the New World (Rivera 1992, 24–8). As Rivera emphasises, while participants in the intense debates which culminated in Valladolid contested the interpretation of specific elements regarding the treatment of the Indians, all sides recognised the papal bulls as the essential framework legitimising the Spanish colonial enterprise (Rivera 1992, 24–41).

If the legitimacy of Spanish colonisation rested on converting the native populations, this in turn hinged on the assumption of their humanity. The system of thought in which appeals to the humanity of the Indians were made was the medieval Christian doctrine based on the teachings of Thomas Aquinas. In this doctrine, humans were distinguished from animals on the basis of their capacity to reason. And the possession of a rational soul indicated the potential for conversion to Christianity. Thus the designation of 'human' entailed the capacity to be baptised and brought into the Catholic faith (Seed 1993, 636–8). The defence of the Indians' *humanity* was the defence of their capacity for conversion to Catholicism, and what was at stake in defending this capacity was the legitimacy of Spanish colonisation of the New World.

Las Casas was not the first or only one to propose substituting African for Indian slave labour: the idea was proposed by many friars – Dominican Pedro de Córdoba in 1516–18, Franciscan Pedro Mexía in 1517, the Jeronomite fathers in 1517, and again in 1518 (Rivera 1992, 184–5). The proposal that Africans were fit for enslavement, in contrast to the Indians, rested on their definition as 'Sarecens and Moors, enemies of Christianity' (Rivera 1992, 190). Africans had been defined in such terms throughout the fifteenth century, in a series of papal bulls (in 1436, 1443, 1452, 1455, 1456, 1481) which endorsed the enslavement of Africans by the Portuguese crown (Rivera 1992; Boxer 1969, 228–48; Mudimbe 1994, 30–7).

The discourses on the humanity of the Indians and the lack of faith of Africans were framed in the theological tradition of Roman Catholic Christianity. Since the thirteenth century this tradition underpinned the absolute political power of the Pope within Europe and hence the religio-political authority of the Spanish and Portuguese monarchs (Rivera 1992, 23–41; Mudimbe 1994, 30–7). From the late fifteenth century, as the Spanish and Portuguese expanded beyond Europe, around the coast of Africa towards Asia and across the ocean to the New World of the

Americas, their colonial ventures and conquests were authorised by this same structure and discourse of religious-political-legal power. The authority of the papal bulls was the ultimate reference for the legitimacy of Spanish colonial rule in the Americas, and Portuguese colonial rule and monopoly of trade in Africa and Asia. This authority defined the purpose of Spanish and Portuguese expansion as the expansion of Christendom: the conversion of infidels to the Christian faith. The debate over the humanity of the Indians was rooted within this same system of knowledge which legitimised the enslavement of Africans as enemies of Christianity, a system of knowledge fundamental to and inseparable from the political structure of Spanish and Portuguese colonisation of the Americas, Africa and Asia.

The legitimating discourse of the transatlantic slave trade and slave-based production in the Americas emerged from systems of thought which specified an 'ontology of difference' between Europeans, Indians and Africans on grounds of humanity and religion, in order to differentially rationalise their political subjugation, dispossession and enslavement. While drawing on established bodies of Christian thought regarding natural law and just war, moral debates about the differential humanity of Indians, Africans and Europeans were conducted essentially in order to legitimise practices of Spanish and Portuguese war, colonisation, slavery and slave trade.

Secular classifications: the methodology of classical and Modern Imperialism

From the late seventeenth century the form and content of racialised international thought began to change. The use of information gathered on the basis of observation and ordered systematically according to a reasoned logic became the foundation for new approaches to knowledge and the distinction of new disciplinary fields. These developments in knowledge emerged in the context of the decline of the political authority of the Catholic church and divine basis of political authority on earth. As relations of political power were reconfigured on secular grounds, scholars sought to defend the secular grounds for authoritative knowledge about the social and natural world. The quest to develop more systematic knowledge became global in scope: the Enlightenment era entailed an ambition to know the whole world and everything in it, manifest in the development of encyclopaedias which rendered the whole world knowable in an ordered and comprehensive manner (Withers 1996). The twin significance of colonial context and epistemological development underpinning the increasingly systematic organisation of the study of non-European peoples was reflected, institutionally, in the establishment during the eighteenth century of scientific-exploratory organisations such as the Society for the Observation of Man established in France in the 1790s (Cohen 1980, 61). Two distinct but related ideas developed from the eighteenth century: scientific ideas about race, and ideas about historical change as the evolutionary progression of societies through distinct stages. Both sets of ideas shared an underlying structure of hierarchy and classification, which informed new modes of colonialism.

From the end of the seventeenth century European scholars began to draw together the information available in the numerous accounts by travellers and explorers of non-European peoples and places. Efforts were made to identify a rational order within the details of empirical diversity gathered in the cosmologies of earlier centuries and embellished by contemporary accounts. During the eighteenth century this was increasingly addressed using techniques of classification arising from the study of plants and animals in the new field of natural history (Bernasconi 2001, 12–13; Hudson 1996, 252–3; Cohen 1980, 60–99; Foucault 1970, 128–32). The Swedish botanist Carl Linnaeus, the French naturalist the Comte de Buffon and the German comparative anatomist Johan Friedrich Blumenbach undertook to sort the diversity of peoples into a coherent system of four or five groups, in a framework based on criteria other than religion (Bernasconi 2001; Hudson 1996; Curran 2011). Peoples were arranged or classified in groups ('races' or 'varieties') according to an array of criteria – moral character; manufacturing capacity; cultural forms and activities; and physical characteristics including skin colour, hair type, shape of body and stature (Jacques 1997).

The eighteenth century was undoubtedly the moment when scientific ideas about race came to be articulated specifically in relation to skin colour, physiology and corporal difference (Curran 2011). However, even as the specification of racial hierarchy was given a new basis in anatomy and biology, the scope of racialised international thought remained far broader, encompassing questions of culture and government. Building on the work of others, German philosopher Immanuel Kant developed a theoretical scheme positioning races in a hierarchy on the basis of cultural and intellectual capacity and civilisation. Kant placed white Europeans at the top, followed by Asians, with black Africans and Native Americans at the bottom, arguing that both Africans and American Indians were incapable of intellectual advance or education to a high level and incapable of self-government (Eze 1995). While Bernasconi (2001) argues that Kant developed the first *theory* of race, his specification of a racial hierarchy articulated ideas reproduced across Enlightenment thought, from Voltaire and Hume through to Hegel (Eze 1997).

The second idea which emerged as a central strand of Enlightenment thought from the eighteenth century was a stadial view of history (Meek 1971; Skinner 2003). This was manifest first in the static identification of different types of society, which could be arranged in a hierarchy on the criteria of more or less sophisticated political institutions (governance), productive activities (economy), or arts and science (culture). The static differentiation of types of society gave way to a teleological understanding of change with the introduction of the idea of progress and a theoretical explanation of historical movement, advance or evolution (Jacques 1997). Societies identified in the vertical hierarchy of civilisation were then positioned horizontally on a temporal trajectory of evolution (Fabian 1983).

These two strands of thought about race and historical progress were formally crystallised in the nineteenth-century discourse about civilisation and employed explicitly to legitimise new imperial ventures. As Anghie and others have highlighted, in the nineteenth century the idea of civilisation was formalised in international law as the criteria of difference by which to regulate differential relations among states (Anghie 2005; Grovogui 1996). The development of international law in the nineteenth century was centrally preoccupied with colonial problems, and "special doctrines and norms had to be devised for the purpose of defining, identifying and placing the uncivilized" (Anghie 2005, 36). Here international law was able to draw upon the resources and 'evolutionary hallucinations' of anthropological knowledge (Mudimbe 1988, 6), which from the mid-nineteenth century renewed an evolutionary approach to the study of the "varieties of man" (Stocking 1987; Burrow 1966; Fabian 1983). The classification of non-European societies according to their level of civilisation, energetically pursued by anthropologists and ethnologists, became a formal requirement of international law and central to the legitimation of different regimes of colonialism.

The discursive construction and definition of African polities through European ethnographic categories was integral to legitimising the expansion of 'informal empire' and formal colonial rule in Africa in the nineteenth and early twentieth century. The binary distinction between civilised and uncivilised states which underpinned the positivist doctrine of international law necessarily expanded to stipulate a more complex graded hierarchy of degrees of civilisation according to diverse forms of colonial rule (protectorates, dominions, crown colonies). In all cases, formal legal and policy discourse was informed by ethnographic categorisations of African societies in terms of civilisation, capacity to govern, and cultural progress (Tilley and Gordon 2007). European ethnographers often produced highly detailed and nuanced studies of African societies, and many held liberal views. Nevertheless anthropologists rarely questioned the underlying premise of colonial rule; indeed many worked as colonial administrators (Sibeud 1994; Wilder 2007). European ethnographic knowledge of African societies was structured by a comparative and hierarchical logic which sought to calibrate African societies on a scale of civilisation. British and French anthropologists and ethnographers studied the political structures of African societies and sought to develop an overall typology through which to give order and classification to the variety and diversity of forms of social and political organisation (Fortes and Evans-Pritchard 1940; Middleton and Tait 1958). One of the central criteria for distinguishing the extent of civilisation and thus positioning African societies in a classificatory system was the existence or lack of centralised structures of political rule. African societies were judged according to a scale of civilisation and positioned in an evolutionary scheme which accorded greater respect to those societies with centralised structures of political authority. African polities with decentralised modes of political and social organisation, categorised by anthropologists as 'stateless', were considered more primitive, lacking in any degree of civilisation. Such classifications directly informed legal debates refining the basis of colonial dispossession across Africa. Thus anthropological classifications and typologies were calibrated with the legal discourse of colonial rule with major consequences. This ethnographic hierarchy informed the formal legal processes of the establishment of European political domination over autonomous African polities, the annexation of territory, dispossession of land, and the construction of new institutions of colonial rule over subject peoples.

From modernisation to failure: rankings and predictions in the era of global finance

Du Bois developed his notion of the colour line at a time when explicit ideas about racial hierarchy were central to the formal institutions of global order, an order which set 'the darker races beyond the pale of democracy and of modern humanity' (1925, 438). The language of race in its modern colonial form – biological theories of racial evolution and the vocabulary of civilisation, savage and tribe – disappeared from legitimate international discourse with the demise of formal colonial rule in the mid-twentieth century. Yet the underlying logics of hierarchy and difference which structured the formal discourse of race have endured, underpinning new technical, ahistorical and apparently race-free vocabularies. Hesse refers to this underlying structuring as *epistemological racialisation*: "the codified organisation of knowledges (e.g. deliberations, expertise, histories, representations, and explanations) based on the adjudication and valorisation of non-Europeanness and the debasement and appropriation of non-Europeanness, *but without explanatory reference to the impact of coloniality*" (2007, 656 – emphasis added). This final section plots the ideological, imperial and epistemological coordinates of contemporary forms of racialised international thought, examining how the discourse of state failure, despite the disappearance of an explicit vocabulary of race, reproduces in new ways features of earlier modes of racialised thought, and how these dimensions are located in the current global conjuncture.

The immediate predecessor to the failed states discourse is not the colonial ideology of racial civilisation but the sanitised language of development and modernisation which emerged in the wake of decolonisation. The discourse of modernisation served to legitimise the practices of western governments and international organisations in providing 'policy advice' and 'technical assistance' in a range of matters of political, economic and social concern to newly independent countries, the new vocabulary helping to disguise essential continuities with colonial relationships. The notion of development embodied a dynamic sense of movement and teleology: the categories of less developed, developing and developed posited in a secular and technical manner the sense of teleological progress earlier expressed through the language of evolution and civilisation. The ahistorical hierarchy and linear dynamism of development through modernisation constituted the reconfiguration of colonial discourse in the specific global conjuncture of decolonisation and the Cold War. The language of development, tradition and modernisation provided a comparative mode of diagnosis and prescription which silenced the history of colonialism in the production of global inequalities, while charting an alternative non-revolutionary path of social and political change and progress for newly independent states in a global order structured by the geopolitics of the Cold War and the threat of revolution.

In this sense the discourse of state failure is situated specifically in the post-Cold War era when the prospect of a revolutionary alternative to liberal capitalism is no longer plausible. The aesthetic form and authoritative basis of the failed states discourse are also rooted in aspects specific to the present. The original hierarchy positioning Africans beneath Amerindians and Europeans during the time of the slave trade was framed by the Christian doctrine underpinning the legitimacy and authority of Spanish and Portuguese colonialism. The colonial conquest of Africa at the end of the nineteenth century was rendered legal through a new racial hierarchy constructed on the secular evolutionary ground of civilisation, with gradations of civilisational status calibrated according to ethnographic knowledge. The new discourse of state failure retains the structuring logic of a hierarchy of gradations, with the criteria for identifying international hierarchy now formulated in terms of a state's institutional forms and capacity to govern. Thus the unit within which the ontology of difference is situated has moved from humanity through races, civilisations and tribes to the institutional form of the state:

> In fragile states, the gap between the model of the rational-legal bureaucratic state of academic literature and development practice and institutional forms on the ground is often very wide.
>
> *(Ingram 2010, 8)*

This inherits the colonial concern with good government, but the judgement of capacity to govern is no longer correlated according to racial or civilisational capacities and maturity. The positions on this new hierarchy of state capacity to govern – from weak to fragile, failing, collapsed and rogue states – are now specified with reference to a general, universal notion of the functional capacity of states. The descriptive vocabulary employed in academic and policy literature to describe and diagnose the process of state failure is proliferous, dramatic and profoundly ahistorical. Just as in the eighteenth-century discourse of racial anatomy, it is "rife with mechanistic metaphors" (Curran 2011, 4) – with states slipping backwards, sliding towards the abyss of collapse, tottering on the brink, before decaying, collapsing or imploding.

Efforts to distinguish different moments of this trajectory invariably entail forms of measurement (Baliamoune-Lutz and McGillivray 2011; Stepputat and Engberg-Pedersen 2008). Several attempts have been made to specify in clear and comprehensive terms the features which make up a failed or fragile state (DFID 2005; Nathan Associates Inc 2006; Stepputat and Engberg-Pedersen 2008; USAID 2005; IRIS Center 2003; World Bank 2002); others have subsequently compiled and compared extant definitions (Di John 2010). These efforts entail breaking the concept of state into a series of constituent elements, each of which can be measured or monitored on the basis of empirical criteria, so as to "operationalise" the concepts for policy-making (Stewart and Brown 2009). The analyses and diagnoses of state fragility/failure thus carry an air of objectivity and precision implied by their basis in empirical observation and measurement. The authority of this discourse is rooted in the broader reign of positivism and quantitative social science which was firmly consolidated in western social science in the twentieth century (Mirowski 2005).

One of the characteristic representational modes through which the failed states discourse is articulated is in the form of tables, rankings and indices. The calculation of the differential capacity to govern among the states of the world today is rendered seemingly objective and ahistorical by the empirical measurement of aspects of government capacity and function. Numerical measurements of discrete governance indicators are compiled to construct a comprehensive framework within which every state can be compared and ranked on a single index of governance and failure, represented visually in tables or maps. Thus all states are positioned with precision in a global ranking, in indices of fragility and failure, many recalculated on an annual basis (Brookings Institute 2011; World Bank 2002). The *Failed States Index*, produced annually by the journal *Foreign Policy* and think tank Fund for Peace, is the most notorious (Fund for Peace 2005; Fund for Peace and Foreign Policy 2011); others include the *State Fragility Index* of the Center for Systemic Peace; *Index of State Weakness in the Developing World* of the Center for Global Development, Brookings Institute; and the World Bank's *Country Policy and Institutional Assessment* (Marshall and Cole 2010; Rice and Patrick 2008; Independent Evaluation Group 2010). In a more optimistic vein, the Mo Ibrahim Foundation has recently developed the Index of Governance which is compiled specifically for African states. While the celebration of 'good governance' suggests a more positive approach than the pathologising diagnoses of fragility and failure, the essential form, structure and method employed faithfully mirrors that of the failure indices (Mo Ibrahim Foundation 2011).

The use of quantification to render qualitative and indeterminate social phenomena into finite and exact numerical form and the use of tables to order and display this precise information, is not new, but these indices assume a form which is arguably specific to the current global conjuncture of neoliberal capitalism and global finance. Visualisation of society and economy using tables, for the purpose of government, was developed in the eighteenth century as society and economy were constituted as fields of scientific enquiry (Frangsmyr et al. 1990). The French physiocrats, led by François Quesnay, were the first to imagine the national economy in the form of numerical information arranged in tables (Roll 1992, 112–14; Buck-Morss 1995), while in Sweden the institutionalised expert production of statistical data for the purpose of government was developed early in the eighteenth century (Johannisson 1990). In the twentieth century, with the demise of colonial empires, these existing practices of quantification and visualisation have been extended to enable international measurement and comparison. The World Bank produced its first annual World Development Report in 1978, while the United Nations Development Programme (UNDP) began publishing its annual Human Development Report in 1990. These reports include measurements of an array of social, economic and political indicators organised by state in the form of tables, graphs and indices. This visual mode of representation furthers the apparent evacuation of race from international knowledge, as the construction of hierarchies of international comparison and judgement now rests on the neutral validity of empirical and numerical facts.

The construction of rankings is also not specific to the international comparison of states; it is a logic of calculation and representation used increasingly in all areas of social life over the past three decades. The expansion of this specific aesthetic form and way of knowing can be historicised not only in relation to the hegemony of positivism but, more specifically, in relation to the growing hegemony of the free market, integral to "audit culture" and neoliberal governmentality (Strathern 2000; Fougner 2008) and, perhaps, characteristic of the era of global finance. The reduction of qualitative and dynamic aspects of social life and process to numerical form is integral to the calculation of risk and thus a central technology of knowledge in global finance, employed in the construction of credit ratings and complex financial products such as derivatives and securities (Langley 2008). Indeed, it was the utility of social accounting for the calculation of insurance that provided one of the early motivations for the development and institutionalisation of statistics in the eighteenth century (Johannisson 1990). And the process of rendering the social world knowable through visualisation in tables, numbers, and through the use of colour and other increasingly more complex forms, has become an important tool in the world of global finance (Pryke 2010).

This is not to suggest that there is any direct relationship between the practices of global finance and the construction of 'failed state' indices, though they might form one component of information in the calculation of national credit ratings. The suggestion is rather that the increasingly normalised use of indices and rankings as a mode of producing comparative international knowledge might be located in the era of the hegemony of the free market and global finance. These aesthetic forms constitute a mode of representing an apparently neutral comparative analysis of capacity to govern and risk of failure. Indices of governance and state failure reproduce hierarchies of international judgement and epistemological racialisation which continue to position the European at the top and the African at the bottom. And, with no reference to race but grounded in the authority of empirical fact, they continue to provide a discursive basis for legitimising western intervention in African and other states. This pseudo-science of international discourse today is one instance of the enduring discursive and historical relations that Du Bois earlier conceived in terms of the colour line.

Conclusion

The global imagination of our times is quick to diagnose failure, determined to predict the onset of collapse, and, at times, willing to applaud success in the governance of African states. Employing a vocabulary and aesthetic form specific to the present, current international thought about good governance and state failure in Africa echoes and resonates with earlier forms of imperial imagination. This chapter has argued that the contemporary discourse of state failure must be recognised as a form of racialised international thought and, as such, situated in a much longer imperial history. While the association of race with skin-colour and the body is rooted more narrowly in eighteenth and nineteenth-century thought, all of the discourses considered here are systems of racialised thought. Following Grovogui and Hesse, the notion of racialised thought is not confined to questions of skin colour or embodiment, but refers to systems of thought about peoples – fundamentally, the European and non-European – which are animated by difference and hierarchy, comparison and judgement, and which legitimise colonial practices and western intervention. As Mudimbe has noted, across all the complexities of changing western ideas about Africa, one thing has remained constant from the sixteenth century to the present day: a moralising attitude of normative judgement (Mudimbe 1994, 6, 14).

From the fifteenth century onwards, ideas about non-European peoples and their relationships with Europe have been organised on the basis of an ontology of difference informing a hierarchical logic which places the European in a position of superiority and which legitimises diverse colonial practices. In the sixteenth century the African was positioned beneath the Indian and European on grounds of humanity and capacity to embrace Christianity. This discourse, rooted in the theological tradition of Roman Catholic Christianity, legitimised Spanish and Portuguese colonial expansion and the enslavement of Africans. The eighteenth century saw profound political and epistemological changes in Europe. Existing ideas about a hierarchy of peoples were reconfigured on the basis of secular reason and empirical observation: the sciences of race and historical evolution were born. These combined to inform the racialised doctrine of civilisation which, in the disciplines of international law and anthropology, was refined into detailed calibrations. The classification of African societies into more or less civilised tribes on the basis of their political organisation and economy directly informed the legitimation of new modes of colonial occupation, dispossession and political rule at the end of the nineteenth century.

With political decolonisation in the twentieth century, the explicit vocabulary of race and civilisation was dropped from international discourse. The superior capacity of western states to govern and the proper form of the western liberal state as a universal model constitute the unspoken and unquestioned assumptions upon which the failed states discourse is erected. Conditions of social, political and economic crises in Africa are diagnosed as resulting from a *failure to govern properly* on the part of African governments. In its ahistorical, apparently neutral descriptive terminology, its focus on the unit of the state, and its technocratic reproduction of international hierarchy this discourse shares much with the earlier language of development and modernisation. Yet, with the possibility of an alternative revolutionary path towards progress now firmly abandoned, the sense of inevitable teleology and forward movement underpinning the discourse of development and modernisation has faded. Today many scholars and policy-makers show little hesitation in resurrecting a form of political analysis and diagnosis which has a far more direct continuity with the ideology of late colonialism.

The construction of international hierarchies remains and continues to develop. The unit of comparison has shifted over the centuries from humanity and religion through biological races and primitive tribes to states. The ontology of difference is now based upon the capacity to govern effectively. And the authority of expert knowledge now derives from the use of empirical description, measurement and quantification. Its hierarchical order is rendered visually explicit and precise in tables and rankings which position African states unrelentingly in the bottom league, the hopeless and desperate. The impulses to collection, compilation, comparison and categorisation, so deeply entrenched in Western thought, recur with renewed energy in the twenty-first century. Facts about African states and conditions, once described with wonder in the *Cosmographies* of the seventeenth century, are now reduced to numerical measurements, to inform and populate the indices, tables and proxy-indicators employed by Western policy-makers for global monitoring, prediction and policy formulation. The think tanks in Washington today have inherited from the eighteenth century Society for the Observation of Man the mantle of producing the knowledge to sustain the imperial imagination.

Bibliography

Alker, H. R. (1992) 'The Humanistic Moment in International Studies: Reflections on Machiavelli and Las Casas: 1992 Presidential Address', *International Studies Quarterly*, 36 (4), 347–71.

Andersen, L. (2010) 'Outsiders inside the State: Post-Conflict Liberia between Trusteeship and Partnership', *Journal of Intervention and Statebuilding*, 4 (2), 129–52.

Anghie, A. (2005) *Imperialism, Sovereignty and the Making of International Law*. Cambridge: Cambridge University Press.

Ayers, A. J. (2010) 'Sudan's Uncivil War: The Global-Historical Constitution of Political Violence', *Review of African Political Economy*, 37 (124), 153–71.

Baliamoune-Lutz, M. and McGillivray, M. (2011) 'State Fragility: Concept and Measurement', in Naudé, W., Santos-Paulino, A. U. and McGillivray, M. (eds), *Fragile States: Causes, Costs, and Responses*, Oxford: Oxford University Press, 33–42.

Bates, R. H. (2008) *When Things Fell Apart: State Failure in Late-Century Africa*. Cambridge: Cambridge University Press.

Bernasconi, R. (2001) 'Who Invented the Concept of Race? Kant's Role in the Enlightenment Construction of Race', in Bernasconi, R. (ed.), *Race*. Oxford: Blackwell, 11–36.

Bøås, M. (2009) 'Making Plans for Liberia: A Trusteeship Approach to Good Governance?', *Third World Quarterly*, 30 (7), 1329–41.

Bøås, M. and Jennings, K. M. (2005) 'Insecurity and Development: The Rhetoric of the "Failed State"', *European Journal of Development Research*, 17 (3), 385–95.

Boxer, C. R. (1969) *The Portuguese Seaborne Empire 1415–1825*. London: Hutchinson.

Branch, D. and Cheeseman, N. (2009) 'Democratization, Sequencing, and State Failure in Africa: Lessons from Kenya', *African Affairs*, 108 (430), 1–26.

Brookings Institute (2011) *Index of State Weakness in the Developing World*. Washington, DC.

Buck-Morss, S. (1995) 'Envisioning Capital: Political Economy on Display', *Critical Inquiry*, 21 (2), 434–67.

Burrow, J. W. (1966) *Evolution and Society: A Study in Victorian Social Theory*. Cambridge: Cambridge University Press.

Call, C. T. (2008) 'The Fallacy of the "Failed State"', *Third World Quarterly*, 29 (8), 1491–1507.

Carozza, P. G. (2003) 'From Conquest to Constitutions: Retrieving a Latin American Tradition of the Idea of Human Rights', *Human Rights Quarterly*, 25 (2), 281–313.

Clayton, L. A. (2009) 'Bartolomé De Las Casas and the African Slave Trade', *History Compass*, 7 (6), 1526–41.

——(2010) *Bartolomé De Las Casas and the Conquest of the Americas*. Chichester: Wiley-Blackwell.

Cohen, W. B. (1980) *The French Encounter with Africans: White Responses to Blacks, 1530–1880*. Bloomington, IN: Indiana University Press.

Curran, A. S. (2011) *The Anatomy of Blackness: Science and Slavery in an Age of Enlightenment.* Baltimore, MD: Johns Hopkins University Press.

DFID (2005) *Why We Need to Work More Effectively in Fragile States.* London: Department for International Development.

Di John, J. (2010) 'The Concept, Causes and Consequences of Failed States: A Critical Review of the Literature and Agenda for Research with Specific Reference to Sub-Saharan Africa', *European Journal of Development Research,* 22 (1), 10–30.

Du Bois, W. E. B. (1925) 'Worlds of Color', *Foreign Affairs,* 3 (3), 423–44.

——(1966 [1946]) *The World and Africa: An Inquiry into the Part which Africa Has Played in World History.* New York: International Publishers.

Eze, E. C. (1995) 'The Color of Reason: The Idea of "Race" in Kant's Anthropology', in Faull, K. M. (ed.), *Anthropology and the German Enlightenment: Perspectives on Humanity.* Lewisburg: Bucknell University Press, 219–20.

Eze, E. C. (ed.) (1997) *Race and the Enlightenment: A Reader.* Oxford: Blackwell.

Fabian, J. (1983) *Time and the Other: How Anthropology Makes Its Object.* New York: Columbia University Press.

Fortes, M. and Evans-Pritchard, E. E. (eds) (1940) *African Political Systems.* London: Oxford University Press.

Foucault, M. (1970) *The Order of Things: An Archaeology of the Human Sciences.* New York: Random House.

Fougner, T. (2008) 'Neoliberal Governance of States: The Role of Competitiveness Indexing and Country Benchmarking', *Millennium – Journal of International Studies,* 37 (2), 303–26.

Frangsmyr, T., Heilbron, J. L. and Rider, R. E. (eds) (1990) *The Quantifying Spirit in the Eighteenth Century.* Berkeley: University of California Press.

Fund for Peace (2005) 'The Failed States Index', *Foreign Policy,* July/August [online]. Available from: www.foreignpolicy.com/story/cms.php?story_id=3098 [accessed 20 December 2005].

Fund for Peace and Foreign Policy (2011) *The Failed States Index 2011,* Foreign Policy [online]. Available from: www.foreignpolicy.com/articles/2011/06/17/2011_failed_sta tes_index_interactive_map_and_rankings [accessed 12 September 2011].

Grovogui, S. N. Z. (1996) *Sovereigns, Quasi Sovereigns, and Africans: Race and Self-Determination in International Law.* Minneapolis: University of Minnesota Press.

——(2001) 'Come to Africa: A Hermeneutic of Race in International Theory', *Alternatives: Global, Local, Political,* 26 (4), 425–48.

——(2002) 'Regimes of Sovereignty: International Morality and the African Condition', *European Journal of International Relations,* 8 (3), 315–38.

Gruffydd Jones, B. (2008) 'The Global Political Economy of Social Crisis: Towards a Critique of the "Failed State" Ideology", *Review of International Political Economy,* 15 (2), 180–205.

Hahn, N. (2011) *The Political Economy of Armed Conflicts in Liberia.* Unpublished Development Studies PhD thesis, SOAS, University of London.

Hanke, L. (1974) *All Mankind Is One: A Study of the Disputation between Bartolome? De Las Casas and Juan Gine?S De Sepu?Lveda in 1550 on the Intellectual and Religious Capacity of the American Indians.* DeKalb: Northern Illinois University Press

Hannaford, I. (1996) *Race: The History of an Idea in the West.* Baltimore, MD: Johns Hopkins University Press.

Hesse, B. (2007) 'Racialized Modernity: An Analytics of White Mythologies', *Ethnic and Racial Studies,* 30 (4), 643–63.

Hill, J. (2005) 'Beyond the Other? A Postcolonial Critique of the Failed State Thesis', *African Identities,* 3 (2), 139–54.

Hudson, N. (1996) 'From "Nation to "Race": The Origin of Racial Classification in Eighteenth-Century Thought', *Eighteenth-Century Studies,* 29 (3), 247–64.

Huxley, G. L. (1980) 'Aristotle, Las Casas and the American Indians', *Proceedings of the Royal Irish Academy,* 80 (C), 57–68.

Independent Evaluation Group (2010) *The World Bank's Country Policy and Institutional Assessment an Evaluation*, Washington, DC: World Bank [online]. Available from: http://siteresources.worldbank.org/EXTCPIA/Resources/CPIA_eval.pdf [accessed 12 September 2011].

Ingram, S. (2010) *State Building: Key Concepts and Operational Implications in Two Fragile States: The Case of Sierra Leone and Liberia*. New York and Geneva: World Bank and UNDP.

International Crisis Group (2004) *Liberia and Sierra Leone: Rebuilding Failed States*. Brussels: ICG Africa Report No. 87.

Iris Center (2003) *Proposed Typology in Order to Classify Countries Based on Performance and State Capacity*, Maryland: Iris center, University of Maryland, and USAID.

Jacques, T. C. (1997) 'From Savages and Barbarians to Primitives: Africa, Social Typologies, and History in Eighteenth-Century French Philosophy', *History and Theory,* 36 (2), 190–215.

Johannisson, K. (1990) 'Society in Numbers: The Debate over Quantification in 18th Century Political Economy', in Frangsmyr, T., Heilbron, J. L. and Rider, R. E. (eds), *The Quantifying Spirit in the Eighteenth Century*. Berkeley: University of California Press, 343–63.

Kieh, G. K. (ed.) (2007) *Beyond State Failure and Collapse: Making the State Relevant in Africa*. Lanham, MD: Lexington Books.

Langley, P. (2008) 'Sub-Prime Mortgage Lending: A Cultural Economy', *Economy and Society,* 37 (4), 469–94.

Levitt, J. I. (2005) *The Evolution of Deadly Conflict in Liberia: From 'Paternaltarianism' to State Collapse*. Durham, NC: Carolina Academic Press.

Mansbach, R. W. and Taylor, K. L. (eds) (2011) *Introduction to Global Politics*. London: Routledge (second edition).

Marshall, M. G. and Cole, B. R. (2010) *State Fragility Index and Matrix 2010*, Polity IV Project [online]. Available from: www.systemicpeace.org/SFImatrix2010c.pdf [accessed 12 September 2011].

McGovern, M. (2005) 'Rebuilding a Failed State: Liberia', *Development in Practice,* 15 (6), 760–6.

Meek, R. L. (1971) 'Smith, Turgot and the Four Stages "Theory"', *History of Political Economy,* 3 (1), 9–27.

Merediz, E. M. and Salles-Reese, V. (2008) 'Addressing the Atlantic Slave Trade: Las Casas and the Legend of the Blacks', in Arias, S. and Merediz, E. M. (eds), *Approaches to Teaching the Writings of Bartolomé De Las Casas*. New York: The Modern Languages Association of America, 177–86.

Middleton, J. and Tait, D. (eds) (1958) *Tribes without Rulers: Studies in African Segmentary Systems*. London: Routledge and Paul.

Mirowski, P. (2005) 'How Positivism Made a Pact with the Postwar Social Sciences in the United States', in Steinmetz, G. (ed.), *The Politics of Method in the Human Sciences: Positivism and its Epistemological Others*. Durham, NC: Duke University Press, 142–72.

Mo Ibrahim Foundation (2011) *2011 Ibrahim Index of African Governance*, Mo Ibrahim Foundation, [online]. Available from: www.moibrahimfoundation.org/en/media/get/20111003_ENG2011-IIAG-SummaryReport-sml.pdf [accessed 12 September 2011].

Morton, A. D. and Bilgin, P. (2002) 'Historicising Representations of "Failed States": Beyond the Cold War Annexation of the Social Sciences?', *Third World Quarterly,* 23 (1), 55–80.

Mudimbe, V. Y. (1988) *The Invention of Africa: Gnosis, Philosophy and the Order of Knowledge*. Bloomington and Indianapolis: Indiana University Press.

——(1994) *The Idea of Africa*. Bloomington and Indianapolis: Indiana University Press.

Nathan Associates Inc (2006) *Fragile States Indicators: A Supplement to the Country Analytical Template*. Washington, DC: USAID.

Ndulo, M. and Grieco, M. (eds) (2010) *Failed and Failing States: The Challenges to African Reconstruction*. Newcastle: Cambridge Scholars Publishing.

Newman, E. (2009) 'Failed States and International Order: Constructing a Post-Westphalian World', *Contemporary Security Policy*, 30 (3), 421–43.

Pryke, M. (2010) 'Money's Eyes: The Visual Preparation of Financial Markets', *Economy and Society*, 39 (4), 427–59.

Rice, S. E. and Patrick, S. (2008) *Index of State Weakness in the Developing World*. Washington, DC: The Brookings Institution.

Rivera, L. N. (1992) *A Violent Evangelism: The Political and Religious Conquest of the Americas*. Louisville, Kentucky: John Knox Press.

Roll, E. (1992) *A History of Economic Thought*. London: Faber and Faber.

Seed, P. (1993) '"Are These Not Also Men?": The Indians' Humanity and Capacity for Spanish Civilisation', *Journal of Latin American Studies*, 25 (3), 629–52.

Seth, V. (2010) *Europe's Indians: Producing Racial Difference, 1500–1900*. Durham, NC: Duke University Press.

Sibeud, E. (1994) 'La Naissance De L'ethnographie Africaniste En France Avant 1914', *Cahiers d'Études Africaines*, 34 (136), 639–58.

Skinner, A. S. (2003) 'Economic Theory', in Broadie, A. (ed.), *The Cambridge Companion to the Scottish Enlightenment*. Cambridge: Cambridge University Press, 178–204.

Stepputat, F. and Engberg-Pedersen, L. (2008) *Fragile States: Definitions, Measurements and Processes*. Copenhagen: Danish Institute for International Studies.

Stewart, F. and Brown, G. (2009) *Fragile States*. Oxford: Centre for Research on Inequality, Human Security and Ethnicity, CRISE Working Paper No. 51.

Stocking, G. W. Jr (1987) *Victorian Anthropology*. New York: Free Press.

Strathern, M. (ed.) (2000) *Audit Cultures: Anthropological Studies in Accountability, Ethics and the Academy*. London: Routledge.

Tilley, H. L. and Gordon, R. J. (eds) (2007) *Ordering Africa: Anthropology, European Imperialism and the Politics of Knowledge*. Manchester: Manchester University Press.

USAID (2005) *Fragile States Strategy*, Washington, DC: United States Agency for International Development [online]. Available from: www.usaid.gov/policy/2005_fragile_states_strategy.pdf [accessed 2 January 2007].

Wilder, G. (2007) 'Colonial Ethnology and Political Rationality in French West Africa', in Tilley, H. L. and Gordon, R. J. (eds), *Ordering Africa: Anthropology, European Imperialism and the Politics of Knowledge*. Manchester: Manchester University Press.

Wilson, R. D. (1957) 'Justifications of Slavery, Past and Present', *Phylon Quarterly*, 18 (4), 407–12.

Withers, C. W. J. (1996) 'Encyclopaedism, Modernism and the Classification of Geographical Knowledge', *Transactions of the Institute of British Geographers*, 21 (1), 275–98.

World Bank (2002) *Index of Failed States and Low Income Countries under Stress*. Washington, DC: World Bank.

5

RE-EMBEDDING THE GLOBAL COLOUR LINE WITHIN POST-1945 INTERNATIONAL THEORY

John M. Hobson

Introduction

The idea of the "global colour line" was bequeathed to us by the famous Black activist, W. E. B. Du Bois. He prophesied around 1900 that the central problem of the twentieth century would be that of the global colour line.[1] Interestingly, in 1950 Harry Hodson claimed that "[t]here are two problems in world politics today which transcend all others. They are the struggle between Communism and liberal democracy, and the problem of race relations. Of the two, I am prepared to argue that the problem of race relations is the more important" (cited in Guilhot 2013). No less interestingly, the editors of this volume point out in their introduction that Du Bois's later writings on the Warsaw Ghetto in 1952 are especially instructive where he entertained the possibility that race was something that was "no longer even solely a matter of color and physical characteristics" but one that "cut across lines of color and physique and belief and status". This brings into play the key question concerning the replacement of racial hierarchy with an equally distorted conception of "cultural hierarchy", in which the racial biology of the pre-1945 world was replaced with a Eurocentric culturalism. And this in turn speaks to the post-scientific racist turn in the social sciences following the 1945 watershed.

The breaking with scientific racism in Western academic thought owes its causes to a number of factors, "internalist" and "externalist", where the latter includes the rhetorical rejection of racism by the nationalist movements and the widespread revulsion of the Nazi Holocaust, while the principal internalist factor comprises the attack on scientific racism from within the Academy that was conducted by the famous anthropologist, Franz Boas (for details see Gossett 1996 [1963], 418–25). Most experts credit Franz Boas with winning an almost single-handed victory over scientific racism (Stocking 1982, Ch. 11; Barkan 1992; Gossett 1997 [1963], 418–25), though this should not obscure the external context that enabled its full

realisation. Either way, though, Boas's achievement was to develop a cultural analysis which trumped the biological conception of difference and which, in turn,
opened the way for the social sciences to develop in a supposedly non-racist way.

Most theorists, especially in international relations (IR), have assumed that it was
this move, which came to the fore in the post-1945 era, that has enabled the
"proper" value-free/positivist analysis of the international system to flourish (notwithstanding the point that one will find only a handful of references to Boas in
the IR literature, all of which are found outside the mainstream). Typical here are
the pronouncements of liberal-inspired scholars who assert that, after 1945, IR
replaced the politics of racial intolerance with a more tolerant and benign discourse
of racial equality (e.g. Gong 1984; Klotz 1995). Such a claim presupposes a binary
construction, where the alternative to scientific racism is racial tolerance and
cultural pluralism. But this necessarily obscures the presence of a third discourse – what
I call subliminal Eurocentric-institutional intolerance. And it is precisely this, I argue,
that came to underpin IR theory during the era of decolonisation (1945–89). Moreover,
it is noteworthy that while scientific racism for the most part locates difference in
terms of biology/genes as well as climate and environment (Lamarckianism being
the partial exception), Eurocentric institutionalism locates difference purely in
terms of culture and institutions – as in the "rational West" versus the "irrational
East" (see Hobson 2012, Ch. 1).

One eloquent testimony to this shift is provided by George Stocking, who
explains the shift from race to the culture concept thus:

> It explained all the same phenomena, but it did so in strictly non-biological
> terms, and its full efficiency as an explanatory concept depended on the
> rejection of the inheritance of acquired characteristics [Lamarckianism]. ... All
> that was necessary to make the adjustment ... was the substitution of a word.
> For 'race' read 'culture' or 'civilisation', for 'racial hierarchy' read 'cultural
> heritage', and the change had taken place. From the implicitly Lamarckian
> 'racial instincts' to an ambiguous 'centuries of racial experience' to a purely
> cultural 'centuries of tradition' was a fairly easy transition – especially when
> the notion of 'racial instincts' had in fact been largely based on centuries of
> experience and tradition.
>
> (Stocking 1982, 265–6)

Here it is important to note that this Boisian assumption concerning the post-1945
transformation is one that fundamentally informs the work of modern critical race
scholars, who assert that cultural Eurocentrism is racism masquerading as a more
tolerant "culturalism" – i.e. "racism in disguise".[1] Thus when speaking of the post-
1945 substitution of cultural difference for racial difference, one such thinker
concludes that "[t]he terms may change, perhaps giving the impression that the old
[racial] problems have disappeared, when in fact they have merely acquired protective coloration through semantic camouflage" (Perry 2007, 216). Or as Thomas
McCarthy expresses it: "the demise of scientific racism in its evolutionary-biological

form did not mean the end of racist thinking in scholarly discourse altogether. A new, post-biological modality of neoracism is now widespread in social science" (McCarthy 2009, 91).

This present volume takes as its point for departure Du Bois's statement about how racism became transmogrified into non-biological realms but that in the process many of the tropes and content of racism were retained. And it seeks to explore how the discourse of race continues to underpin the practice of IR, both in its theoretical and empirical domains. This chapter will advance this key theme by interrogating IR theory in the post-1945 era; a task that I see as urgent given that arguably IR remains the last frontier insofar as it has remained egregiously impervious to the claims made by Du Bois as well as those by critical race theorists and postcolonial/non-Eurocentric IR scholars. One caveat is worth noting however. For I want to argue that we need to be sensitive to the *different* forms that Western-centrism and Western-hierarchical thinking have taken within the discipline; a theme that weaves its way throughout this chapter.

One of the sensitivities that is somewhat elided by the Boisian/critical race assertion is its assumption that scientific racism pervaded IR and international thought before 1945. But this, I believe, elides the many thinkers who embraced what I call "Eurocentric institutionalism" (i.e. the "culture conception") between 1760 and 1945. Such a discourse co-existed with scientific racist international thought in this period. And while these discourses certainly overlapped in numerous ways, I argue that they cannot be reduced one to the other (see Hobson 2012, chs 1 and 13). Given that I am in agreement with the claim that after 1945 Eurocentric institutionalism became the default metanarrative of IR, this necessarily means that post-1945 international theory has, in effect, linked up with its Eurocentric forebears rather than constituting something entirely new. That said, though, two points follow: first, that after 1945 what we witness is the end of scientific racist thought in IR, with Eurocentric institutionalism expanding (rather than emerging) to fill the void that the exit of scientific racism left behind;[2] and second, that there was indeed a transformation that was effected but it was one that applied to the modality of Eurocentric institutionalism. Before 1945 it took on an explicit form, what I call "manifest" Eurocentrism, but after 1945 it transmogrified into a much more subliminal form – or what I call "subliminal Eurocentrism". By this I mean that all the old manifest Eurocentric-institutional (and scientific racist) tropes, civilisation, barbarism, savagery and imperialism, were whitewashed but reappeared in terms (or what Nicolas Guilhot (2013) calls "conceptual proxies") that dare not speak their name, such as "tradition versus modernity" or "core versus periphery", US hegemony or international financial institution (IFI) intervention and, not least, following 1989, humanitarian interventionism, rogue states and quasi-states/failed states.

It warrants pausing for a moment to consider the context which led to this transformation. The principal reason for the emergence of subliminal Eurocentrism after 1945 lies with the West's "colonial-racist guilt syndrome". In turn, the emergence of this syndrome was due in part to a series of intra-Western developments that I mentioned earlier concerning the Nazi Holocaust and the work done by Franz Boas, as well as the "rhetorical entrapment" and resistance that was deployed by the anti-colonialist nationalist movements as they managed to discredit both scientific racism and formal empire.[3] And here it is noteworthy that characterising the 1945–89 era as the era of the Cold War, which was essentially an *international* intra-Western civil war, deflects attention or focus away from the *global* battle for decolonisation between East and West that was equally as significant and in which the Cold War became firmly embedded. For it was this global battle in particular that comprised an important milieu or crucible within which *subliminal Eurocentric* international theory was primarily forged.

In general, the upshot of the emergent Western racist-imperial guilt complex was not so much a turn away from Eurocentrism and normative Western imperialism, given that both the Western superpowers continued it in a variety of ways between 1945 and 1989 – even if it reined in Europe's imperialist politics – but a desire to hide or obscure imperialism from view in the body of international theory while often according it progressive functional sanction. More generally, in subliminal Eurocentrism *all* the monikers of manifest Eurocentrism are present but obscured or hidden from immediate view. In essence, all talk of "civilisation versus barbarism" or "whites versus non-whites" was given a wide berth on the grounds that it smacked of the old racist idea of white racial – and Western imperial – supremacy. Such a sensibility seemed more outwardly acceptable and seemed to appease the Western racist-imperial guilt syndrome. In such self-deluded ways was subliminal Eurocentrism advanced. So to sum up thus far, then, I argue that subliminal Eurocentrism in effect turns manifest Eurocentrism inside out. And because international theory's subliminal Eurocentrism is much more hidden and sublimated, I shall need to move onto different terrain when revealing its key categories and *modus operandi* compared to the much easier task of deconstructing pre-1945 manifest Eurocentrism and scientific racism.

How then has subliminal Eurocentrism underpinned post-1945 IR theory? The first section considers how IR theory has whitewashed Europe's imperial past while often providing a kind of functional and even moral retrospective sanctioning of imperialism, much as the following section reveals how neo-imperialism has been whitewashed while offering a similar functional sanctioning of this phenomenon. The final section reveals how North–South or East–West relations have been elided while (re)presenting world politics as effectively intra-Western politics, which is coupled with an elision of Eastern agency in the making of both Western and world politics.

Post-1945 IR theory and the whitewashing of Western *imperialism* from world politics

One of the ways in which subliminal Eurocentrism has operated is to sanitise or whitewash Western imperialism from the historical record of world politics while, paradoxically, at the same time according it a progressive functional sanction. Perhaps the most poignant example of this manoeuvre lies in Hans Morgenthau's classical realist text *Politics Among Nations* (Morgenthau 1967 [1948]), in which imperialism is reimagined not as a policy that the West had long deployed vis-à-vis the East but as a *normal* universal strategy of aspiring great powers in relation to each other. (Re) presented in this way, Morgenthau is able to downplay the role that Western imperialism played within the international system in the last half of the millennium.

In Morgenthau's vision imperialism becomes defined in opposition to a "status quo policy", where the latter refers to a state that seeks to preserve the existing distribution of power in the inter-state system. Imperialism, by contrast, constitutes a foreign policy that aims at "acquiring more power than [a great power] actually has, through a reversal of existing power relations" (Morgenthau 1967 [1948], 36–7). This definition is superior to all previous ones, he insists, because earlier definitions lacked ethical neutrality and objectivity given that the term tended to be deployed as a pejorative and is "indiscriminately applied to any foreign policy, regardless of its actual character, to which the user happens to be opposed" (Morgenthau 1967 [1948], 41). The paradox here is that Morgenthau produces a definition which can be applied to any foreign policy that seeks to challenge the status quo, even if this has no relevance to colonies, formal or informal, thereby rendering the term far less precise than he would have us believe. Indeed, as one critic put it, Morgenthau "dilutes the term beyond utility. Imperialism becomes the default action of any powerful state that is not pursuing a status quo policy" (Salter 2002, 117; also Guilhot 2013). One obvious difficulty of this move emerges from the point that when a great power maintains its empire but does not seek to expand it, it is following a policy of the status quo rather than an imperialist one. Thus, with the exception of various key moments between *c.*1492 and 1960/1980 – mainly between 1888 and 1910 when the imperial powers did not significantly expand their colonial territory – *ipso facto* the majority of the formal-imperial era logically drops from view.

By effectively inverting the pre-1945 Eurocentric formulations of imperialism, the paradox emerges wherein Morgenthau's universalised definition sanitises or empties the concept of its European/Western particularities (Morgenthau 1967 [1948], chs 4 and 5). This has the effect of not only letting the West off the moral hook but relegating one of the crucial dynamics of world politics after 1492 to a stagnant backwater in the vibrant and mainstream Western story. This is a striking move given that the pre-1945 Eurocentric tendency was to explicitly treat Western imperialism as *the* story of international politics. In this way, then, the East–West dynamic of world politics becomes obscured by an overwhelming focus on intra-Western relations. Thus, in strong contrast to the *c.*1830–1945 era of international theory, the likes of Carr and Morgenthau's emphasis on empire has been conspicuous for its absence.[4] But in the process, such a *lacuna* performs an important task in naturalising the East/West imperial division while also revealing the self-deluded aspect of subliminal Eurocentrism.

Following on immediately from this is another major subliminal Eurocentric trope that goes hand in hand with the naturalisation of imperialism. This entails the claim that decolonisation did not emerge via East–West contestations but was a benign gift that was graciously bequeathed by Western civilisation. Significantly, the first four editions of Morgenthau's key text were published at a time when the politics of empire and of decolonisation were reaching their climax. It is true that Morgenthau discusses the "colonial revolution" but it is accorded a mere 1 per cent of the total text (Morgenthau 1967 [1948], 340–5)[5]; and, moreover, it is described in typically subliminal Eurocentric terms. Instead of awarding the East a substantial degree of agency in the overthrow of empire, he ends up by reimagining the story as a pristine moment of Western triumphalism. Decolonisation becomes reimagined as a result of the "triumph of the moral ideas of the West", specifically the principles of national self-determination and social justice. And this is encapsulated within a subliminal paternalist-Eurocentric frame in which Western ideas were paternalistically taught to, and passively endogenised by, a so-called passive and *emulative* East. Thus, he claims:

> [i]n the wake of its conquests, the West brought to Asia not only its technology and political institutions, but also its principles of political morality. The nations of the West taught the peoples of Asia by their own example that the full development of the individual's faculties depends upon the ability of the nation to which he belongs to determine of its own free will its political and cultural destinies, and that this national freedom is worth fighting for; and the peoples of Asia learned that lesson.
>
> *(Morgenthau 1967 [1948], 344–5)*

This story of Eastern emulation and learning in the face of the benign "Western teacher" is a fundamental property of the paternalist wing of Eurocentrism; an idiom that was originally articulated by writers ranging from Karl Marx and Friedrich Engels to J. A. Hobson and Leonard Hobhouse, through to the likes of John Stuart Mill, Norman Angell and Alfred Zimmern (see Hobson 2012, chs 2 and 7).

Then again, this process of "whitewashing Western imperialism" can take a different, albeit complementary, form, wherein Western imperialism becomes justified, if not celebrated, as a gift of Western civilisation – thereby entirely eliding its dark side. One example can be found in the works of Hedley Bull and Adam Watson's liberal "pluralist" English School theory, where we encounter a retrospective justification of pre-1945 Western imperialism as a benign process that graciously diffused civilisation across the world (Bull and Watson 1984). But while the rationale of Western colonialism and imperialism was supported by pluralism in the context of the pre-1945 world, nevertheless it was not explicitly stated as such. Instead we are treated to a happy story in which the West diffused its "rational" civilisational institutions and practices outwards so that the East too could come to enjoy the benefits of residing within civilised international society. In the past, manifest Eurocentric liberals referred to this civilising process as the "civilising mission" or simply "liberal empire"; terms that have now been replaced by the more innocent-sounding phrase, the "expansion of (Western) international society". Indeed, Bull in particular railed against the proposition that such Western expansion was in any way coercive or imperialistic, arguing that it was instead entirely necessary if civilisation was spread to the benefit of all non-Western societies that lacked such ingredients – in the absence of which they should not be awarded membership in international society since backward (barbaric and savage) polities are deemed to be incapable of fully reciprocating (e.g. Bull 1984, 122; 2000 [1980], 181). In this way we return directly to the manifest paternalist-Eurocentric justification for European imperialism that was forcefully advocated by John Stuart Mill:

> To suppose that the same international customs, and the same rules of international morality, can obtain between one civilised nation and another, and between civilised nations and barbarians, is a grave error … . In the first place, the rules of ordinary international morality imply reciprocity. But barbarians will not reciprocate. They cannot be depended on for observing any rules. … In the next place, nations which are still barbarous have not got beyond the period during which it is likely to be for their benefit that they should be conquered and held in subjection by foreigners.
>
> *(Mill 1984 [1859], 118).*

However, the point that Third World countries sought to acquire these institutions neither as a means to promote world order nor as a sign of their desire to voluntarily join the European club but as protection, pure and simple, against an imperialist and marauding West is conspicuous only for its absence, with any sensitivity to the coercive actions of the West all but absent. Relevant here is William Callahan's important discussion of the Chinese "century of humiliation" (*c.*1839–1943). For this imperialist engagement with China "did not lead to order but to massive social dislocation, and ultimately violent revolution" (Callahan 2004, 313; see also Kayaoglu 2010). Thus Bull's silence on such issues once again has the effect of naturalising and sanctioning the imperial expansion of European international society. However, it is certainly the case that the classical English School scholar, Gerrit Gong, emphasises the imperialist notion of the standard of civilisation and reveals, often in genuinely sympathetic fashion, the many ways in which its imposition was resisted by non-Western states and viewed as an affront to their dignity. But he too ends up by invoking Bull and Watson's functionalist-imperial argument when he asserts that China's resistance to Europe's impositions of unequal territories and extraterritoriality led her to challenge them "in international legal terms [which thereby] underscored the extent to which [China] had accepted the principles and practices of the European international society" (Gong 1984, 183).

All in all, then, it turns out that Bull and Watson effect a *bipolar* construction of hierarchy in international society, where the "liberal principle" of non-interventionism turns out to apply only to relations between civilised states (i.e. within Europe), whereas imperial-hierarchy was the acceptable relationship between Western and Eastern societies. It is this move, therefore, that serves to convert the focus of English School pluralism from the "anarchical society" within Europe to the "hierarchical society" within the global realm, thereby transforming "pluralism" into English School (Eurocentric) "monism" (see Keene 2002; Kayaoglu 2010).

Post-1945 IR theory and the whitewashing of Western *neo-imperialism* from world politics

A further subliminal strategy has been the normative prescription of a "benign" *neo*-imperial politics that also goes by a whitewashed or sanitised name. Thus neorealist hegemonic stability theory (HST) elevates the exercise of (Anglo-Saxon) *hegemony* to the implicit status of a civilising mission (e.g. Gilpin 1981), while neoliberal institutionalism does much the same with respect to the role played by Western international institutions, especially the IFIs (Keohane 1984). In both visions, a major rationale of Western hegemons and their international institutions is to *culturally convert* Third World states along Western civilisational lines: the very essence of the old liberal mantra of the civilising mission. And both approaches echo the manifest paternalist Eurocentric formula of awarding "pioneering" progressive agency to the West and "conditional agency" to the East. These two terms refer to the point that for paternalist forms of Eurocentrism the West is assumed to have the "fully rational" capability to self-generate into modernity (the "Eurocentric logic of immanence"), while the East is said to be blocked from doing so on account of its "irrational institutions". This led to the paternalist-imperial formula in which Eastern development *can* occur but only *on condition* that the rational institutions of the civilised West are delivered courtesy of the benign-paternalist Western civilising mission. Thus for HST and Keohane's neoliberal institutionalism, hegemony and international institutions respectively come to replace the terminology of the liberal civilising mission, even if these former terms perform the exact same logic as the latter.

The route into this alternative reading of HST lies with the point that in order to celebrate British and American hegemony Gilpin is forced to suspend some of the cardinal axioms of neorealism. For a key property of hegemony is that it must secure world order and development for all states but in the process this leads inevitably to the relative decline of the hegemon via the "free rider problem". The immediate problem here is that neorealism, especially in its "offensive" variant that Gilpin supported in the period when he constructed HST (i.e. 1975 through 1987),[6] asserts that states seek to *maximise* their relative gains over others (Gilpin 1975, 23, 34–6, 85–92). But it is clear that in HST this principle applies to all states *bar the hegemon*. Or, put differently, in this vision we are treated to a story in which the leading great power not only does *not* seek to enhance its relative power over others but instead *sacrifices its power for the benefit of others*, thereby contradicting the cardinal realist axiom – that "the strong do what they can and the weak suffer what they must". Thus in Gilpin's HST this cardinal realist axiom is precisely inverted: "The weak do what they can and the strongest does what it must."

That the hegemon is exceptional is clear, though why it is so is not explained other than through a circularity as well as through a structural-functionalist mode of reasoning: specifically, that the hegemon self-sacrifices because "that is what hegemons do" (i.e. the circularity); and that without the presence of a hegemon the world economy descends into recession and rising inter-state competition because the *international system requires* a hegemon to promote stability and world order (i.e. the structural-functionalist assertion). But simply asserting that the system "requires" a hegemon for ensuring world order and stability does not explain *why a leading great power chooses* to become a hegemon in the first place, especially as all it can look forward to is its decline relative to those that it "helps". In essence, then, there is no recourse within neorealist logic to explain the highly anomalous altruistic status that HST ascribes to the United States in the 1945–73 period or to Britain in 1845–73.

Explaining this gap in the theory requires focussing on the presence of a sub-conscious American ethnocentrism and subliminal paternalist Eurocentrism which, I want to suggest, lies at the very base of HST. That is, US hegemony reflects the nineteenth-century discourse of "American exceptionalism" and its accompanying neo-imperialist idiom of America's "manifest destiny", much as "British excep-tionalism" and "manifest destiny" underpinned the idea of the British Empire. For the notion of helping all other states, especially those in the Third World, conjures up the idiom of the "civilising mission" and the "white man's burden". Thus I want to suggest that within Gilpin's theory it is precisely this Eurocentric-imperialist sensibility that underpins the real explanation for why leading Anglo-Saxon great powers choose to become hegemons and why they supposedly sacrifice themselves for the good of others.

Still, while my reading thus far is based on logical deduction, nevertheless there is a clear slippage in Gilpin's "positivist play of mimetic universalism" where he makes explicit reference to hegemony as a benign imperial civilising mission. As is well known, Gilpin begins by differentiating hegemons from imperial powers. Although Gilpin argues that, with the exception of the Soviet Union, the modern world is governed by the progressive non-imperialist politics of liberal hegemons whereas the pre-modern world was based on the cyclical and stultifying/regressive politics of despotic Eastern empires, this distinction is problematised by the obvious point that Britain was the greatest imperial power prior to 1945, as much as the United States has been the greatest neo-imperial power in the post-1945 era. The critical point is that Gilpin attempts to circumvent this obvious inconsistency by explicitly resorting, paradoxically, to the nineteenth-century imperialist trope of the liberal civilising mission. To this end he invokes Karl Marx's paternalist civilis-ing mission conception whereby modern European imperial powers transferred capital and technologies to the colonies not to exploit but to *uplift* them (Gilpin 1981, 142–3); or again, that

> the dominant power helps to create challenging powers. Ironically, as Marx himself appreciated, one of the greatest forces for diffusion has been imperi-alism … . The imperial power has stimulated the colonized peoples to learn its ways and frequently has taught them advanced military, political, and economic techniques.
>
> *(Gilpin 1981, 176)*

Here, then, we encounter the key "paternalist-imperial" civilising mission trope, in which liberal empires take on the guise of a benevolent father who teaches his children – both directly and by way of example – to embrace and develop what he has already pioneered so that they can grow up and one day prosper.

Thus in defending his "non-imperialist" reading of hegemony it seems clear that Gilpin, like Hedley Bull, is addressing the wrong target. For his assumption is that imperialism is defined by the *exploitation* of the weak by the strong. But in Marx's vision – as well as that of the paternalist Eurocentric liberal – imperialism is conceptualised as a *civilising mission* precisely because it entails the West engaging in the "paternalist uplift", rather than the coercive exploitation, of the East.

Post-1945 IR theory and the elision of North–South or East–West relations from world politics

Another generic aspect of subliminal Eurocentric IR theory in the post-1945 era, which stands in marked contrast to the manifest Eurocentrism and scientific racism of the previous era, is a shift in focus away from North/South relations or East/ West relations in favour of a near-exclusive focus on intra-Western relations in which the provincial West masquerades as the universal. This is indeed a profound and marked change given that the headlining focus of attention in scientific racist and manifest Eurocentric-institutionalist international theory was precisely a rigid focus on North–South or East–West relations. One might assume at first glance that such an elision might be symptomatic of a non-Eurocentric approach. But the move is entirely consistent with subliminal Eurocentrism given that this vision presents the West as endowed with hyper-agency while Eastern agency is downgraded, if not erased altogether. That is, all developments within world politics are explained through Western hyper-agency, with the West being presented as the universal and Eastern agency blipping off the ontological radar screen altogether. This is a typical feature of classical realism and Waltzian neorealism and it is to a certain extent reproduced in neorealist HST. Because of the importance of this ontological strategy and the centrality that these realist theories have long enjoyed within the discipline of IR, it is useful to consider this in a little more detail to illustrate my case.

Hegemonic stability theory effectively instructs the student that she can learn all she needs to know about world politics/economics by simply focussing all her attention on the actions of the Anglo-Saxon hegemons. Significantly, one of the theory's prominent advocates replied to a question posed by an audience member (presumably a Luxembourg national) at the 1990 APSA conference: "Sure, people in Luxembourg have good ideas. But who gives a damn? Luxembourg ain't hegemonic" (Stephen Krasner, cited in Hobson 2012, 195). Such a narrow focus necessarily precludes the actions of small Western states (as in American ethnocentrism) and Third World states (as in paternalist Eurocentrism). Analogous to "World Series Baseball" that involves only North American teams, so for HST America *is* the world, much as Britain *was* the world in the nineteenth century.

This exclusive focus is predicated on the fact that the hegemon graciously provides the key services to ensure the development of the world economy under conditions of relative peace and stability. For in the absence of hegemony the world plunges headlong into certain disaster through a reversion to the Dark Age of the interwar period. Accordingly, the theory encapsulates perfectly the well-known words of Madeleine Albright, uttered in a 1998 UN speech: "We [the United States] are the indispensable nation. We stand tall. We see further into the future." And this in turn propels us back to the point originally made in Stanley Hoffmann's famous essay, "An American Social Science: International Relations", where he pointed out that American students were drawn to the study of IR because "[t]o study United States foreign policy was to study the international system. To study the international system could not fail to bring one back to the role of the United States" (Hoffmann 2001 [1977], 35). Indeed, no other modern theory of IR conforms so closely to this American ethnocentric and Eurocentric idiom than does HST.

Waltzian neorealism, which has dominated the discipline in one way or another since 1979, is conventionally thought of as the universalist theory *par excellence* given that it has supposedly done away with issues concerning civilisational/societal difference. But if we dig deep beneath the veneered surface of this representation, a number of important signs of Eurocentrism reappear. First and foremost, Waltzian neorealism elides altogether the agency of Eastern actors. Kenneth Waltz expressed this idiom thus: "[i]t would be … ridiculous to construct a theory of international politics based on Malaysia and Costa Rica … . To focus on great powers is not to lose sight of lesser ones. Concern with the latter's fate requires paying more attention to the former" (Waltz 1979, 72–3). Nor was this some kind of ad hoc one-off statement, for the elision of Eastern agency was fundamentally inscribed within the heart of his theory given its exclusive focus on the (Western) great powers. As Waltz put it,

> theory, like the story of international politics, is written in terms of the great power of an era. … . In international politics, as in any self-help system, the units of greatest capability set the scene of action for others as well as for themselves. In systems theory, structure is a generative notion, and the structure of a system is generated by the interaction of its principal parts.
>
> *(Waltz 1979, 72)*

Though this statement avoids deploying the adjective "Western" before great powers, it seems to me that this is what he has in mind; or at least this is in effect what transpires given that his focus is on the post-1648 era.[7] But this elision of Eastern agency is problematic for various reasons, all of which in effect disturb the foundations of his theory, both directly and indirectly.

It is often thought that the end of the Cold War caught Waltz's theory off guard, revealing its inability to explain international change on the one hand while simultaneously problematising Waltz's belief that Cold War bipolarity was a particularly stable system on the other. But what is usually ignored at this juncture is the point that some appreciation of Eastern agency is necessary if we are to begin to construct an adequate explanation of the end of Cold War bipolarity. Such a point is, however, explicitly denied by Waltz. Thus, writing on the eve of the Second Cold War he announced that

> the waning of hegemonic competition in an era of détente and the increased prominence of north–south relations led many to believe that the world could no longer be defined in bipolar terms. But the waning of American-Russian competition and the *increased importance of third-world problems* do not imply the end of bipolarity.
>
> *(Waltz 1979, 204 – my emphasis)*

However, while the Second Cold War was initiated by the Soviet invasion of Afghanistan in December 1979, nevertheless it was in Afghanistan that the Soviets experienced their own "Vietnam", with an exhaustive decade-long war ending in defeat at the hands of the Mujahideen fighters. While defeat at the hands of "small-scale" Eastern agents could not in turn wholly account for the end of the Soviet Union, it certainly played a part in the unfolding drama. Thus the end of bipolarity, which entailed a fundamental change in the distribution of power in the international system, was at least in part brought about by Eastern agency, none of which registers on Waltz's theoretical radar screen.

Equally, the defeat of the United States in Vietnam in the face of intransigent Vietnamese resistance agency gave rise to the "Vietnam Syndrome", which in turn significantly affected American military thinking in the aftermath of 1975 and placed certain limits on potential future US military actions. Critically, that such Eastern resistance agency has had a profound impact on the American superpower refutes Waltz's claim that "[t]he United States need worry little about wayward movements and unwanted events in weak states … . The principal pains of a great power, if they are not self-inflicted, arise from the effects of policies pursued by other great powers" (Waltz 1979, 202). Thus, we need to amend Waltz's various statements that have been cited already so as to factor in Eastern agency. Accordingly, his words could be rephrased to the effect that "Eastern agents (in part) set the scene of action for the Western superpowers", and "the structure of the system is partly generated by the interactions of East and West". And equally we might amend his earlier claim by stating that "it would be ridiculous to construct a theory of international politics based exclusively on the United States and the USSR. To focus on small Eastern powers and actors is not to lose sight of the bigger ones. Concern with the latter's fate requires paying at least some attention to the former."

Critically, East–West interactions or North–South relations are obscured in Waltz's theory. Nevertheless, at this juncture Waltz might well invoke one of his defensive delimiting arguments – in this case the defence that "interaction relations" should be ignored when constructing a proper *structural theory* of international politics. Such interactions are dismissed as but irrelevant "unit-level" attributes, the inclusion of which would only blur the strict parsimonious definition of international structure that he polices with vigilance. As he put it:

> Abstracting relations means leaving aside questions about the cultural, eco-
> nomic, political, and military interactions of states … . To define a structure
> requires ignoring how units relate with one another (how they interact) and
> concentrating on how they stand in relation to one another (how they are
> arranged or positioned). Interactions … take place at the level of the units.
>
> *(Waltz 1979, 80)*

While such a move might well enable Waltz to conveniently restrict the parameters of his theory in order to shield him from such criticism, this does not enable
an escape from the Eurocentric charge. For it is precisely *this* move that elides or
dismisses the many East/West interactions that shape the actions and the inner
constitution of the Western great powers that in turn informs their outward tra-
jectories (Hobson 2004; 2007). Ignoring this dimension leads to a reified conception
of Western great powers as self-constituting, autonomous entities, whose societies
and economies develop entirely independently of non-Western economic, military,
political and cultural interactions – the very *leitmotif* of Eurocentric theory.

Nevertheless, the sceptical reader might well object to my overall claim about
the dominance of subliminal Eurocentrism by offering up liberal modernisation
theory and dependency/world-systems theory as examples of theories that focus
explicitly on North/South or East/West relations. But they turn out to be the
exceptions that prove the subliminal Eurocentric rule. The Eurocentric cues are
found either in the guise of the reification of Western agency and the erasure of
Eastern agency, as in world-systems theory (Wallerstein 1974; 1984), or in liberal
modernisation theory's vision wherein the East is awarded "derivative" agency
insofar as it *can* develop but only by replicating the Western development path, the
five stages of which weave a linear line that begins with replicating British indus-
trialisation and culminates with the American age of high-mass consumption
(Rostow 1960).[8] Moreover, the old, manifestly Eurocentric trope of "civilisation
versus barbarism" came to be effectively replaced by the subliminal Eurocentric
tropes of "tradition versus modernity" or "core versus periphery". I shall take
Wallerstein's approach by way of illustration since this is clearly a counter-intuitive
example.

While there are a variety of factors in Wallerstein's theory of world politics that
betray a subliminal Eurocentric predisposition, I shall single out two that are most
relevant here. First, although the standard secondary reportage of world-systems
theory asserts that European capitalism developed only because it was able to
exploit the South, thereby supposedly overcoming the predominant Eurocentric
trope of the endogenous "logic of immanence" (in which European societies self-
generate in a linear fashion as a result of their exceptional institutions), nevertheless
it turns out that this trope precisely underpins Wallerstein's explanation of the rise
of European capitalism. Here he focuses on a range of *intra-European* factors as

being responsible for Europe's breakthrough into modernity. These include the fact that Europe was an *exceptional* anarchic multi-state system (as opposed to Eastern "world empires" which constituted single-state systems), with the resulting problem of incessant warfare forcing European rulers to court the capitalist class in order to derive sufficient revenues to meet these geopolitical challenges. Other factors include the flight of the peasantry from the land owing to the higher rates of exploitation that were imposed by the nobility in the aftermath of the Black Death; the rise of the towns as nodal points in long-distance *intra*-European trading circuits and, above all, as refuge harbours for the over-exploited peasantry; the primitive accumulation of capital through the beginning of the enclosure movement; and various technological innovations that enhanced agrarian production (Wallerstein 1974). In short, then, Wallerstein's explanation of the rise of modern European capitalism is situated squarely within the Eurocentric method that places the endogenous "logic of immanence" at its heart.

The second aspect of Wallerstein's Eurocentrism lies in his analysis of how Northern capitalism today prospers by exploiting the periphery. Again, this might seem to be symptomatic of a non-Eurocentric analysis where Western neo-imperial hierarchy is given pride of place. Undoubtedly this aspect of the approach feeds into a non-Eurocentric approach and provides a vital corrective to Bull's representation of the expansion of Europe in highly consensual and "naturalised" terms. But the problem here is that in correcting for this deficiency Wallerstein bends the polemical stick the other way to produce a vision of a Leviathanesque, marauding imperial hyper-agential West and a victimised agency-less East. Thus, in conjuring up an image of a Western vampire that sucks the lifeblood out of its entrapped Eastern victim, Wallerstein effectively consigns all traces of Eastern agency to the dustbin of history – past, present and future. And so while the West's superior economic power today rests on its exploitation of the East, nevertheless in erasing Eastern agency from the story of the global political economy, so we are treated to another tale of why the West is the sole agent in world politics and will remain so indefinitely. Indeed, because Wallerstein denies the prospects of Eastern agency so he too, in effect, *naturalises* and *eternalises* this Western-dominated capitalist world economy (what I call the problem of "Eurofetishism").

It is also notable and deeply concerning that much of critical IR theory beyond world-systems theory reverts us back into the Eurocentric cul-de-sac with its reified and fetishised conception of Western domination and its downplaying or erasure of Eastern agency. It can be found in the standard Gramscian analysis (Hobson 2012, 242–52), though it is also true that there has developed an important strand of "postcolonial Gramscianism" that reverses us back out of the Eurocentric cul-de-sac (e.g. Slater 2004; Pasha 2006). Equally, parts of feminism have exhibited Eurocentric and imperialist properties, as black and brown feminists have argued (e.g. Spivak 1985; Mohanty 1986), though there is a rising tide of non-Eurocentric feminism that has emerged inside and outside of IR (e.g. Agathangelou and Ling 2009; Jabri 2012; Loomba 1998; Harding 1998). Arguably too, significant parts of postmodernism and poststructuralism have exhibited Eurocentrism (Hobson 2007), the final upshot of which being that critical theory does not constitute a ready-made antidote to the problem of Eurocentrism that pervades the mainstream – though there are moves afoot to rectify this problem, even if there is still a long way to go before it can be said to be resolved.

Conclusion

This chapter reveals how the Boasian epistemic revolution led not to an end to Western-centrism but, most paradoxically, propelled us into the very cul-de-sac that Du Bois had feared, wherein scientific racism and manifest Eurocentrism merely transmogrified into a much more insidious form in the guise of subliminal Eurocentrism. And its insidious nature derives from the fact that IR theory's subliminal Eurocentrism is cloaked or camouflaged by the rhetoric of value-free positivism. At least pre-1945 manifest-Eurocentric international theory did not hide behind such obfuscatory semantics but was open about its Western-centrism. Nevertheless, a further irony emerges here in that the global colour line has not only been re-embedded within IR as we proceed through the twenty-first century, just as it was throughout the twentieth, but it finds its place within significant swathes of critical – as much as mainstream – IR theory today (though, of course, positivism is not invoked by critical theorists).

It would, however, be remiss not to mention my claim that I develop elsewhere wherein after 1989 mainstream international theory has in some ways returned us to the past of "manifest" Eurocentrism (Hobson 2012, chs 11 and 12). Liberal cosmopolitans and what I call "Western-liberals" (such as John Rawls, David Rothkopf, Anne-Marie Slaughter and John Ikenberry), as well as what I call "Western-realists" (such as Niall Ferguson, Robert Kagan, Paul Kennedy and Robert Kaplan) have explicitly reinvoked the C-word (civilisation), while the E-word (empire) has been rehabilitated by many such thinkers as the post-1945 racist-imperial guilt syndrome has given way to a renewed messianic Western-imperialist sensibility. This, then, constitutes another twist in the story of the development of Eurocentrism since 1945, all of which reinforces the claims that I have developed in this chapter while simultaneously warning us to be sensitive to the shape-shifting nature of Eurocentrism and the various *modus operandi* that this Western-centric discourse has taken. For this requires constant vigilance if we are to develop a truly alternative, progressive conception of world politics that can move us beyond the tragic performative-Eurocentric story of wars, clashes, imperialism and conflict that have infected inter-civilisational relations for far too long.

Notes

1 See especially Barker (1981); Hunt (1987); Balibar (1991); Miles (1993); Füredi (1998); MacMaster (2001); Perry (2007); McCarthy (2009).
2 Nevertheless, there was a small minority of realist writers who retained various racist sensibilities; see Guilhot (2013).
3 Hunt (1987); Lauren (1996); Füredi (1998).

4 Although other post-1945 realists embraced a pro-imperialist sensibility (see Guilhot 2013).
5 For a wider discussion of how realists were silent on the issue of decolonization see Guilhot (2013).
6 Though he later qualifies this assertion; see Gilpin (2001: 79).
7 Though even this is symptomatic of Eurocentrism given that the Ottoman and Safavid Empires, India, Japan and China were much more significant powers than were the leading imperial powers of Europe right down to the nineteenth century; see Hobson (2004: chs. 2–4).
8 Though Rostow notes that the replication process is not one of photocopying Britain's industrialization given the role of state intervention in late-development.

Bibliography

Agathangelou, A. M. and Ling, L. H. M. (2009) *Transforming World Politics* (London: Routledge).
Balibar, E. (1991) Is There a Neo-Racism? In Balibar, E. and Wallerstein, I. (eds) *Race, Nation, Class: Ambiguous Identities* (London: Verso), 17–28.
Barkan, E. (1992) *The Retreat of Scientific Racism* (Cambridge: Cambridge University Press).
Barker, M. (1981) *The New Racism* (London: Junction Books).
Bull, H. (2000 [1980]) The European International Order. In Alderson, K. and Hurrell, A. (eds) *Hedley Bull on International Society* (London: Palgrave Macmillan), 170–87.
——(1984) The Emergence of Universal International Society. In Bull, H. and Watson, A. (eds) *The Expansion of International Society* (Oxford: Oxford University Press), 119–26.
Bull, H. and Watson, A. (eds) (1984) *The Expansion of International Society* (Oxford: Oxford University Press).
Callahan, W. A. (2004) Nationalising International Theory: Race, Class, and the English School. *Global Society*, 18 (4), 305–23.
Du Bois, W. E. B. (1900) The Present Outlook for the Dark Races of Mankind. *AME Church Review*, 17 (2), 95–110.
——(1903) *The Souls of Black Folk* (Chicago, IL: A. C. McClurg).
Füredi, F. (1998) *The Silent War* (London: Pluto).
Gilpin, R. (1975) *US Power and the Multinational Corporation* (New York, NY: Basic Books).
——(1981) *War and Change in World Politics* (Cambridge: Cambridge University Press).
——(2001) *Global Political Economy* (Princeton, NJ: Princeton University Press).
Gong, G. W. (1984) *The Standard of 'Civilisation' in International Society* (Oxford: Clarendon).
Gossett, T. F. (1997 [1963]) *Race: The History of an Idea in America* (Oxford: Oxford University Press).
Guilhot, N. (2013) Imperial Realism: Post-War IR Theory and Decolonisation. *International History Review*, forthcoming.
Harding, S. (1998) *Is Science Multicultural?* (Bloomington, IN: Indiana University Press).
Hobson, J. M. (2004) *The Eastern Origins of Western Civilisation* (Cambridge: Cambridge University Press).
——(2007) Is Critical Theory always for the White West and for Western Imperialism? Beyond Westphalian towards a Post-Racist Critical International Relations. *Review of International Studies*, 33 (S1), 91–116.
——(2012) *The Eurocentric Conception of World Politics: Western International Theory, 1760–2010* (Cambridge: Cambridge University Press).
Hoffmann, S. (2001 [1977]) An American Social Science: International Relations. In Crawford, R. M. A. and Jarvis, D. S. L. (eds) *International Relations – Still an American Social Science?* (Albany, NY: SUNY Press), 27–51.
Hunt, M. H. (1987) *Ideology and US Foreign Policy* (London: Yale University Press).
Jabri, V. (2013) *The Postcolonial Subject* (London: Routledge).

Kayaoglu, T. (2010) *Legal Imperialism* (Cambridge: Cambridge University Press).

Keene, E. (2002) *Beyond the Anarchical Society* (Cambridge: Cambridge University Press).

Keohane, R.O. (1984) *After Hegemony* (Princeton, NJ: Princeton University Press).

Klotz, A. (1995) *Norms in International Relations* (Ithaca, NY: Cornell University Press).

Lauren, P. G. (1996) *Power and Prejudice* (Boulder, CO: Westview Press).

Loomba, A. (1998) *Colonialism/Postcolonialism* (New York, NY: Routledge).

MacMaster, N. (2001) *Racism in Europe* (Houndmills: Palgrave).

McCarthy, T. L. (2009) *Race, Empire, and the Idea of Human Development* (Cambridge: Cambridge University Press).

Mill, J. S. (1984 [1859]) A Few Words on Non-Intervention. In Robson, J. M. (ed.) *Collected Works of John Stuart Mill*, Vol. XXI (Toronto: Toronto University Press), 111–24.

Miles, R. (1993) *Racism after 'Race Relations'* (London: Routledge).

Mohanty, C. T. (1986) Under Western Eyes: Feminist Scholarship and Colonial Discourses. *Boundary 2*, 12 (3), 333–58.

Morgenthau, H. J. (1967 [1948]) *Politics Among Nations* (New York, NY: Alfred A. Knopf).

Pasha, M. K. (2006) Islam, 'Soft' Orientalism and Hegemony: A Gramscian Rereading. In Bieler, A. and Morton, A. D. (eds) *Images of Gramsci* (London: Routledge), 149–64.

Perry, R. J. (2007) *'Race' and Racism* (New York, NY: Palgrave Macmillan).

Rostow, W. W. (1960) *The Stages of Economic Growth* (Cambridge: Cambridge University Press).

Salter, M. B. (2002) *Barbarians & Civilization in International Relations* (London: Pluto).

Slater, D. (2004) *Geopolitics and the Post-Colonial* (Oxford: Blackwell).

Spivak, G. C. (1985) Three Women's Texts and a Critique of Imperialism. *Critical Inquiry*, 12 (1), 243–61.

Stocking, G. W. (1982) *Race, Culture and Evolution* (Chicago, IL: University of Chicago Press).

Vitalis, R. (2008) From International Relations – Back When 'International Relations Meant Race Relations' – to Area Studies, ISA Annual Convention (San Francisco).

Wallerstein, I. (1974) *The Modern World-System*, Vol. I (London: Academic Press).

——(1984) *The Politics of the World-Economy* (Cambridge: Cambridge University Press).

Waltz, K. N. (1979) *Theory of International Politics* (New York, NY: McGraw Hill).

6

AGAINST RACE TABOOS

The global colour line in philosophical discourse

Srdjan Vucetic

Introduction

As the editors explain in the introduction, the roles played by race and racism belong to some of the least explored topics in International Relations (IR), in spite of having profound implications for the understanding of the field's origins, research questions, concepts and theories as well as ethical considerations.[1] The term global colour line, inaugurated a century ago by W. E. B. Du Bois, is a case in point. Even as a mere trope it recasts almost everything IR has said through its mainstream theories and other dominant semiotic codes. How, indeed, did the lines that groups of people draw between themselves become both 'global' and 'coloured' – attributed to humans and their bodies in a way that qualitatively differs from virtually all other ideas and practices of the inside/outside difference? This question, like virtually all questions involving race and racism, falls outside the mainstream IR discourse; it is ignored in equal measure by introductory textbooks as well as leading journals. At a superficial reading, this is puzzling. If IR's scholarly production revolves around the study of all lines that bind human beings to the global and/or the international, then the discipline ought to have dealt with the causes and effects of historical and contemporary colour lines head-on. Errol Henderson's chapter argues that IR's silence on race is a function of past and present disciplinary cultures, especially the culture of white privilege. This culture tends to elide all race-talk, and in turn efface the problem of the global colour line. By way of a hypothesis, one could suggest that this elision is a conscious, as well as philosophically and politically legitimate, reaction to the racist crimes of the not-too-distant yesteryear. But this argument would be self-serving. Reflecting on the Brixton uprisings of 1981 in *International Affairs*, R. J. Vincent, one of the key figures of the 'English School', wrote this:

Like sex in Victorian England, it has been said, race is a taboo subject in contemporary polite society. Conflicts or attitudes that to the simpleminded might appear to be self-evidently racial are explained away as class-based, or as difficulties attending immigration, or as responses to special local circumstances. Certainly, race relations are not an area in which political reputations are easily made, and outspokenness on the subject seems to be the preserve of those who have little to lose, their having either departed the scene or not yet arrived at it.

Yet beneath this wish to talk about something else, and perhaps in part explaining it, lurk the largest of claims for the factor of race in politics, and the direst of forebodings about the future of race relations. As early as 1903 W. E. B. Du Bois was already expressing the problem of the twentieth century as the problem of 'the colour-line', and this has been a theme of pan-African congresses to the present day.

(R. J. Vincent 1982, 658)

He then went on to reclaim the concept of race over class, ethnicity and nation ('The difficulty with the rejection of the concept of race is that it would afford us no purchase on the popular notion of race as part of everyday belief and experience, and therefore a piece of political data whether we like it or not') and suggest, citing Frantz Fanon, K. M. Pannikar, Edward Said and Ali Mazrui that race *must* be used in the analysis of hierarchies in world politics ('rich white states are said to exploit poor non-white ones, or, beyond the state, a white bourgeoisie is said to exploit a black proletarian'), especially in IR textbooks ('it may be said that textbooks tend to be written by those near the top rather than the bottom of the world hierarchy, and that they are for that reason less sensitive to the factor of race than if they were written from underneath looking up'). Accounts of the role of race in international life, Vincent concluded, are important because they can help the fight for global justice.[2]

Vincent's reflections are as relevant today as they were three decades ago. The race taboo makes it difficult to deal with the enduring lived experience of racism everywhere. What I would like to add is that these difficulties might in fact be compounded within post-colonial, anti-racist, and post-racial structures such as IR. While post-racialist ideals must be defended – how can a humanistic scholarly field be against full equality for all? – one must also recognise that any tabooisation of race works against these ideals because it solidifies the position of those who have benefited from the historical distribution of power and authority, both in world politics and in the academic study thereof. Indeed, if this volume is anything to go by, what distinguishes IR from both humanistic and social scientific fields of which it is a part is a systematic and persistent inability and unwillingness to dilute its dominant whiteness – here used to refer to all those socio-intellectual structures that privilege and protect people of (principally) European descent at the expense of everyone else. There are good reasons why exchanges about what it is that scholars should be studying are passionate, but in this case I believe there is a major political and moral argument to be made on why IR cannot treat the problem of the global colour line as a historical issue or, worse, an issue that has been resolved in a postracial era.[3]

Mainstream ideas on the role of race in international life have long been contested, starting with Du Bois, and often very effectively. As the introduction to this volume suggests, nothing destabilises mainstream approaches to world politics like analyses of the conditions under which the pursuit of state sovereignty relies on racist definitions of political membership or histories of phenomena like 'race war', 'race alliance', and 'race suicide'. But even as many IR-ists have made significant inroads into the problems of race and racism in world politics, their efforts remain relatively peripheral in the field and, no less important, sparsely connected within and across their putative peripheries. One problem that hobbles the scholarship of the global colour line – and I do not claim it is *the* problem – is conceptualisation; more specifically, how best to situate the concept of race vis-à-vis a broader philosophical discourse, or what in the IR context is sometimes known as meta-theory.

To appreciate the multiplicity of parallel and occasionally competing conceptual and theoretical approaches on race and racism, many of which are yet to be fully integrated into IR discourse, and their relationship to meta-theory, consider the following list of questions. If race is known to be scientifically illegitimate, why does it keep mobilising public power so well in so many contexts? What is the relationship between real and illusory orders of superordination and subordination? Is, to borrow from Du Bois, the 'relation of the darker to the lighter men in Asia and Africa, in America and the islands of the sea' produced by institutional allocation of economic resources, or is it primarily about discourses and practices that force individuals and groups into acting subjects? What role does human psychology play, if any? Can race even be treated separately from class, ethnicity, gender and other social forces that give rise to social orders? Can individual societies transgress the boundaries of race, or will various colour lines always arise from larger, more enduring and possibly 'hidden' structures upon which the modern international society rests? And if all these dichotomies are false, should we bring all these parts back into a single explanatory whole and, if so, how? In short, how can we conceptually grapple with the ways in which ideas, discourses, institutions and practices come together to colour so many social divisions at a global scale? The way I see it, we cannot help but access each of these questions by means of philosophy.

Once again, there are many next steps in the project to make IR 'less white'. But while we fight to remedy the status quo – getting at least some textbook writings to admit that Du Bois made legitimate and insightful points about world politics would constitute a major victory – we should also keep unpacking the conceptual and theoretical relationships that have made and continue to make the study of the global colour line at once possible and impossible. In this chapter, I consider *some* dimensions of these long-standing questions through the lenses of two debates in the philosophy of race: the 'onto-semantic' debate on the meaning of race, and whether it is real; and the 'normative' debate on how race serves political and moral purposes, and whether we should conserve or eliminate it from our discourse.

I should like to say at the outset that my overview of philosophy compresses a number of distinct debates and nuanced arguments, while putting aside others (epistemology, for example). This is because my work lies in IR, not philosophy. But while there is room for consideration of interpretations other than the one offered here, I believe that that this exercise follows the general purpose of this volume, which is to encourage reflection and critical self-awareness about the multi-layered nature of the research agenda on the global colour line. Put another way: 'they' (philosophers) can help 'us' (IR-ists) think harder about the principal assumptions and conceptual relationships we use to understand the processes of inclusion/exclusion that affect millions of people.

This proposition is subject to an important caveat. Not so long ago Charles W. Mills described philosophy as 'one of the very "whitest" of the humanities' (Mills 1998, 13). I am not sure what Mills would say about philosophy today, but I do wish to note that his field is now richer for a new subfield called the 'philosophy of race'. And it is this body of scholarship that most clearly points out distinctions among different approaches to race, while also identifying options and opportunities that have not yet been realised in IR scholarship.

What is race?

In the first instance, this is a semantic question. It foregrounds the relationship between the concept and the linguistics forms used to transmit it, and can therefore be rewritten as 'What do we mean by race?'. Because of the concept's uneasy presence in the public domain, the definition of the concept of race cannot just 'follow' the desiderata of research puzzles or theoretical frameworks; indeed, it is simply next to impossible to write about race without at least implicitly engaging the political questions concerning development, multiculturalism, affirmative action, colour blindness and many other aspects of contemporary politics and social justice. (In the case of IR, this issue is compounded by the long shadow that the concept casts over the discipline's history and its relationship to public power.)

This dimension of race has led philosophers to pay close attention to ordinary language reasoning and popular intuitions on the concept. Following a pattern established in the philosophy of language, two camps have emerged, 'neo-descriptivism' and the 'emergence' school. Where these two schools meet is in the idea that the ordinary language approach can be helpful in identifying the 'parameters' of race-talk within a linguistic community, as in the broad question of whether race-talk refers to a natural biological or social kind. In the words of Joshua Glasgow, '[i]t is hard to overstate the importance of this question. … [O]nce we know what race is *supposed* to be, we can figure out whether there is, in fact, any such thing' (Glasgow 2009, 6–7, italics in the original). Another meeting point is this: everyone agrees that race is supposed to be a social kind. This point takes us into 'onto-semantics', a coinage that is meant to underscore the dialectical nature of the concept.

In ordinary usage, 'racism' refers to a belief that some races are in some sense inferior to others. A series of great twentieth-century transformations – the war against Nazism, decolonisation, second wave feminism, various scientific advances, civil rights and human rights movements, and other forces – have delegitimised this type of thinking and acting. Scholarly definitions of racism, however, often go beyond expressed beliefs and examine assorted 'social realities' of racism, its discourse and ideologies, choices and interactions, behaviours and outcomes, institutions and institutionalised orders, practices and habits and so on. I will discuss metaphysical matters below, but the simple point here is that, while race-talk may or may not lead to racism, it is almost certain that racism need not be related to talk.

The contention that race is (or is supposed to be) a social kind suggests that at some point in history people did not see race. From this perspective, genealogies on 'What made race possible?' are especially important in the study of the global colour line because many groups commonly identified as races in contemporary ordinary language were once regarded as actual races at different stages of development. Among historians, the emergent consensus holds that race and racism are products of European/Western modernity; the practice of assigning properties of the human body onto 'character', which began with seventeenth-century European travellers, paved the way for the later emergence of race as a biological fact and a social problem. Pre-modern peoples also engaged in colonialism, but this type of colonialism did not produce, and was not produced by, race-based hierarchies. So while the ancient Aztecs, Athenians and Azande were sexist, slave-holding and xenophobic in matters of citizenship, religion and language, they were probably not racist in either the ordinary or scholarly sense of the term. In contrast, modern-era Europeans, whose expanding empires moved to establish boundaries between the superior whites and the inferior non-whites, were certainly racist because they purposefully ordered and re-ordered people on the basis of assorted physical (biological) traits such as skin colour, hair and nose.

How, where and when the social contract became what Mills (1997) calls the 'racial contract' remains to be more fully examined, but most historians would probably agree that racial thought reached a peak in the late nineteenth and early twentieth century, when colonial empires were the order of the day and when few self-identified whites questioned social Darwinian, Galtonian, Spencerian or Lamarckian ideas of race as a permanent or semi-permanent category that determined the worth and potential of everyone everywhere.[4] In this 'racialist' discourse, human collectives were coded by geography and/or physiognomy and these codes signalled the presence of heritable psychological, cultural and behavioural traits.[5] It was racialism that authorised the racist management of allegedly backward peoples through enslavements, genocide, ghettos, land-grabs and apartheid.

The majority of contemporary state and nonstate actors in the world are officially post-colonial and anti-racist, yet they are also 'racial' because they continue to rely on race in order to articulate representations of difference and manage cultural and political diversity (Omi and Winant 1986). In fact, it is often argued that it is the mainstreaming of anti-racism in both state and nonstate institutions, policies and decisions that have (seemingly paradoxically) kept racial exclusions alive, albeit in non-supremacist, separate-but-equal terms. These observations have moved a number of scholars to call for an analytical shift away from 'protoracism' and towards a more critical study of 'culture' (Balibar 1991; Goldberg 1993) and (again, seemingly paradoxical) 'new racism' (Barker 1981) phenomena such as 'racism and its doubles' (Taguieff 2001 [1988]), 'racism without racists' (Bonilla-Silva 2006, 1–4), 'racism without races' (Balibar 1991, 21) and even 'racism without racism' (Goldberg 2009, 361).

Arguably, each of these perspectives to various degrees owes something to Michel Foucault's teachings on political modernity, including his notion of 'state racism' – 'a racism that society will direct against itself, against its own elements and its own products' (Foucault 2003 [1975–6], 62). 'State racism' is a loose term, but one implication is that modern states are both 'racial' and 'racist' in the sense that they function by 'purifying' their populations by identifying, and subsequently isolating, the poor, the deviant, the criminal and other 'degenerate' elements (Foucault 2003 [1975–6], 62; see also 81, 254–5). Crudely interpreting Foucault's scattered writings on race further, we could also say that his own genealogy would conclude that racial representations of difference became meaningful only once European colonialism coalesced with anthropology, biology and other modern regimes of truth. This reading of history also accords with Foucauldian categories like biopolitics and governmentality, which together motivate the analysis of race and racism as one set of relations among subjects, bodies and the state which became contractually established in modern times. (Whether Foucault was as interested in the global colour line as in racialised Europe remains a matter of some debate.)

All of these new ways of talking about race and the varieties of racisms clearly go beyond 'mere' semantics: what processes created folk theories of race for the first time? Under what conditions can they and do they change? In what ways do they vary in history and geography? And so on. According to Glasgow, this line of reasoning is precisely what gives unity to the philosophy of race as a field (Glasgow 2009, 124–25). What we mean by the word 'race' depends on how we think about it in ontological terms, namely, whether we believe that race is real or illusory. If one is to judge by ordinary language practices, affirmative action policies, national census questionnaires, forensic DNA assessments or personalised genetic genealogies, race clearly exists. The same goes for the lived experience of those, to go back to Vincent, at the 'bottom of the world hierarchy'. But if we were to ask natural scientists whether race existed most of them would answer in the negative – and in sharp contrast to their nineteenth-century counterparts. The idea that phenotypes and genotypes – for example, body hair gene – are indicative of some biological or genetic fixity has been proven to be wrong.[6]

The failure of science to find evidence of the natural (biological) foundations of the idea of human races paved the way for the rise of 'constructivist' or 'constructionist' (sometimes prefaced with the adjectives 'social' or 'political') explanations of race. Here, race is a social kind – constructed, contingent and contestable, but '*nonetheless real*' (Mills 1997, 126, italics in the original). For philosophers like Ron Mallon (2006), this view constitutes an 'ontological consensus'. One could amass citations, but it would be pointless: entire research programmes in political science, sociology, anthropology, cultural studies and so on are today devoted to the study of how race articulates and legitimises intragroup unity and intergroup incommensurability, while influencing the differentiated distributions of wealth, worth, resources, entitlement and opportunity in broader social systems that social scientists study under the rubrics of the 'sovereign state', 'freedom of movement' or 'division of labour'. Indeed, constructivists tend to treat race as an explanandum, not explanans, or at least primarily as an explanandum, meaning that in this ontology 'blacks', 'Caucasian majority', 'Chadians', or 'visible minorities' do not exist independently of the acts of categorisation in specific contexts.

While there are many constructivist conceptualisations of race, current trends seem to favour 'racialisation' or 'racialised identity'. Introduced into English from the late 1970s in different contexts and via different conceptual histories by sociologists Michael Banton, Robert Miles and Michael Omi and Howard Winant, 'racialisation' refers to a social and political *process* by which race is inscribed and projected onto the human body. Philosopher Sally Haslanger has provided the most precise definition of the term yet:

> A group is *racialized* (in context C) if and only if (by definition) its members are (or would be) socially positioned as subordinate or privileged along some dimension (economic, political, legal, social, etc.) (in C), and the group is 'marked' as a target for this treatment by observed or imagined bodily features presumed to be evidence of ancestral links to a certain geographical region.
>
> *(Haslanger 2008, 65, italics in the original; see also 2000, 44)*

As a category of analysis, racialisation applies to objects and situations, but its focus is on agency, subjects, and identity formation. In turn, racialisation is closely tied to different theories and analyses of power within modern societies. In my reading, Haslanger's definition accords even with the notion of Foucauldian power, according to which the very process by which race is inscribed and projected onto the human body constitutes an exercise of power, rather than a reflection of some pre-existing social hierarchy. In addition to foregrounding power analysis, the concept of racialisation invites researchers to explore the differential processes of race-making in relation to one another, across multiple sites. What this means, considering the previous point, is that actors authorised to draw and redraw colour lines must be regarded as at once an effect of a global system of racialised power and agents of that power at the regional, national or local level.[7]

In IR studies of race, broadly constructivist viewpoints can be found in the 1970s and even earlier,[8] but a more-or-less unified constructivist research agenda is of more recent vintage or only just being put together. As other chapters in this volume demonstrate, apart from carefully scrutinising their discipline's richly racist past, constructivist IR theorists – originally labelled 'poststructuralist', 'critical' and 'postcolonial' – have so far interrogated the making and breaking of racialised identities in North–South relations, the US-led Global War on Terror, immigration controls, the management of cultural diversity and the like. This line of research has a distinct record, but it has so far struggled to come up with a framework or frameworks for theorising the global – or at least the international – from the perspective of race. States, nations, social movements and other 'units' are all said to operate within a racialised global system, but what remains to be analysed is how this macro-structural feature affects patterns of privilege, protection, control and inequality among them.

An important exception is the Marxist tradition (Wallerstein, 1991), which in IR often positions itself against constructivist and poststructuralist approaches in explicitly ontological terms. Instructive is a recent argument by Branwen Gruffydd Jones (2008). When analysing the (re)production of race and various racisms, poststructuralists typically use the bracketed '(re)' to emphasise the fluidity of racialised subjects that are (re)produced by discourses and practices that emerge from the constructed, contingent and contestable background knowledge of what constitutes social and political reality. Here, racial power is about (re)producing racialised subjects that appear to possess fixed materiality. For Gruffydd Jones, accounts of this type are 'vital but incomplete' (Gruffydd Jones 2008, 911). For her, racial power is material in the sense that it is routinely reproduced – note no bracketed '(re)' – through the relations structuring societal interaction with nature; specifically, through the regulation of nature as private property within the development of global capitalism, which carries the legacies of imperial conquest and colonial dispossession of non-European, non-white peoples (Gruffydd Jones 2008, 917–22).

Thus viewed, a more complete understanding of racial power requires a new social ontology, namely critical realism's preference for the so-called 'depth ontology'. A review of this position is not needed since, as far as IR is concerned, the 2000s can be regarded as a 'critical realism awareness decade'. For the purposes of this chapter, the most important part of the critical realist position concerns the existence of a mind-independent external reality. At the risk of oversimplifying matters, it can be said that critical realism assumes that social phenomena operate at multiple levels or layers of reality. At deeper levels, entities exist regardless of our knowledge claims about them; at the 'empirical' level, however, we can directly observe them thanks to their 'causal effects' (powers, mechanisms, properties, etc). Here, causation is broadly conceptualised to describe a reality as an open system in which 'racialised oppression' emerges as a consequence of a deeper and prior interaction of the 'enabling/constraining' entities and mechanisms such as 'human rights/wrongs', 'collective entitlements/obligations' or 'private/public property'. In other words, we cannot understand race as a meaningful social category without first understanding how capitalist society (or some functional 'deeper' equivalent) structures human beings into specific roles and ranks. Suffice it say, this line of argumentation unsettles poststructuralists because it appears to minimise their contribution to the study of racialised structures of oppression. Can one accept that the experience of being assigned or 'ascribed' to categories such as whiteness *causes* people to think and act as if they are white – that is, individual persons who share a privileged and protected collective identity – without also accepting that racialised identities cannot exist outside certain material hierarchies?

Like many other IR debates, this debate on the nature of racialised reality has followed paths blazed by others, this time by Marxist methodologists. One of the questions they examined was the extent to which critical realism emerged as 'Marxism by stealth' and a way to continue to study how, for example, race serves to convince the poor that they are a certain colour and that defending their relatively privileged status within a broader global order is in their best interest. Arguably, one of the ways in which critical realism harmonises Marxist politics is by fostering research centred on the concept of class and, in turn, facilitating politically engaged critiques of poverty, exploitation and other unjust manifestations of social power, many of which are often dismissed in contemporary academia as antiquarian 'Marxian' or 'Marxoid' topics. Related, and equally relevant to IR, is the debate between (cultural) sociologists and (cultural) anthropologists on what comes first, 'social structure' or 'culture'. As I will show in the next section, the question that has kept moral and political philosophers (among others) awake at night is whether the category of race is 'empty' or at the very least 'derivative' of some other category, such as class politics.

There are two bodies of research that complicate the standard discursive-materialist dichotomies. The first goes under the rubric 'racial habits', which begins with an observation that racialised outcomes are not necessarily contingent on racists actors. The goal of this line of research – which draws inspiration from Freudian, Deweyan, Bourdiean and other social-theoretical frameworks as well as, increasingly, from social neuroscience – is to demonstrate how individuals and groups become racialised through embodied habits, which can be defined as preconscious or unconscious engines of action co-constituted with culture and social structures already dominant in society. For example, the habitualised aesthetics of appropriating Native or African American spiritual traditions as an antidote to consumerist and materialist conformities in the contemporary US has less to do with engaged history and more to do with subconscious desires of people designated as white to continue to pursue their privileges and protections. If race-making indeed occurs through a plethora of informal, illicit and, importantly, implicit practices, then there is little wonder that communities can be at once antiracist and ethnocentric (Alcoff 2006, chapters 7 and 8). This insight applies to 'Obamerica' (Bonilla-Silva 2010, Chapter 9) as much as it applies to academic fields like IR (Hobson 2012).

Separate, but directly relevant to the study of racial habits is the research programme on 'racial cognition', which is an umbrella term that unites studies in cognitive and evolutionary psychology, as well as (and to a lesser extent) in evolutionary anthropology. On the basis of a whole variety of experimental research, social psychologists have now for decades argued that racial prejudice – prejudice related to skin colour and/or body appearance – can be present even among those who consistently reject the existence of races (or believe that there is a single human race) and otherwise hold reliable anti-racist attitudes. That race may be a by-product of evolved cognition of the human brain is a more recent contention. Philosophers Daniel Kelly, Edouard Machery and Ron Mallon (2010, 450) summarise this body of research thus:

> Racial categorization develops early and reliably across cultures; it does not depend entirely on social learning; it is, in some respects, similar to our folk biology. Thus, racial categorization seems to be neither the product of socialization alone nor of the perceptual saliency of skin color. It does not appear to result from a general tendency toward group prejudice, either. Rather, this body of evidence is best explained by the hypothesis that racial categorization results from some species-typical, canalized cognitive system. Because it is species-typical, environmentally canalized, and complex, this supposed cognitive system is plausibly the product of evolution by natural selection. Given the specific properties of racial categorization, this cognitive system is also plausibly domain-specific, treating race differently than other categories (including some other social categories). All this is grist for the mill of evolutionary psychologists.

Viewed from the perspective of the 'psy sciences' taken together, race often appears less contingent and contestable than constructivists have intimated. But if evolved cognition is even partly behind folk theory of race, then its academic analogue ought to invite further reflection on the psychological microfoundations of racial categorisation.

Now it is constructivists' turn to feel uneasy. Social and cognitive psychology, experimental and otherwise, is often dismissed for being subjectivist and ahistorical to the point that it is almost taboo in some circles. The criticism is all too familiar: what constructivists are meant to study instead are cultural and social structures that make race possible in different contexts, not what goes on inside people's heads. For pragmatically minded philosophers, this attitude leads to a lost opportunity. A rapprochement between constructivism and psychological disciplines is desirable because each approach has weaknesses that can potentially be offset through some form of combined and eclectic reasoning. Moves to accommodate psychological insights into constructivist viewpoints do not necessarily upset the ontological consensus on race; in fact, it might induce constructivist race scholars to further work out their ontological commitments on the mutual constitution of agents and structures, which would be important since the question of how cultural and social structures of race systematically influence individuals is no less pressing than the one of how individuals create and resist those structures.

While it is true that the wild variation in meanings of race continues to puzzle evolutionary psychology, it is equally true that constructivism struggles with the apparent pervasiveness of certain forms of racialism. Put aside Mill's 'racial contract' or define racialism broadly and the historical consensus on the origins of race dissipates. The ancients understood human subjectivity differently from the moderns, yet they both sometimes drew rather similarly coloured lines between 'us' and 'them' (Isaac 2004). This possibility warrants pause and reflection: if race is a product of universal evolved cognitive mechanisms, then it might well be that race (or at least race-like) categories delineated human population even in pre-modernity – an idea that of course would run contrary to the teachings of most standard genealogies as well as most historical materialist readings of race. Conversely, why is it that race and its cognates persist in the face of overwhelming evidence that the natural bio-logical concept is false? One answer, to go back to the 'new racism' scholarship, is that race and racism are sufficiently different phenomena such that the elimination of the latter need not eliminate the former. Another answer, coming from the psy sciences, is that the greatest barriers in battling racism may not be legal, social or political, as hitherto understood, but psychological.

At a minimum, these possibilities give philosophers ground from which to cri-ticise the systematic 'disregard' of psychology in constructivist approaches on race (Kelly et al. 2010, 468; compare Appiah 2006). This disregard is a problem because it continues to cement the purposive and representational biases of contemporary race theory, which is an ontological issue as well. If race-making is not simply a function of linguistic practices (both ordinary and extraordinary) but also one of the routines of thought, perception and activities in everyday contexts, then the cur-rent analysis of the global colour line will remain 'vital, but incomplete' for yet another reason.

Importantly, racial habits are never theorised as 'false' ideas but as a part of broader reality structured around social institutions and organised relations that are at once 'reproduced' and '(re)produced' because most humans in most contexts indeed do not reflect on their course of action; instead, they automatically act and interact in accordance with the cultures and/or social structures of conduct into which they were socialised or which they learned implicitly. Along the same lines, virtually all students of race working in psychological disciplines would agree: race and other identities cannot be examined by separating environmental factors from intrapyschic ones. Indeed, both relational psychoanalysts and cognitive-cum-evolutionary psy-chologists would now agree that the social environment in which cognitive, affective, Freudian or any other mechanisms in the human psyche operate is as important as the structure and function of the mechanisms themselves. This point also accords with a Foucauldian teaching that the privileged and the oppressed cannot change the system of power in which they find themselves, they can only tweak its modalities (Brah 2005; Hook 2007). And so we reach a question implied in Foucault's power/knowledge nexus: what if the scholarship on race, too, constitutes part of the operation of power that makes it difficult to challenge racism?

Should we do away with race?

Every scholar of the global colour line must come to terms with the politics of antiracism: What role, if any, should race play in the pursuit of social justice?

Should we abandon racially divided societies and move toward colour blindness? How ought we to approach development or multiculturalism? This inevitability of politics can be stated more broadly. According to Mallon (2006), rather than being about semantics or ontology, the philosophical debate on race is mainly normative. This is to say that the ontological consensus still leaves us with a dissensus regarding moral, practical, prudential and, indeed, political implications of race-talk. The relevance of this debate is self-evident: what concept – or concepts – best suits our anti-racist aims? To paraphrase Mallon, the penultimate question in the philosophy of race is neither 'What do we mean by race?' nor 'Is race an illusion?' but 'What do we want race to be?' (Mallon 2006, 550).

In lieu of an answer, Mallon urges us to consider the basic normative parameters such as the epistemic and political value of race-talk (whether its meanings could be more effectively subsumed under a different kind, namely ethnicity, and whether it helps in dealing with racism and its legacies) and the degree of entrenchment of race-talk in everyday discourse, both public and private. On these parameters, scholars tend to be divided into two main camps. 'Conservationists' maintain that racial categories should be conserved for the purposes of public policy analysis, social reform and/or identity-based politics (Mills 1997). In contrast, 'eliminativists' – a catch-all term that sometimes includes political liberals, postcolonial theorists and conservative polemicists – contend that race is an illusion laden with disagreeable claims and, as such, should be eliminated from public discourse.

The problem with the eliminativist position from the perspective of the study of the global colour line is that it erases the philosophical and theoretical basis for anti-racist politics that is supposed to motivate scholarship in the first place. This is a major normative argument for conserving race that goes back to Du Bois: critical confrontation with race is the necessary step in the possibilities of overcoming the problem of race. What also needs emphasising is that conservationist race-talk consciously seeks to avoid any reference to nineteenth-century racial meanings or, for that matter, the language emerging from contemporary genomics. The concept of racialisation serves so many philosophers well – think of Lawrence Blum's (2002) racialised groups, Linda Martín Alcoff's (2006) racialised identities, Glasgow's (2009) asterisked 'race★' and even Appiah's (1996) racial identities – precisely because it so clearly emphasises the fact that race is a socially and politically constructed phenomenon. The normative goal here is not to 'conserve' race so much as to 'substitute' it with race-like discourse.

One candidate is class. This substitutionist move has a long pedigree. Robert Miles (1989), for example, has long demanded that race be replaced with racism defined as an ideological struggle within contemporary capitalism. Miles developed his concept of racialisation precisely in order to explain the political conflicts arising from twentieth-century tensions between the capitalist need for massive free movements of labour, on the one hand, and the nationalist need for loyal citizens, on the other. Another candidate is ethnicity. Its *prima facie* advantage lies in the successful replacement of 'race' in global ordinary language usage concerning certain groups in certain location such as Roma in Europe or Chadians in the Gulf.

There are conceptual advantages as well: constructivist definitions of race usually encompass a reference to real or fictive 'ancestral links' as a necessary condition for racialisation. This is of course a standard definition of ethnicity – membership based on discourses, perceptions, practices, etc. of shared ancestry. Given that the costs of race-talk (intellectual incoherence, essentialism and reification) generally outweigh the potential benefits (for example, enabling group-based social justice claims), argues philosopher J. Angelo Corlett (2003), this overlap is an opportune reason to 'replace' the former with the latter.

The problem with the substitutionist strategies is that they erase the fact that race is both more global and more directly enmeshed in power relations. The race-to-class move imposes a high price on theoretical and empirical work because it disregards a world of ideas and practices that precede – some would say supersede – the modern nation-state (to say nothing of the international labour market). Class relations become much more complex once people see each other not as rich/poor but as indelibly different from one another on some seemingly natural (biological) dimensions. A vast body of sociological research on access to opportunities in a variety of contexts shows that that, controlling for education and income, non-whites almost always face greater challenges than whites. The same applies to ethnicity. When ethnic differences are 'tagged' onto the body, the hierarchy between ethnic actors is constructed as self-evident and indelible, thus revitalising the racialised structure of oppression.

At stake here is both analysis and ethics: ethnicity not only misses the full gamut of (bio)power relations that made race historically possible but is also poorly equipped to address the judgments about justice based on colonial and postcolonial struggles along the blackness/whiteness boundary. It can also be argued that the race-to-ethnicity move would in fact go against the semantic teachings on the role of ordinary language and the folk theories of identity. Going back to Mallon (2006, 550), public policies dealing with different inter-generational groups will work best if the communities of language targeted by those policies themselves recognise differences between race and ethnicity in their everyday discourse, both public and private. All being equal, in general conversations and popular intuitions race-talk operates on a higher degree of abstraction than ethnicity-talk. For example, while ethnic meanings typically derive from contextual knowledge claims (and disclaims) regarding the subject's genealogy ('Her ancestors are from X'), race-talk usually requires a broader and more abstract background knowledge about the human body and/or the ways in which identities have been racialised ('Her ancestors are black' or 'Her ancestors were mistreated by the colour of their skin'). It is also worth pointing out that ordinary language does not recognise 'ethnicism' as a functional equivalent of racism.

Yet another self-consciously normative position against substitutionism arises from intersectionality theory, which is based on the idea that categories of difference such race, class, ethnicity and sexuality always have simultaneous and interacting effects on the social and political world. This perspective, associated with Kimberly Crenshaw, María Lugones, Elizabeth Spelman and other feminist theorists writing in the 1970s and 1980s, is precisely what drives journals with double titles like the venerable *Race & Class* or the newer *Race/Ethnicity*, as well as numerous research programmes in both social sciences and humanities. Here, we do not want race to be either class or ethnicity because any replacement move ignores the ontological fact that the intersections, interlockings and assemblages of these categories are always greater than the sum of their parts.

Perhaps the latest and related attempt to capture overlap, intersection and interlocking between race and ethnicity – or between racialisation and ethnicisation – is the concept of 'ethnorace'. Building on Goldberg (1993; 2009), Alcoff defines 'ethnorace' as

> pertaining to groups who have both ethnic and racialized characteristics, who are a historical people with customs and conventions developed out of collective agency, but who are also identified and identifiable by bodily morphology that allows for both group affinity as well as group exclusion and denigration.
>
> *(Alcoff 2009, 22)*

Like racialisation, ethnorace is unlikely to enter ordinary conversations soon (to say nothing of helping shift people's self-conceptions in them), but it can help theorise the dynamic nature of social divisions based on kinship. In addition to describing pan-ethnic categories or caste orders that in certain contexts can have ideas of race embedded within them (to use contemporary examples: Caucasians in Moscow, Copts in Cairo, Dalits in Punjab, Latinos in the US, etc.), the concept of ethnorace might be part of the answer to long-standing research puzzles on how ethnic groups in different contexts become racialised, deracialised or re-racialised.

There is indeed no shortage of reasons why most philosophers of race prefer to 'reconstruct' or 'ameliorate' race-talk rather than outright replacing it with some other discourse (Glasgow 2009, 147–54; compare Alcoff 2006, Chapter 10). Once again, the philosophical debates considered in this article are dialectical in the sense that theories on how we ought to talk about the world always depend on theories on what is in the world. The question 'What do we want race to be?' always and by necessity depends on 'What can we want?' and vice versa – the facts regarding human diversity cannot be separated from the political and normative interpretation of that diversity. So while some philosophers might explore how the latest research on the peculiar evolution of human cognition may be relevant for eliminativist, substitionist and reconstructionist desires alike (Kelly et al. 2010), IR-ists might investigate what political and normative positions made race so taboo not only in their discipline in general but also within their research programmes in specific. When Vincent wrote about IR's race taboo in 1982, IR had barely begun to reflect on the role of Eurocentrism in theory-building. Although the situation has improved since (Hobson 2012), the question of how various forms of whiteness are (re)produced in the discipline is yet to become central to the analysis of practices of power and, in turn, politically engaged critiques of the international/global.

Conclusions

As an object of reflection in IR, race has waxed and waned over time, yet one would be hard-pressed to deny its centrality to the origins of the discipline or its relevance in the development of the modern international. Race is also a mercurial concept: debates over its ontology, epistemological status, and legitimacy are necessary precisely because race is a moving target – its manifestations vary in history and geography. In this chapter, I have addressed some of these debates via a quick tour of the philosophy of race. My main argument is that students of the global colour line should consider using the categories racialisation and racialised identity over the category race.

When it comes to onto-semantics, nearly all philosophers of race agree that race is a social kind as opposed to something that exists in nature. But race is real in the sense that it produces, and is produced by, social structures: Xs become racialised when their perceived ancestral or morphological differences are invested with intersubjective meanings that position them as subordinate to Ys in context C. Embedded into this conceptualisation is an emphasis on the multidimensionality of power. Rather than just coercion, racialisation also refers to diffuse political construction of difference such that the identity X comes to be viewed as indelible and therefore antithetical to the project built and established by Y. The near-universal agreement that racism now has a negative moral quality means that coercive power is less effective in producing racialised oppression than ever before, and claims that some Xs are unassimilable continue to succeed everywhere.

I have also suggested that the concept of racialisation may be well equipped to incorporate the theoretical frameworks on racial habits and racial cognition in addition to assorted social and cultural structures. To use the previous example, the fact that discourses on the degrees of ethnic assimilability and entitlement contain forms of 'new racism' is evidence that racialisation occurs even in the absence of expressed racist purposes or conscious beliefs that X are inferior to Y. This opens up new ontological and theoretical vistas: if race-making is partly (or also) a function of the evolution of human psychology, then we may have an easier task explaining why phenotype and ancestry were built into so many political orders in modern history, including the modern international. IR has good 'foundational' reasons to be reticent about exploring evolutionary explanations of the social and political world, but reticence should not turn into 'disregard', much less into a taboo. To the extent that philosophers discussed in this chapter are right, the tensions over what race means, what race is and what do/can we want race to be will prove to be an asset in the transdisciplinary conversations that will take place in the next generation of studies of the global colour line.

Notes

1 For the written comments, I am grateful to Zoltán Búzás, John Hobson, J. Anne Tickner, and Dvora Yanow. All errors remain mine. Parts of this chapter draw on my 'Black

Banker, White Banker: Philosophies of the Global Colour Line', *Cambridge Review of International Affairs* 25 (1), 27–48 (2013).

2 Quotes are from Vincent (1982, 660, 666, 669). This article also offers some antiquated ideas with respect to race. According to Hobson, like so many other post-1945 Euro-centric international theorists Vincent posited that the mainstreaming of decolonial antiracism would be sufficient for achieving racial equality (2012, 310, 319).

3 On past and current oppressions within IR that condition the lived experience of people identified by themselves and others as non-white, see, *inter alia*, Persaud and Walker (2001), Vitalis (2000) and Hobson (2012).

4 For effective overviews of key personalities and events that made these ideas possible and pertinent bibliographies, see, *inter alia*, Blum (2002) and Zack (2002).

5 In this context, 'colour' referred not only to skin tone, but also to facial and in fact most other bodily features that were understood to be naturally constituted in relation to race. Philosophers like to qualify racialism as 'thick racialism', 'biobehavioral essentialism' and 'racial naturalism' (Mallon 2006; Blum 2002; Zack 2002).

6 Versions of the biology-diversity link remain preserved in some fields, such as genomic medicine in the United States context. There, research appears to be primarily, though not exclusively, driven by new economic opportunities as identified by the powerful pharmaceutical industry. Glasgow (2009, 97–108), Mallon (2006, 543), Marks (2008, 27) and Rose (2007, 155–171).

7 As far as ordinary language goes, the word racialization has little traction, but it helps to remember that the same quality applied to the concept of gender not so long ago (Haslanger 2005).

8 For example, Robert Vitalis' book manuscript (forthcoming with Oxford University Press), *The End of Empire in American International Relations*, finds 'broadly constructivist' viewpoints on race and racism in the writings of Ralph Bunche, Alain Locke, and other members of the 'Howard School of International Relations'.

Bibliography

Alcoff, Linda (2006) *Visible Identities: Race, Gender, and the Self* (New York, NY: Oxford University Press).

——(2009) Latinos Beyond the Binary. *Southern Journal of Philosophy*, 157 (1), 112–28.

Appiah, K. Anthony (1996) Race, Culture, Identity: Misunderstood Connections. In Appiah, K Anthony and Guttman, Amy (eds) *Color Conscious* (Princeton, NJ: Princeton University Press), 30–105.

——(2006) How to Decide if Races Exist. *Proceedings of the Aristotelian Society*, 106 (3), 363–80.

Balibar, Etienne (1991) Racism and Nationalism. In Balibar, Etienne and Wallerstein, Immanuel (eds) *Race, Nation, Class: Ambiguous Identities* (London: Verso), 37–67.

Barker, Martin (1981) *The New Racism* (London: Junction Books).

Blum, Lawrence (2002) *'I'm Not a Racist, but … ': The Moral Quandary of Race* (Ithaca, NY: Cornell University Press).

Bonilla-Silva, Eduardo (2006) *Racism without Racists: Color-blind Racism and the Persistence of Racial Inequality in the United States* (New York, NY: Rowman & Littlefield).

Brah, Avtar (2005) Ambivalent Documents/Fugitive Pieces: Author, Text, Subject. In Murji, Karim and Solomos, John (eds) *Racialization: Studies in Theory and Practice* (Oxford: Oxford University Press), 69–86.

Corlett, J. Angelo (2003) *Race, Racism, and Reparations* (Ithaca, NY: Cornell University Press).

Du Bois, W. E. B. (1901) The Freedmen's Bureau. *The Atlantic Monthly*, March. Available at: www. theatlantic.com/past/docs/issues/01mar/dubois.htm (accessed 1 March 2011).

Foucault, Michel (2003 [1975–76]) *Society must be Defended: Lectures at the Collège de France 1975–1976* (New York, NY: Picador).

Glasgow, Joshua (2009) *A Theory of Race* (New York, NY: Routledge).

Goldberg, David Theo (1993) *Racist Culture: Philosophy and the Politics of Meaning* (Oxford: Basil Blackwell).

——(2009) *The Threat of Race: Reflections on Racial Neoliberalism* (Oxford: Blackwell).

Gruffydd Jones, Branwen (2008) Race in the Ontology of International Order. *Political Studies*, 56 (4), 907–27.

Haslanger, Sally (2000) Gender and Race: (What) Are They? (What) Do We Want Them to Be? *Nous*, 34 (1), 31–55.

——(2005) What are we Talking About? The Semantics and Politics of Social Kinds. *Hypatia*, 20 (4), 10–26.

——(2008) A Social Constructionist Analysis of Race. In Koenig, Barbara A. Lee, Sandra Soo-Jin and Richardson, Sarah S. (eds) *Revisiting Race in a Genomic Age* (New Brunswick, NJ: Rutgers University Press), 56–69.

Hobson, John M. (2012) The Eurocentric Conception of World Politics: Western International Theory, 1760–2010 (Cambridge: Cambridge University Press).

Hook, Derek (2007) *Foucault, Psychology and the Analytics of Power* (Houndmills: Palgrave Macmillan).

Isaac, Benjamin (2004) *The Invention of Racism in Classical Antiquity* (Princeton, NJ: Princeton University Press).

Kelly, Daniel, Machery, Edouard and Mallon, Ron (2010) Race and Racial Cognition. In John Doris (ed.) *The Moral Psychology Handbook* (New York, NY: Oxford University Press), 432–71.

Lewontin, Richard (1972) The Apportionment of Human Diversity. *Evolutionary Biology*, 6, 391–8.

Mallon, Ron (2004) Passing, Traveling, and Reality: Social Construction and the Metaphysics of Race. *Nous*, 38 (4), 644–73.

——(2006) 'Race': Normative, Not Metaphysical or Semantic. *Ethics*, 116 (3), 525–51.

Marks, Jonathan (2008) Race: Past, Present, and Future. In Koenig, Barbara A., Lee, Sandra Soo-Jin and Richardson, Sarah S. (eds) *Revisiting Race in a Genomic Age* (New Brunswick, NJ: Rutgers University Press), 21–38.

Miles, Robert (1989) *Racism* (New York, NY: Routledge).

Mills, Charles W. (1997) *The Racial Contract* (Ithaca, New York, NY: Cornell University Press).

——(1998) The Racial Polity. In Babbitt, Susan and Campbell, Sue (eds) *Racism and Philosophy* (Malden, MA: Blackwell), 13–31.

Omi, Michael and Winant, Howard (1986) *Racial Formation in the United States: From the 1960s to the 1980s* (New York, NY: Routledge & Kegan Paul).

Persaud, Randolph and Walker, R. B. J. (2001) Apertura: Race in International Relations. *Alternatives*, 26 (4), 373–76.

Rose, Nikolas S. (2007) *The Politics of Life Itself: Biomedicine, Power, and Subjectivity in the Twenty-first Century* (Princeton, NJ: Princeton University Press).

Taguieff, Pierre André (2001 [1988]) *The Force of Prejudice: Racism and its Doubles*. Hassan Melehy (transl.) (Minneapolis, MN: University of Minnesota Press).

Vincent, R. J. (1982) Race in International Relations. *International Affairs*, 4 (1), 658–70.

Vitalis, Robert (2000) The Graceful and Generous Liberal Gesture: Making Racism Invisible in American International Relations. *Millennium*, 29 (2), 331–56.

Vucetic, Srdjan (2013) Black Banker, White Banker: Philosophies of the Global Color Line: *Cambridge Review of International Affairs* 25 (1): 27–48.

Wallerstein, Immanuel (1991) The Construction of Peoplehood: Racism, Nationalism, Ethnicity. In Balibar, Etienne and Wallerstein, Immanuel (eds) *Race, Nation, Class: Ambiguous Identities* (London: Verso), 71–85.

Zack, Naomi (2002) *Philosophy of Science and Race* (New York, NY: Routledge).

PART II

International practices of race and racism

7

COLONIAL VIOLENCE

Race and gender on the sugar plantations of British Guiana

Randolph B. Persaud

> Standing there, drinking in the perfume, and soothed by the soft and silent breeze, your eyes gazing upon flowers and plants and lawns trimmed neat and in order, you begin to realise that the "luxuriance" of tropical life has been brought within the bounds of law and order. Nature here is no longer wild and wanton, but civilized and chaste.
>
> Rev. L. Crookall, 1898, at the Botanical Garden
> in Georgetown, British Guiana

Introduction

Analyses of the historical connections between race and international relations have been developing with gathering momentum for some time now, and by all indications, the sub-field which has emerged is here to stay. There are many areas where new work needs to be done but two in particular stand out. First, a lot more attention needs to be paid to the administration or, more accurately, the techniques and practices of colonial rulership with significant emphasis on the routine forms of 'governance'. In doing so, even more effort needs to be spent investigating the quotidian character of violence. Second, despite frequent acknowledgement of the racio-gendered character of colonial violence, academic production in the area has room for development. These areas of investigation may be in the broad social science form of historical analysis, a kind of structuralism, or the more grounded 'history from below' perspectives. Put differently, the gendered character of violence in administration of colonialism may be tackled both synchronically and diachronically. By studying the racio-gendered violence tied to sugar production in a nineteenth-century colony, this chapter hopes to make a small contribution in that direction. Further, given that the analysis here is fundamentally informed by the work of Franz Fanon, the opportunity arises to impress the problematic of gendered violence in the dynamic of colonialism.

Sugar has a sweet but violent history. Sugar is also deeply connected to the making of the modern world, and specifically to the emergence of global capitalism and the modern inter-state system. In this sense, 'King Sugar' is one of the major contributors to modernity, and certainly one of the first global commodities with the signature of globalisation (Williams 1964, Wolf 1982, Mintz 1986). The history of sugar is also associated with slavery and some of the worst forms of colonial domination, racial oppression, predatory sexual relations, labour exploitation, civilisational marginalisation, paternalism, and various forms and levels of violence (Hyam 1990; Banivabua-Mar, 2007).

Most studies of violence and colonialism actually focus on the *direct violence* done *by the colonizers* during the periods of conquest and through the centuries of administering the colonial project. Adam Hochschild's excellent work on violence in colonial Africa, *King Leopold's Ghost* (1999), is an outstanding instance of this approach. Yet we know from Frantz Fanon, and others, that colonial violence was truly complicated, since it was at once direct and indirect; pervasive and localised; mundane and targeted; physical and psychological; chaotic and directed; centralised and dispersed; and both criticised and embraced. Colonial violence, we can say further, was massively overdetermined in its institutional forms and multiply organised in its strategic and tactical delivery. The multilayered complexity of colonial violence demands closer attention so that we can go beyond the more instrumentalist explanations based on theories of frontal opposition.

The examination of colonial violence brings into focus an acknowledgment made by Du Bois and signalled by the editors in their introduction as worthy of more investigation – that of the racialised *and gendered* nature of practices of colonial domination. These practices have been receiving increasing attention in international relations, this being the case particularly in the postcolonial and feminist approaches (Doty 1996, Mohammed 1998, Pasha 1998, Vitalis 2000, Persaud and Walker 2001, Shepherd 2002, Inayatullah and Blaney 2003, Agathangelou 2004, Chowdhry and Nair 2004, Gruffydd Jones 2006, Das 2010, Shilliam 2010, Sajed 2013, Seth 2013). While solid ground has been made in understanding race and gender in international relations, however, the two forms of domination are still too separated in their treatment. The editors also note that Du Bois was keen to frame analyses of the colour line through what Fanon would later call the "lived experience" of those who lived behind its "veil". As a matter of lived experience, race and gender are bound up with each other, this being so both for the coloniser and the colonised. In this chapter I therefore argue that race was the anchoring principle in the structured totality of the colonial system, and that gender was one social force that mediated the forms of violence employed for reproduction of the system as a whole. Specific case studies can shed significant light on these relations of violence.

This chapter takes up the task of examining how the process of accumulation in a colonial sugar economy, in this case British Guiana, generated multiple forms of violence. Much of this violence was delivered directly by the agents of colonialism (what I see as vertical violence) in order to establish order and stability, but a good deal of the violence was also *among* the dominated populations themselves (horizontal violence). I argue here that horizontal violence was a *derivative* of the vertical form, where the latter was *the* integral aspect in the maintenance and reproduction of colonial-plantocratic power. The chapter focuses specifically on the murder of indentured women by indentured men, a form of localised violence that demands further elaboration. Much like slavery, and in fact because of the end of slavery, the violence examined here is linked to the supply, management and reproduction of labour power. Without necessarily falling into economic determinism, I must insist that to understand this (colonial) violence, it is necessary to go beyond the corporal body, itself an object of pain, to the general body politic, including the systems of political and cultural power, and economic accumulation. Michel Foucault has demonstrated in convincing fashion how different techniques, apparatuses and regimes of punishment are consistent with the general socio-economic and political order. Thus, up to the end of the eighteenth century, inflicting pain on the body, in public and as a spectacle, was central to the production of order. This *supplice*, which is 'corporal punishment, painful to a more or less horrible degree', was itself a technology of political power, as much as it was a form of punishment for crimes committed (Foucault 1979, 33). By the early nineteenth century changes in the political and economic order saw the decline of torture and the introduction of more panoptic strategies of surveillance accompanied by penal reform. In the second phase the panoptic strategies were "not for power itself, nor for the immediate salvation of a threatened society; its aim [was] to strengthen the social forces – to increase production, to develop the economy, spread education, raise the level of public morality", all of these being necessary requirements of a rising industrial capitalism (Foucault 1979, 208).

In the case under study, indentured women were widely abused, and more tellingly, dozens were maimed or murdered on the sugar plantations in British Guiana and Trinidad and Tobago (Reddock 1985; Mohapatra 1995). The historian Basdeo Mangru (1987, 217) reports that "[t]he official statistics showed 23 murders of Indian women by their husbands or reputed husbands in the period 1859–64, 11 between 1865–70, 36 between 1884–95 and 17 between 1901–7. There were also 35 cases of cutting and wounding of Indian wives with the hoe and cutlass between 1886 and 1890." There is little doubt that many cases of wounding were never brought to the attention of the authorities, since, to begin with, the violence was employed to punish and control. Further, suicides, which were rife, have not been taken into consideration in the extant literature on violence in the colony. It is important to note that the violence against indentured women by male partners had identifiable patterns of public display. As Prabhu P. Mohapatra (1995, 240) has noted, "In most instances, the women were hacked to death by cutlasses, issued to men for cutting cane." This will be examined later. It is first necessary to map the objective economic, political, and social conditions of the colony leading up to the period under consideration.

Between 1838 and 1917 the political economy, society and culture of British Guiana was structurally transformed. These transformations began almost immediately in the post-emancipation period. In broad terms, the structural reconfiguration of Guianese society in this period might be understood as a set of complex and interconnected processes involving the simultaneous withering away of the institutions of slavery and the implantation of a new system of labour power based upon both relations of incorporation and coercion. Put simply, the social and political relations governing accumulation were restructured in such a way as to maintain control, including violent control, over the new labour regime in the sugar industry. This new regime based upon indentured labour saw some 240,000 East Indians and several thousand Chinese taken to the colony in the period under consideration (Mandle, 1973).

Analysis of violence against indentured women in the colony has been focused in three areas.[1] First, the research has solidly established the distorted ratio of women to men – an average of 35:100 for the entire period – and much has been rightfully made of the planters' refusal to increase the female population. Second, considerable attention has been paid to the 'quality' of women recruited in India, as well as the methods of recruitment. Third, almost all writers on the subject devote some space to the widespread phenomenon of wife murders by indentured men. Reports from various officials in the colony have produced valuable information on women. The issue, however, is not so much whether women have been included or excluded, but *how* they have been incorporated in the analyses of indentureship and in the structures of violence in the decades after emancipation. Put differently, the question at hand pertains to the epistemological status of gender in accounting for the emergence of the post-emancipation social formation as well as the structural location of violence embedded in the plantation form of accumulation. A fourth strand can be found in the brilliant analysis of Prabhu P. Mohapatra (2010) who has examined the legal response to 'wife murder' in terms of a general colonial strategy of 'returning' the Indian family to its supposed original condition in order to set up the infrastructure for the reproduction of labour power.

This chapter engages the ways in which the system of indentureship was built simultaneously upon both a coercive regime of surplus extraction *and* a gendered division of labour. These latter elements themselves must be understood in the broader racialised assumptions and practices, which attended the colonial social formation. Further, a concerted effort is made to demonstrate that some of the explanations for violence against women are mere extensions of basic Eurocentric division of the world between the Saved and the Dammed (Persaud and Walker 2001, Hobson 2011). In general, much is made of the intrinsic nature of Indian culture, Indian men and women, and 'oriental' religion (more Hinduism than Islam) in accounting for the macabre practices of violence against women in nineteenth-century plantation life. Indentured labourers were racially constituted in two ways. On the one hand they were seen as 'hard working' and 'thrifty' (Hoefte 1998, 103; Rodway 1998), a construction that itself was inter-textually derived from the supposed dialectical opposite of the African. The Indian was also seen *principally* through his religion, thus the near universal colonial appellation of the Hindustani.

This essential characteristics of the Hindustani by the colonizer, as Hoefte (1998, 103) reminds us, were "bloodthirsty", "querulous", "cantankerous", "exacting", "revengeful" and so excessively frugal as to be able "to kill somebody for a dime" and eat dirt to save money". The violence against women was not only reduced to crimes of *passion* but considered natural and, therefore, understandable violence. James Rodway (1912, 208) gives us a typical Orientalised pronouncement, what I see as patriarchal thuggery on the subject:

> From the legal standpoint, perhaps the greatest difficulty with the coolie-man is his jealousy. Unfortunately, the number of women brought from India is insufficient; some of them leave their husbands when offers of rich jewellery are made by other men. In such cases the husband does not hesitate to chop the faithless woman to pieces. Possibly he wonders that the law takes cognisance of such a thing and wants to hang him, for after all it is one of the primary laws of nature to kill a woman under such circumstances. We can hardly help admiring this trait in his character … ."

Rodway's observation above was typical of the times, meaning that racio-gendered hegemony was both deeply and widely embedded in the colonial mind. It was based on the eurocentricism of the late nineteenth century, a period when colonial expansion actually accelerated in territorial terms and deepened in terms of its Orientalist repertoire (Prashad 2007). The danger of this separating indentureship from the legacy of slavery has been noted by Nalini Mohabir (2010), who "looks at indentureship and its dialogic relationship to the institution of slavery in Guyana". Most importantly, Mohabir "moves away from binaries towards a relational account," and "complicates neat divisions" that exist in some of the scholarship on the subject.[2]

The post-emancipation conundrum of race: The voice of a landowner

In the immediate aftermath of emancipation the colony faced real problems with labour supply. Planters were caught between the anti-slavery policies of the British Government in London and the requirements of labour on the plantations. The years after emancipation also revealed cultural contradictions of a deeply radicalised system of accumulation. Simply put, the Africans that were long constructed as inferior and uncivilised were the very *people* that the planters would do anything to get as labourers. These contradictions were forcefully expressed in a book published by T. Bosworth in London in 1853 under the authorship of 'A Landowner'.

In the words of the Landowner (1853, 65), "The Negro (*sic*) character has been often described as a compound of cunning and suspicion; but, perhaps its chief distinguishing trait is the most insufferable self-conceit; this is the greatest obstacle to the improvement of the race … ." He continues, "Utterly unaware of the extent of his own ignorance, and supremely happy in it, the negro neither seeks, nor even admits, the advantages of instruction" (Landowner 1853, 66). This 'spokesman' for the planters goes on to quote a letter sent in 1839 to London by Sir C. T. Metcalfe, the Governor of Jamaica. According to Metcalfe,

> The labourers, if they shall be induced to prefer the mere means of life, to the wages and earning of a comfortable subsistence, will yearly decline in civilisation, become an ignorant, degraded class in society, and lose all the advantages which may be secured by a moderate degree of industry and exertion.
>
> *(Landowner 1853, 66)*

These were devastating words and particularly truculent representations of newly emancipated Africans. But the story about race here is far more complicated and the plot is extraordinarily sophisticated. For in fact, the Landowner admits in his own report that the 'negro' "has been painted blacker than really is". The reason for this is that he wants the Crown to take responsibility for abolishing slavery because the planters believed that it is emancipation that produced a culture of labour withdrawal. The Landowner (1853, 78) thus writes,

> But having thus plainly stated the present condition of the emancipated negroes, far be it for me to assert, that their vices and failings are inherent in the race, and not to be eradicated; on the contrary, they would seem to be merely the natural consequences of the great change from slavery to freedom, which the present generation has undergone.

Having established in his own terms that emancipation has facilitated the near collapse of the colony due to labour shortage, the Landowner then goes on to make a comprehensive case for labourers from Africa. The case had to be not only comprehensive, but extraordinary, because bonded labour, or any immigration from Africa to the West Indies, was at the time strongly protested by the Anti-Slavery Society. Accordingly, the following arguments were made: (1) that Africans would be better off in the colony rather than staying in Africa and suffering (2) that immigrants are free men and women and should be allowed to exercise their own judgment rather than be subjected to the paternalism of the Anti-Slavery Society; (3) that the new African immigrants would 'civilise' the newly emancipated Africans in British Guiana who, since emancipation have declined in work ethic and morality, and who are an 'indolent and volatile race"; (4) that the new African indentured immigrants may return to Africa and civilise their own people who did not enjoy the supposed civilizing effects of labour in the West Indies; and (5) that African women would have the opportunity to earn their own incomes since, "as with most slave nations, women are accustomed to toil as hard, if not harder than the men" (Kale 1998, 88–90).

The complexity of this radicalised discourse could be found in the ways in which there are simultaneous and multiple constructions of Africans. Thus the

African is first constructed through the usual language of laziness and lacking culture, a construction that began at the inception of slavery. Then, these same constructions are taken and argued that they are not innate, but *the result of emancipation*. Finally, the African is nonchalantly returned to backwardness through the argument that new African immigrants from Africa can go back to their homelands and civilise their people who have not yet been fully exposed to colonialism. Similar operations were made regarding the 'coolie'.

The problem of scarcity

The importation of 'Coolie' labour in British Guiana resulted from a complex mixture of economic, political and ideological circumstances. It should be stated forthwith that the decision to turn to indentured labourers was not simply a matter of the *shortage* of labour. This is a central point and it moves away from the pre-dominant understanding that it was shortage *per se* that warranted indentured immigrants. There was not, in other words, an absolute labour shortage, but a relative one, a point that the British and Foreign Anti-Slavery Society made with great determination through its publication the Anti-Slavery *Reporter*.[3] The labour supply in the colony was *precarious*. The difference between the two is not a matter of head count, but essentially political in nature. J. R. Mandle has shown that from the onset of emancipation, British Guiana entered a labour supply crisis. Mandle correctly argues that examination of output data for the main products gives a vivid picture of the extent of the crisis. Thus, "[b]y 1836–40 coffee output was only about one-third of the 1816–20 level, and cotton output had fallen from about nine million pounds in 1812–15-to about 500,000 pounds" (Mandle 1973, 18). Sugar output, though it had been on an upward movement since 1812–15, fell by some 19 per cent during the *second half* of the 1830s. The accepted explanation for the decline in output is that there was widespread withdrawal of labour from the sugar estates, and that this combined with a high death rate, disrupted the econ-omy, and in the end made it necessary to find a reliable source of labour outside the colony.

Posing the problem as one only of *shortage*, however, is of limited value, not least because it does not tell you specifically why *indentured labour* was subsequently sought. There was indeed a labour supply problem, but the real issue for the planters, as Walter Rodney argues, was one of *control* of the labour process, and more broadly, the attempt to protect the privileges which obtained in the extant race-class and state-society institutions (Rodney 1981; see also Persaud 2001; Mohapatra 2007). Kale (1998, 60–1) also reminds us that the real issue for the planters was the fact that their hitherto unchallenged authority with respect to wages and work condi-tions had come to an end. If the issue was one of shortage defined in terms of head count, why did the planters not embark on labour imports earlier, say after 1807, when curtailment of the slave trade exerted labour supply pressures? The decline in coffee and cotton production actually was the result of the sectoral rationalisation. Sugar, as Mandle argues, became firmly entrenched. Sugar production actually increased by 214 per cent from 1815 through 1835. Since sugar is a labour intensive industry the significant increase in production in such a short period would not sustain an argument of chronic shortage. The year 1829 in fact, was one of the most profitable years in the colony, when 109 million pounds of sugar was produced.

While emancipation did in and of itself lead to labour withdrawal, the equally pressing matter was that *a labour market* had actually emerged. The ex-slaves were now in a position to bargain for wages and better working conditions. *Task gangs* were formed as a strategy of strengthening the bargaining position of workers with the planters. Significantly, the *task gangs* broke the absolute control the planters, managers and overseers had in controlling every aspect of estate work. As far back as 1897 W. Alleyne Ireland (2009 [1897], 2) had noted that "Three years after Emancipation it was proved by returns from sixty estates that a hogshead of sugar, which sold for eighty-nine dollars, cost ninety-eight dollars to produce. [Under these conditions], the planter sought salvation by introducing labourers from other countries." While cost must have been uppermost in the minds of the planters, they were equally keen on the reinstutionalisation of a labour regime which, once established through the indenture system, simultaneously marginalised the ex-slaves, provided labour supply stability (after 1851), and in the long term, prevented any revolutionary political developments. An unqualified acceptance of labour shortage would have problems in explaining the strikes of 1842, which swept through Demerara and Essequibo. The protests were in fact *against* labour imports from the other West Indian Islands, as well as Portuguese, English, Irish, and even American workers (Seecharan 1997, 2–3). As late as 1890, H. V. P. Bronkhurst (1890, 70) would note that "The importation of so many thousands of Asiatic labourers to till the soil of the country is a standing reproach to the labouring Creole population."

The historical evidence is clear concerning the political dimension of labour shortage. Simply put, while there was a shortage, the bigger picture was one of authority and control of the labour process and, more broadly, a defence against further erosion of the political power of the planters. It is important to understand that the vilification of emancipated Africans was not confined to British Guiana but to other British West Indian territories. Drawing on the work of Shepherd, Amar Wahab (2007, 3) notes that "planters in Jamaica resorted rather unsuccessfully to coercive tactics and unacceptable labour terms such as anti-settler laws, lower wages, destruction of ex-slaves' property, and prevention of ex-slaves' land purchases to keep African ex-slaves bound to the plantation." Writing in 1871, John Edward Jenkins, a 'progressive' lawyer from the UK who went to the colony, was explicit in his observation that the importation of indentured labour was not simply a matter of labour shortage but one that may be understood as the politics of industrial discipline. Jenkins (2010, 262) thus noted that the emancipated African labour force has been "taught a *lesson* which though 'very severe' was doubtless wholesome and just". The lesson, of course, was that the imported labour 'flooded' the local labour market, one in which the 'coolie' was paid half the wages of African labour. Finally, the newly arrived indentured labourers did not display the same industrial militancy as the newly emancipated Africans. As Mohapatra (2007, 111) notes, "the key point of these migration systems was not mainly coercion at the point of recruitment … but the effective control exercised by employers over labourers and the lowering of wages below the market rates." It is well to remember, as does Nalini Mohabir (2010, 238), that "indentureship was shaped by prior geographical, historical, and racialised colonial practices which saw the survival of 'massa' (master) "backraman" and overseer roles in relation to a post-emancipation indentured work force".

It was under these circumstances that in January 1836 John Gladstone, father of Prime Minister Gladstone and expatriate Demerara planter, anticipating an end to the apprenticeship system in 1840 (which actually occurred on 1 August 1838) wrote to Gillanders, Arbuthnot & Co. in Calcutta inquiring about Indian labour. After acknowledging the significance of the impending end of apprenticeships, Gladstone was careful to note that the key objective in securing labour from the Indian subcontinent was to create a labour supply pool *independent of our negro population*" (Scoble 1840, 4). He specifically asked about 'bound labour'. Gillanders wrote back to Gladstone with good news. The company noted that they had been in supply of bound labour and that they would indeed be in a position to meet the labour order of the Demerara planter. Moreover, Gillanders 'informed' Gladstone that the Indians he had in mind were "more akin to the monkey" and that they had paltry needs. It was clear from the texture of the communication that the labour company was operating with some notion of the racial suitability of the labourers for the type of back-breaking and 'bound labour' being discussed.

The sex dimension of the request was equally clear. On 10 March 1837, Gladstone, along with another expatriate planter from Liverpool, one John Moss, wrote again to Gillanders and Co.:

> [I]f the female Coolies will engage to work there, a larger proportion may be sent, say two women to three men, or, if desired, equal numbers; but if *they will not engage to work there*, then the proportion … of *one female to nine or ten men*, for cooking and washing, is enough!
>
> Scoble (1840, 6)

The planters were keen to instruct the recruiters that children, in the amount of 15–20, were welcome. Following the labour order, appropriate ordinances were passed in London to define the juridical terms governing the conditions of engagement, transfer, and insertion of the new 'immigrants'. Two ships, the *Hesperus* and *Whitby* were dispatched to India. The Caribbean thus took another major turn in its history and by 1888 Pieter Marinus Netscher (1888, 146) would write that "through the advent of those competing labourers, the people have made themselves completely independent of the caprices and extravagant demands of the Creole workmen".

Gender composition

From the very beginning the sex composition of the indentured immigrants was severely distorted. Estate records show, upon arrival, further aggravation of the

TABLE 7.1 Male/Female assignment of first batch of Indian indentured workers

Estate	Males	Females
Vreed-en-Hoop	65	5
Vriedestein	31	0
Anna Regina	46	3
Belle Vue	79	3
Waterloo	47	0
Highbury	117	11
Total	385	22

Source: Adapted from Scoble (1840)

distortion. The assignment of the first 407 immigrants to the estates makes this case easy to understand, as demonstrated by the data in Table 7.1.

The ships sailed with 405 men, 12 women and 20 children; there were thus 34 men per 1 woman. The overall ratio of adult men to grown women actually assigned was 17.5 males to one female, but as the table above indicates, some estates had no females of any age. This distortion became a definitive aspect of the social reproduction of the indentured system. Through the period in question the Crown and the planters engaged in a running dispute over the male/female ratio. Until 1857 there was no mandatory stipulation affecting the gender distribution, but even after ordinances (the first in 1857) were put in place to govern the same, the problem remained. Table 7.2 below shows the male/female ratio for the period 1838 through 1914.

Clem Seecharan shows that there were major fluctuations in the male/female ratio through the period of indentureship. The period 1845–70 saw an intake of 32:100, but that went up to 40:100 after 1870. What is interesting to note here is that this gendered system actually resembled that of slavery, which generally had a 2/3 to 1/3 female/male intake. This is an important point because it allows for critical reflection on the ways in which the extant literature has dealt with women. In general the arguments have been that the sex distortion resulted from the

TABLE 7.2 Number of Indian women to 100 men, selected years 1838–1914

Year	Women to 100 men	Year	Women to 100 men	Year	Women to 100 men
1838	3	1881	40	1911	39
1845	18	1888	41	1914	34
1846	25	1889	40		
1847	19	1891	46		
1848	25	1893	41		
1851	25	1894	40		
1857	57	1895	43		
1863	24	1896	49		
1864	24	1900	50		

Source: Seecharan (1997, 28)

cultural propensity of East Indians to "keep women at home", and that women who did make the voyage must have been of what I shall call "fallen status". Seecharan (1997, 29) makes the astute observation that the fallen status thesis has "hardened into an unexamined dogma", and that "[s]cholarly opinion is in its infancy, often hovering around robust speculations".

The fallen status thesis is partly buoyed on by the fact that some 73 per cent of the women who went to the colony were single. Given Indian marriage patterns – namely, the tendency for Indian girls to get married at an early age – the extremely high proportion of single women who migrated was indicative of some kind of problem. The reasoning is that it would have been unbecoming for a woman of good standing (and caste) to have agreed to migrate (Shepherd 2002; Bahadur 2011). Those who did leave, it is believed, were prompted by the opportunity to escape various forms of caste, class and cultural marginalisation, or from domestic oppression supposedly embedded in the Indian family tradition of patriarchal hegemony. Basdeo Mangru (1987, 22) expresses this position with clarity. He writes:

> Indian women who regularly boarded emigrant vessels comprised principally young widow and married and single women who have already gone astray, and are therefore not only most anxious to avoid their homes and conceal their antecedents, but were also at the same time the least likely to be received back into their families. Prostitutes from Calcutta and other large Indian cities were shipped largely to augment the numerical shortage and minimize demurrage."

The behavioural attributes of the women themselves are often combined with the *process* of recruiting females. *Arkatis* were instructed to find good-looking women of character, and for this they were paid more per head, than for each male recruit (Beaumont 1871). There is evidence that many women were forced into the holding depots and kept there under strict surveillance, and that, as noted above, many were kidnapped (Bahadur 2011, 54–56). The literature also tends to stress deception as a strategy of the *arkatis*. Mangru (1987, 22), for example, argues that the recruiters had a strong "psychological hold" over the prospective immigrants, and that "[w]omen in particular were vulnerable and liable to be deceived". Seecharan (1997, 18) is suspicious of this emphasis on deception, and instead suggests that stronger economic motives might have been at play. Notwithstanding these disputes, sufficient evidence exists to posit that, at a minimum, some level of coercion was employed in the recruitment process.

Against the behavioural factors which no doubt affected migration, there were developments in the world economy which called for cheap labour and, accordingly, for population transfers. British Guiana and India were connected to that world economy through the imperial system of Britain, and through the processes of global accumulation, grounded in this case in the sugar economy. As Seecharan (1997) has shown, in the case of India there was already significant internal migration on account of the development of industry in Calcutta and Assam.

Indian workers were also shipped off to the tea plantations of Shri Lanka. In fact, it was the competition from other sources of labour – Mauritius, Malaya, and Shri Lanka – that pushed the *arkatis* into the northern United Provinces, specifically eastern Utter Paradesh and western Bihar after 1860. This part of India, at the time, was increasingly being penetrated by British capital, which caused dislocations, including accelerated commodification of labour and the making of a wage-dependent population. There was also a severe depression in India from the late 1820s through the 1850s (Levine 2007, 70). The caste configuration of the social formation entailed land concentration in the hands of the Brahmains, Kshattriyas, Bhuinhars, Banias, etc. Seecharan (1997, 24) states that these upper castes con-trolled 79.8 per cent of the land in the Bhojpuri districts, which were the major immigrant sources after the 1860s: "For those who were deeply indebted or whose families were perennially indebted, overseas migration offered escape from this bondage which blighted effort and strangled initiative." In contradistinction to the proximate circumstances that 'pushed' or 'pulled' indentured labour migration, some writers (for example, Mohapatra 1995) insist that developments within global capitalism were central to the mobility of labour.

Indentured women in colonial society

It might be useful to review some of the major explanations of the violence against women during the period under consideration. K. O. Laurence has usefully iden-tified the major arguments. What follows immediately is an overview of these arguments. First, there is the jealousy contention. In this explanation, the shortage of women caused great sexual jealousies and it was this that led to violence. The shortage of women gave many options, not the least of which was the one of moving from one relationship to another. Many women were 'kept' and there were instances of women engaging in multiple marriages. The logic of this expla-nation is that shortage set up the objective conditions for intense competition, 'betrayal', shame, and then violence. Laurence (1994, 241) puts it thus:

> Moreover, an estate wife in the later nineteenth century was an important symbol of status and of masculinity, extremely important to the husband's self esteem as well as to his standing in his own society. Her departure for another man was a source of fundamental shame, a major blow to the husband's pride, indicative of failure both to keep his wife in appropriate subjection according to the ancestral culture and to sustain his own self-respect.

Second, and in contradistinction to the shortage argument, is the idea that the *quality* of women who came was the real issue, a construction which itself reflects aggravated social and class compartmentalisation. In this respect, the argument is that the male/female ratio had little bearing on violence. Rather, the violence was on account of the *behaviour* of the women, and that their behaviour was a matter of their low caste or marginalised existence in India. Some colonial officials felt "that the women were of such 'low class' that the men regarded them as chattels and treated them as such" (quoted in Laurence 1994, 239).

A third explanation focuses on the supposed low value that 'Asiatics' placed on female life (Laurence 1994, 240). There is indeed considerable evidence of under-valuing women in some Asian societies, India being one of them. The question though is the extent to which this disposition had a bearing on the violence in the *colony*. One important fact to consider is that there were far fewer murders among non-indentured and 'freed' Indians who were not living on plantations.

Fourth, and continuing along an orientalised trajectory, is the notion that it was a national attribute of India that men chopped "women as a way of resolving sexual differences" (Laurence 1994, 241) Another way of saying this is that chopping was a custom of Indian culture. Again, there was less chopping in the *villages* compared to the *estates*. If indeed chopping is a cultural attribute, it would be hard to explain how it is prevalent on the estates, but not so frequent with those enjoying greater civic freedoms.

A fifth argument focuses on a combination of race and religion, in this case, Hinduism. In earlier times men such as Henry Mitchell insisted that the Hindu religion was propitious for the violence visited upon women in the colony. One version of this thesis was that the violence was simply an expression of the ways of the uncivilised. Thus, Sir Clinton Murdoch in 1876 advanced the idea that much of the violence was "attributable to the want of respect for the sacredness of life which everywhere prevails among ignorant and pagan populations" (Laurence 1994, 241).

K. O. Laurence himself offers a seventh, and different, argument. In his view the radicalised and orientalised notions of Indian culture or religion are misplaced. Yet Laurence himself falls in the trap of these same tendencies. He (1994, 241) thus states that "in linking the vulnerability of women to the cultural pattern of the immigrants Murdoch was entirely right". The basis for Laurence's conclusion seems to be the way Indian men treated their unfaithful wives. There is no doubt that men treated their unfaithful wives with 'sternness', as Laurence notes. But was that peculiar to Indian men, or can the answer be found in broader patterns of both patriarchal and colonial violence? I join Mohapatra, Wahab, and others who see the construction of violence against indentured women reduced to 'wife murder' as deeply Orientalised.

A structural view of colonial violence

There may indeed be a correlation between 'wife murder' and the sex composition of indentured estate life, but for the latter to be understood properly it is important to recognise that *generalised violence* was a feature of colonial society as a whole. The institution of slavery was formed, maintained and reproduced through systematic violence, and this to the very end as the increased use of the cat-o'-nine tails *after* emancipation makes clear. Here for instance is what an eye-witness reported about slave work in Cuba in 1847:

> It was crop time; the mills went round night and day. On every estate (I scarcely
> hope to be believed when I state the fact) every slave was worked under the
> whip 18 hours out of 24, and in the boiling-houses from 5 A.M. to 6 P.M.,
> and from 11 A.M. to midnight the sound of the hellish lash was incessant;
> indeed, it was necessary to keep the overtasked wretches awake. The six
> hours during which they rested were spent in a barracoon – a strong, foul,
> close sty, where they wallowed without distinction of age and sex.
>
> *Dalton (1855, 21)*

The testimony of eye-witness also establishes in convincing fashion the way in
which the administration of violence on a daily basis was tied into the emasculatory
violence of the planters against the slaves and then the indentured. Here is the
eye-witness on that subject – "There was no marrying amongst the slaves on
plantations; breeding was discouraged; it was cheaper and less troublesome to buy
than to breed. On many estates females were entirely excluded" (Dalton 1855, 21).
Mohapatra (1995) made almost exactly the same observation with regards to the
availability of women on the sugar plantations. He argues that only in the later
stages of the indentured labour regime did the planters become interested in
expanding the labour pool from within the colony. Mohapatra goes on to
demonstrate the ways in which the attempts to deal with violence against women
as 'wife murder' was connected to an attempt to reinvent the Indian family.

Violence, therefore, was embedded in indentureship from the very recruiting
grounds and depots in India (where many of the women recruited were tricked or
kidnapped), across the *kala pani,* and finally in the system of labour and social
control on the sugar estates. Court records show significantly disproportionate
numbers of indentured immigrants convicted for crimes relating to the labour laws
and to matters in 'civil society' (Trotman 1986).

In addition to the use of force for the effect of direct submission, colonial violence may also be understood as a kind of public spectacle intended to demonstrate
to the slave, and then the 'coolie', the capacity and willingness to visit pain on the
'subject races'. The techniques of violence themselves had to be known, since
colonial administrators had come to the conclusion that "the Indian, as the African
slaves before him, would walk without protest to the gallows, but was terrified of
the Cat-O'-Nine".

The spectacle of violence was alive and well during the period of indentureship.
This was not confined to 'wife murderers' but was broadly applied to all those
sentenced to death. The *supplice* in British Guiana in the nineteenth century (just
when it was in recession in Europe) can be gleaned from a Demerara sheriff, who
later recorded these acts that he himself presided over. Here is one instance from
Henry Kirke's account:

> At an execution at Suddie, in February, 1873, when the bolt was drawn
> the man dropped so that his feet touched the ground, and in that position
> the poor wretch writhed and struggled until he was raised up by some of the

prisoners (present to witness the execution as a moral object-lesson) high enough to allow Hamlet, the executioner, to take a few turns of the slack of the rope round a pin in the cross beam of the gallows. This supplementary work done, the man was dropped again to hang until life was slowly choked out of him. In the confusion the cap dropped off his face, and the awful contortions of the exposed features during the death-struggle were utterly indescribable.

Kirke (1898, 305)

And here another:

His struggles were so fearful to observe, and his agony appeared to be intense. "It's all right," said Hamlet; but when the man's struggles ceased and life seemed to be extinct, the knot gave way, and Butler fell to the ground. He was still alive, and on being lifted up exclaimed, "Oh, my God!" They carried the wretched man up again on to the scaffold, and, with most mistaken kindness, gave him brandy, so that he became conscious, and exclaimed, "For God's sake, make haste and finish it." He was then hanged a second time this time, fortunately, with effect.

Kirke (1898, 306)

Noteworthy is the fact that even those colonial administrators who were supposedly sympathetic to the conditions of indentureship were not necessarily removed from the general system of violence. Take for instance the testimony of Mr De Vouex, a magistrate who filed an official report in 1869 and noted:

No magistrate was, I believe, ever more severe on proved crime and misconduct, and in proof I may mention that in the eleven months during which I held office in the first district named I ordered more flogging than had ever taken place before in a similar time, and out of a population of twenty thousand … I sentenced twelve hundred to imprisonment *with hard labour*, and of these probably two-fifths were indentured immigrants convicted chiefly of breach of contract.

Quoted in Jenkins (2010 [1871], 254).

Mohapatra underlines the integral strategy of violence in the colony (British Guiana and Trinidad), demonstrating how in fact the magnitude and techniques of this violence was an outcome of the debasement of the indentured. He notes that despite severe punishment for 'wife murder', "persistence of the murder through the 1870s and the spurt in the 1880s strengthened the belief that the Indian men were immune to the terrors of capital punishment" (Mohapatra 1995, 238). There was a public call from various quarters of the colonial administration to intensify the pain visited on the bodies of the men: "In 1873 an exasperated *Royal Gazette of British Guiana* went so far as to suggest mutilation of the body of the hanged criminal render the terror of capital punishment a deterrent" (Mohapatra 1995, 238). No-one was to be outdone and so even a H. V. P Bronkhurst, a Wesleyan missionary, insisted on the intensification of brutality and the display of this writhing pain which Foucault dramatises in *Discipline and Punish*. As Mohapatra notes, the missionary considered hanging too mild a form of death, and in my own view, too routine. Instead, Bronkhurst wanted not only death but a sort of ceremonial destruction of the body, the latter demanded because of Bronkhurst's interpretation of the eastern man. Here is Bronkhurst himself:

> It is a well known fact that the great majority of our coolies believe that whenever a man dies on the gallows in a strange land he goes back to his native land immediately after death, consequently hanging is no punishment whatever ... I would recommend public decapitation. ... The partial dismemberment of the bodies of the murderer after they are hanged, recommended by some, will not remove from the minds of the coolies the notion that death by hanging on the gallows is but a safe and sure passage to their native land. ... I would strongly recommend beheading or decapitation of the murderer *in the presence of all spectators.*
>
> *(Quoted in Mohapatra 1995, 239, my emphasis)*

Bronkhurst's celebration of violence not only brings to mind Fanon's (1967, 90) observation that "European civilization and its best representatives are responsible for colonial racism." But his celebration also forcefully underlines the argument here that colonialism did not simply use violence as an instrument of law and order but one that would at once systematise violence as part of normal day-to-day life and exorcise the colonised of their assumed cultural backwardness, their habits and tendencies, and even their gods (Fanon 1967, 90). It is well to keep in mind that this is the same Mr De Vouex who expressed concern about an unwritten rule where the indentured worker should only be in three places during working hours, namely, actually at work, in hospital, or in jail (Jenkins 2010 [1871], 247). The culture of colonialism, therefore, was a culture of violence.

A more structural approach to violence also takes cognisance of the spatial formation of plantation societies, and specifically, the living arrangements on the sugar estates. In general, the white planters and their managers lived in fenced-off compounds that were protected by armed guards. The emancipated Africans moved to villages or to the city, and the indentured servants were placed in *logies*. The *logies* were really nothing more than a shed with walls as they lacked plumbing of any sort. The workers had to share bathing and latrine facilities. Following Fanon, we can posit that the spatial configuration of the society was intentionally compartmentalised, and that this led to a general sense of isolation, if not quarantine (see Doty 1996, 59). Put differently, the coloniser effectively employed spatial techniques of discipline and regulation of daily life on the plantations. It is well to keep in mind that the indentured servant, as a matter of routine, had to get a pass to move from one estate to another. Fanon argues that the colonial world was 'cut in two' quarters, two separate zones, and that these relations of separation were the breeding grounds for violence (Fanon 1967, 36–41).

The culture of violence also manifested itself in an amalgam of deprivations and consequent squalor in which people lived their lives out. Here is the testimony of Joseph Beaumont (1871, 65), former chief justice of the colony:

> I never could have believed that such beings could exist had I not seen them in Demerara; but I have seen some there who presented such sights of terror that now, after the lapse of years, they haunt me – creatures so worn by illness and starvation as to appear at first sight actual skeletons, every bone visible, perfectly fleshless, their legs appearing like long stilts, their very buttocks almost entirely exposed and worn to the bone, and the faces showing the terrible appearance of a skeleton's head, only lighted up in their great hollow orbits by eyes that yet reflected a dull glimmer.

The destitution of the indentured, combined with the culture of violence present, may indeed have shaped the way in which people resolved social problems. Along these lines Mohabir (2010, 245) writes that "any freedom of movement through indenture contracts operated with the strictures of white supremacy; i.e. economic imperatives which required racial subordination". Violence against women may be understood in this context, with 'wife shortage' as the proximate cause.

One thing that there is no dispute about is that indentured women paid heavily with their lives and bodies, not to mention the culture of fear which must have attended their daily existence. The social (rather than behavioural) character of the violence may be understood through *how* the acts of violence, namely, the techniques employed and the parts of the bodies targeted. By all accounts the violence was usually ghastly. Parts of the body were cut off, including nose, breasts and hands. The violence was also often conducted in public, sometimes preceded by a 'ritual' sharpening of a cutlass in a public area. Many women were murdered in full view of the public, as if the man was exacting some sort of socially acceptable justice (Kirke 1898, 218–19). In effect, these public murders of indentured women amounted not only to executions but also to *public spectacles* intended to discipline the conduct of women in the general economy of sexual practices. Wahab (2007, 8) also makes the important observation that "dominant white patriarchal authority emasculated East Indian men by eroding their patriarchal authority which competed to regulate women's respectability".

Conclusion

It should be obvious that the violence meted out to women in the colonial plantations was not solipsistic; rather that this violence was a *continuation* of a system of violence against African men and women during the period of slavery. Mohabir (2010, 246) puts this thematic rather well when she states that the challenge "is not only how to rethink delimited past narratives, but how to hold the fabric of overlap together with the tension of separate experiences". The attempt to link violence in the colony to the supposed cultural backwardness of the indentured labourers, or the slaves before them, is difficult to sustain. This is especially so given the fact that other immigrant groups were also harshly treated, or more accurately, brutalised on the plantations. Chinese indentured immigrants were also at the receiving end of brutal whippings and other forms of violence administered by the planters, their overseers and their agents. Clearly, structural and direct violence were integral elements in the maintenance of the colonial socio-economic order.

Four central arguments of the chapter may be reiterated. First, while there is a voluminous literature on violence by the colonisers against the colonised, there is not nearly enough about the violence among the colonised themselves. This is obviously understandable given the utter brutalities of the coloniser, as happened in Leopold's Congo, and also on account of strands of revisionism which construct a more benign history of what occurred during several centuries of colonial dom-ination spread across the globe. While there is great need for further study of the violence of the coloniser, as well as the imperialists and neo-imperialists, much may be gained by also studying violence in broader terms, including violence among and between the colonised themselves. The gendered character of this violence is also clearly visible.

Second, in this particular instance while we have examined how violence against indentured women by indentured men was in and of itself a macabre state of affairs, we have also had the occasion to push beyond the proximate circumstances and situate this violence into the very 'body politic' of colonial society. We were able to see that four elements of the colonial system worked in tight formation to sustain and reproduce colonial-plantocratic power, these being (a) the necessity of *vulnerable* labour power after emancipation as a response to the emergence of a labour market and labour militancy; (b) the dire conditions of the indentured servants, including 'spectacular' violence against indentured women; (c) the adminis-tration of law and order including forms of public punishment and even suggested decapitation and mutilation of the body of the criminal (the 'wife murderer'); and (d) a system of Orientalised knowledge that sutured these elements together into a coherent and structured totality.

Thirdly, central to the ghastly murders was an economy of sex, hatched as it were, specifically for the labour requirements of the sugar plantations and combined with the gendered assumptions of industrial sugar production. The sex ratio which has been widely seen as the *cause* of the murders was actually a form of violence itself, a gendered form of violence – that is, an emasculatory form of violence against indentured men. Moreover, this economy of sex was also built on the racialised assumptions of both Indian indentured men and women. The women were all assumed to be of 'loose morals' and as such, a smaller number of them would be suffice to 'service' the surplus of men. The English also routinely carried around in their heads the idea that Indian men are effeminate, a formulation that must have translated into assumptions about the relationship between desire and the modes of satisfaction.

Fourth and finally, for the system to have sustained itself as long as it did, it was necessary that colonial officials and the planter class work hand in hand, a necessity occasioned by the constant threat of popular uprisings. There were several lines of possible violence, all of them of course real threats to production and privilege. These included the possible violence *among* the freed slaves, the indentured, and the Portuguese 'shopkeepers' (which actually happened in 1846, 1877, 1889); intra-indentured violence including 'wife murder'; and popular uprisings (ex-slaves and the indentured) against the colonial state and planter class. The management of these multiple threats, both to white privilege and to colonial production, employed both the *supplice* (of terror) and the kind of panoptic apparatuses discussed by Foucault. In his analysis of the transformations of punishment and penal forms, Foucault (1979, 207) himself goes to great length to demonstrate that "the panoptic schema, without disappearing as such or losing any of its properties, was destined to spread throughout the social body; its vocation was to become a generalized function". The same may be said of British Guiana here, namely, that gendered violence was generalised throughout the system. This is another way to understand the catastrophic violence against indentured women on the sugar plantation.

Notes

1 Nalini Mohabir (2010, 243) identifies three strands, namely, indentureship as a result of coercion; (2) as voluntary immigration; and (3) as an "oppressive system stained by exploitative and cross-cutting processes of capitalism and racism".
2 For an outstanding critique of colonial texts on nineteenth-century British Guiana, see Persaud (1991).
3 In July 1842 a Select Committee report was released. The major findings include labour shortage in terms of 'head-count' but it also noted two other problems that had nothing to do with shortage per se. First, the planters found that the former slaves were demanding very high wages on what would be an open labour market. Second, the report also stated that many of the former slaves had gone into work other than in the sugar industry. The report thus pointed to a crisis of industrial relations in the post-emancipation period. See Ireland (2009 [1897]).

Bibliography

Abadeer, Adel S. (2008) *The Entrapment of the Poor Into Involuntary Labor: Understanding the Worldwide Practice of Modern-Day Slavery* (Lewiston, NY: The Edwin Mellen Press).

Agathangelou, Anna M. (2004) "Power, Borders, Security, Wealth: Lessons of Violence and Desire from September 11," *International Studies Quarterly*, 48 (3), 517–38.

Bahadur, Gaiutra (2011) "Coolie Women Are in Demand Here", *The Virginia Quarterly Review*, Spring, 48–61.

Ballagh, James C. (1969) *White Servitude in the Colony of Virginia: A Study of the System of Indentured Labor in the American Colonies* (New York: Burt Franklin Publishers).

Banivabua-Mar, Tracey (2007) *Violence and Colonial Dialogue: The Australian-Pacific Indentured Labor Trade* (Honolulu: University of Hawaii Press).

Beaumont, Joseph (1871) *The New Slavery: An Account of the Indian and Chinese Immigrants in British Guiana* (London: W. Ridgway).

Bronkhurst, H. V. P. (1890) *Description and Historical Geography of British Guiana and West India Islands* (Demerara: Argosy Press).

Brummell, John (1853) *British Guiana: Demerara After Fifteen Years of Freedom. By a Landowner.* http://books.google.com/books/about/British_Guiana_Demerara_after_fifteen_ye.html? id=ZRVcAAAAQAAJ.

Chowdhry, Geeta and Nair, S. (eds) (2004) *Power, Postcolonialism and International Relations: Reading race, gender and class.* London: Routledge.

Dabydeen, D. and Samaroo, B. (eds) (1987) *India in the Caribbean* (London: Hansib).

Dalton, Henry G. (1855) *The History of British Guiana* (London: Longman, Brown, Green and Longmans).

Das, R. (2010) "Colonial legacies, post-colonial (in)securities, and gender(ed) representations in South Asia's nuclear policies", *Social Identities: Journal for the Study of Race, Nation and Culture*, Vol. 16, Issue 6.

Des Voeux, William (1903) *My Colonial Service in British Guiana, St. Lucia, Trinidad, Fiji, Australia, New Foundland, and Hong Kong, With Interludes* (London: John Murray)

Doty, Roxanne Lynn (1996) *Imperial Encounters* (Minneapolis: University of Minnesota Press).

Duff, Robert (1866) *British Guiana: Natural Productions, Industrial Occupations, and Social Institutions* (Glasgow: Thomas Murray and Son).

Epstein, Charlotte (2005) *The Power of Words in International Relations: Birth of an Anti-Whaling Discourse* (Cambridge: Cambridge)

Fanon, Frantz, (1967) *Black Skin White Mask* (New York, Grove Press).

Foucault, M. (1979) *Discipline & Punish: The Birth of the Prison* (New York: Vintage Books).

Grovogui, Siba N. (2001) 'Come to Africa: A Hermeneutics of Race in International Theory', *Alternatives*, Vol. 26, No. 1, pp. 425–448.

Grovogui, Siba N'atioula (2006) "Mind, Body, and Gut! Elements of Postcolonial Human Rights Discourse", in B. G. Jones (ed.) *Decolonizing International Relations* (Lanham, MD: Rowan and Littlefield).

Hobson, John M. (2012) *The Eurocentric Conception of World Politics: Western International Theory, 1760–2010* (New York: Cambridge University Press).

Hochschild, Adam (1999) *King Leopold's Ghost: A Story of Greed, Terror, and Heroism in Colonial Africa* (New York: Mariner Books).

Hoefte, R. (1998) *In Place of Slavery: A Social History of British Indian and Javanese Labourers in Suriname* (Gainesville, Florida: University Press of Florida).

Hyam, Ronald (1990) *Empire and Sexuality: The British Experience* (Manchester: University of Manchester Press).

Inayatullah, Naeem and Blaney, David L. (2003) *International Relations and the Problem of Difference* (New York: Routledge).

Ireland, W. Alleyne (2009 [1897]) *Tropical Colonization: An Introduction to the Study of the Subject* (Ann Arbor: University of Michigan Library).

Jenkins, J. E. (2010 [1871]) *The Coolie: His Rights and Wrongs* (The Caribbean Press).

Jones, Branwen Gruffydd (2006) *Decolonizing International Relations* (Lanham, MD: Rowan and Littlefield).

Kale, Madhavi (1998) *Fragments of Empire: Capital, Slavery, and Indian Indentured Labor Migration in the British Caribbean* (Philadelphia: University of Pennsylvania Press).

Kirke, Henry (1898) *Twenty-Five Years in British Guiana* (London: Sampson Low, Marston & Co. Ltd.).

Krishna, Sankaran (2009) *Globalization and Postcolonialism.* (Lanham, MD: Rowan & Littlefield).

Laurence, K. O. (1994) *A Question of Labour: Indentured Immigration into Trinidad and British Guiana 1875–1917* (New York: St Martin's Press).

Levine, Philippa (2007) *The British Empire: Sunrise to Sunset* (Edinburgh Gate: Pearson)

Majumdar, Roma B. et al. (1976) *Bonded Labour in India* (Calcutta: India Book Exchange).

Mandle, Jay R. (1973) *The Plantation Economy: Population and Economic Change in Guyana 1838–1960* (Philadelphia: Temple University Press).

Mangru, Basdeo (1987) *Benevolent Neutrality: Indian Government Policy and Labour Migration to British Guiana 1854–1884* (London: Hansib Press).

Mintz, Sidney (1986) *Sweetness and Power: The Place of Sugar in Modern History* (New York: Penguin).

Mohabir, Nalini (2010) "Servitude in the Shadow of Slavery? Towards a Relational Account of Indenture", in Raphael Hormann and Gesa Mackenthun (eds) *Human Bondage in the Cultural Contact Zone: Transdisciplinary Perspectives and its Discourses* (Germany: Waxman Verlag GmbH).

Mohammed, Patricia (1994)"Gender as a Primary Signifier in the Construction of Community and State among Indians in Trinidad", *Caribbean Quarterly*, 40 9 (3/4), 32–43.

Mohammed, P. (1998) "Towards Indigenous Feminist Theorizing in the Caribbean", *Feminist Review*, 59 (1), 6–33.

Mohapatra, Prabhu P. (1995) "Restoring the Family': Wife Murders and the Making of a Sexual Contract for Indian Immigrant Labour in the British Caribbean Colonies, 1860–1920", *Studies in History*, 11 (2), 227–60.

Mohapatra, Prabhu, (2007) "Eurocentrism, Forced Labour, and Global Migration: A Critical Assessment", *IRSH*, 52 (1), 110–15.

Momsen, Janet H. (1988) "Gender Roles in Caribbean Agricultural Labor", in Malcom Cross and Gad Heuman (eds) *Labour in the Caribbean* (London: Macmillan).

Netscher, P. M. (1888) *History of the Colonies: Essequibo, Demerary & Berbice – From the Dutch Establishment to the Present Day* ('s-Gravenhage: Martinus Nijhoff).

Pasha, Mustapha K. (1998) *Colonial Political Economy: Recruitment and underdevelopment in the Punjab* (New York: Oxford University Press).

Persaud, Randolph B. (2001) "Racial Assumptions in Global Labor Recruitment and Supply", *Alternatives*, 26 (4), 377–99.

Persaud, Randolph B. and Walker, R. B. J. (eds) (2001) "Race and International Relations", *Alternatives*, Special Issue, 26 (1).

Persaud, Walter H. (1991) "Benevolent Neutrality: A Foucaudian Reading of the Historiography of East Indians in Nineteenth Century British Guiana", in Diaz, H. P., Rummens, J. W. A. and Taylor, P. D. M. (eds) *Forging Identities and Patterns of Development in Latin America and the Caribbean* (Toronto: Canadian Scholars Press), 298–311.

Peterson, Spike V. (2003) *A Critical Rewriting of Global Political Economy: Integrating Reproductive, Productive, and Virtual Economies* (London: Routledge).

Prashad, Vivay (2007) *The Darker Nations: A People's History of the Third World* (New York: The New Press).

Pointing, Jeremy (1987) "East Indian Women in the Caribbean: Experience and Voice", in Dadydeen, D. and Samaroo, B. (eds) *India in the Caribbean* (Warwick, UK: Hansib/University of Warwick Press).

Quijano, Anibal (2000) "Coloniality of Power, Eurocentrism, and Latin America", *Nepantla: Views from South*, 1 (3), 533–580.

Reddock, Rhoda (1985) "Fredom Denied: Indian Women and Indentureship in Trinidad and Tobago, 1845–1917", *Economic and Political Weekly*, 20 (43).

Rodney, Walter (1981) *A History of the Guyanese Working People, 1881–1905* (Baltimore: The Johns Hopkins University Press).

Rodway, James (1912) *History of British Guiana: From the Year 1668 to the Present Time* (Georgetown: J. Thomson).

Ruhomon, Peter (1988) *History of the East Indians in British Guiana, 1838–1938*.

Schomburgk, Robert H. (1970 [1840]) *A Description of British Guiana: Geographical and Statistical* (New York: Augustus M. Kelley Publishers).

Scoble, John (1840) *Hill Coolies: A Brief Exposure of the Deplorable Condition of the Hill Collie in British Guiana* (London: Harvey and Darton).

Seecharan, Clem, (1997) *'Tiger in the Stars': The Anatomy of Indian Achievement in British Guiana, 1919–1929* (London: Macmillan Press).

Seth, Sanjay (2013) *Postcolonial Theory and International Relations: A Critical Introduction* (London: Routledge).

Shepherd, Verne A. (2002) *Maharani's Misery: Narratives of a Passage from India to the Caribbean* (Jamaica: University of West Indies Press).

Shilliam, R. (ed.) (2010) *International Relations and Non-Western Thought: Imperialism, Colonialism, and investigation of global modernity* (London: Routledge).

Taussig, Michael (1987) *Shamanism, Colonialism, and the Wild Man: A Study in Terror and Healing* (Chicago: University of Chicago Press)

Tinker, Hugh (1974) *A New System of Slavery: The Export of Indian Labour Overseas 1830–1920* (New York: Oxford University Press).

Trotman, David V. (1986) *Crime in Trinidad: Conflict and Control in a plantation society, 1838–1900* (Knoxville: University of Tennessee Press).

Trotz, Alissa D. (2003) "Behind the Banner of Culture? Gender, 'Race' and the Family in Guyana", *New West Indian Guide/ Nieuwe West-Indische Gids*, 77 (1/2), 5–29.

Vitalis, Robert (2000) "The Graceful and Generous Liberal Gesture: Making Racism Invisible in American International Relations," *Millennium – Journal of International Studies*, 29 (2), 331–56.

Wahab, Amar, (2007) "Mapping West Indian Orientalism: Race, Gender and Representations of Indentured Coolies in the Nineteenth-Century British West Indies," *Journal of Asian American Studies*, 10 (3), 283–311.

Williams, Eric (1964) *Capitalism and Slavery* (London: Andre Deutsch).

Wolf, Eric R. (1982) *Europe and the People Without History* (Berkeley: University of California Press).

8

A POSTCOLONIAL RACIAL/SPATIAL ORDER

Gandhi, Ambedkar, and the construction of the international

Sankaran Krishna

Introduction

Rachel Buchanan (2011) objects to a statue of Mohandas K. Gandhi that stands outside Wellington Railway Station in the capital of Aotearoa (New Zealand).[1] A statue of Kupe, his wife Hine-te-Aparangi, and a healer named Pekahourangi, the first Maori who discovered Aotearoa over a thousand years ago, occupied the site from about 1940 to 1986, when it was vandalized. It was later bronzed and moved to the Taranaki Wharf. Buchanan is particularly exercised by the replacement of Aotearoa's founders by someone who has become iconic of the anti-political, vacuous and benign evocation of peace and non-violence – Gandhi. The latter has come to represent "an easy, ahistorical peace and love" and "a global non-violent superstar (who) is so much easier to accommodate, recall and unveil than … difficult little indigenous nobodies and their white-feathered followers …" (Buchanan 2011, 1079).

In many ways, the Gandhi statue at Wellington Railway Station is very similar to the role Gandhi the man plays in the discipline of international relations. Based on selective and thin appropriations of his voluminous writings and political actions, he is idealized as an icon of peaceful political change.[2] In this essay I would like to problematize such pacific figurations of Gandhi and locate his politics at the intersection of race, caste, and the international system. Binary categories such as black/white, western/nonwestern, and global north and south tend to draw our eyes away from the complexities within each of them and desensitize us to ways in they are themselves hierarchized. W. E. B. Du Bois' invocation of the color line, wittingly or otherwise, reifies distinctions that are far more malleable, problematic and internally racist and casteist than we might otherwise suppose.

I argue that Gandhi was instrumental in a particular postcolonial rendition of race and space in our world, one that is hostile to ideals of equality and democracy, non-violence and peace. By focusing on two periods in his long political life – his engagement with a certain racial order in South Africa and his encounters with the Dalit[3] leader Bhim Rao Ambedkar in the 1930s – I show how a certain post-colonial rendition of the racial and spatial order of the international system formed the backdrop of Gandhi's life and was powerfully reinforced by his politics. This racial/spatial order was highly evident during the UN World Conference Against Racism held in 2001. At that conference the Indian government successfully deflected efforts by India's Dalits to have casteism equated with racism and to have untouchability discussed as part of the proceedings. Getting beyond this racial/spatial world order necessitates a reevaluation of signifiers like Gandhi and politicizing their static solidity.

South Africa and India: then and now

In August–September, 2001, the 3rd United Nations World Conference Against Racism, Racial Discrimination, Xenophobia, and Related Intolerance took place in Durban, South Africa. India's Dalits organized an energetic campaign to have caste-based discrimination included in the UN Conference as a form of racism, since they were both descent-based forms of discrimination, and to leverage international opprobrium to accelerate the glacial pace of change within India. They listed the long and still-continuing atrocities against Dalits and marshaled evidence to show the impact of discrimination against them and their status at the bottom of most developmental indices in that largely poor country. They pointed out that the government was a signatory to the Universal Declaration of Human Rights (1948), the International Convention on the Elimination of All Forms of Racial Discrimination (ICERD, 1965) and the UN's International Covenant on Civil and Political Rights (ICCPR, 1979) that proscribe descent-based discrimination, and hence a legal case could be made that it was negligent in living up to its obligations (see Louis 2003; Natarajan and Greenough (2009).[4]

The Government of India's response was swift and predictable: it averred that casteism was not racism and that caste was a domestic matter, so any attempts at an international conference to pronounce on it would be tantamount to an infringement on state sovereignty. Further, since the Constitution of India had outlawed untouchability and caste-based discrimination, besides enacting policies of reservations (or affirmative action) for lower castes and ex-untouchables, there was nothing there to be raised at the Conference. While admitting progress had been slow, it pointed out that hierarchy and discrimination dating millennia could not be changed overnight. Reflecting the new geopolitics after the end of the Cold War, India made common cause with the United States and Israel (both similarly interested in keeping their 'domestic' racial issues off the agenda at Durban) in blocking such efforts.

India's *quid pro quo* with these two countries was seemingly in contrast to its decades-long leadership of the global south in the struggle against apartheid and on the Palestinian issue. India's role in the Non-Aligned Movement and other international initiatives between 1947 and the early 1990s had been a powerful source of legitimacy for its postcolonial state and a source of pride for many in the nation's public sphere. The extent to which this perception is shared by India's Dalits, or by others in the global south, is not something many in the Indian middle class pause to think about. This perception is reflected in the overarching tropes of non-alignment and third-world leadership that animate so much of the literature on international relations emerging from and on India. Indeed, one might argue that the Indian variant of the discipline of international relations is a (un)critical part of the hegemony of a certain upper-caste, middle-class view of the world and India's place in it that I describe here as the postcolonial racial/spatial order.

That Durban was the site of the Indian government's actions may seem ironic to many: it was there that Gandhi had spent his formative political years (1893–1914) and it was there that he invented and honed his unique method of non-violent resistance. Yet, I argue that there are important continuities rather than rupture between Gandhi and the Indian government's actions at the Conference.

Writing in 1938, the founder of the National Association for the Advancement of Colored People (NAACP) and the premier African-American intellectual of his era, W. E. B. Du Bois, observed the tendency of India and Indians to "stand apart from the darker peoples and seek her affinities among whites. She has long wished to regard herself as 'Aryan,' rather than 'colored' and to think of herself as much nearer physically and spiritually to Germany and England than to Africa, China or the South Seas'" (cited in Prashad 2000, viii–ix).

Where did this self-fashioning by certain Indians as 'Aryans,' as racially and culturally closer to the west, and as different from and superior to niggers, coolies, chinks, and others come from? It is a long story that involves colonial anthropology, the pseudoscience of race, linguistic families, Orientalist knowledge systems, upper-caste Hindu interlocutors 'explaining' and 'translating' India to European ethnographers, and the interaction of all these with certain extant systems of endogamy and caste hierarchy in the subcontinent. By the second half of the nineteenth century, an emerging middle-class intelligentsia in colonial India saw itself as racially and culturally the equals of the west and even sharing a genealogy or ancestry with them (see Trautmann 1997; Robb 2003).

As Subho Basu (2010) summarizes, a novel geographic information system emerged in the latter half of the nineteenth century to produce a racial mapping of the world in which this upper-caste Hindu intelligentsia distanced itself from 'domestic others' (Muslims, aboriginal groups, Dalits, 'criminal' tribes) as well as inferior 'foreign others' (anchored at bottom by dark-skinned Africans), while simultaneously affiliating itself with 'Aryan' Caucasians. In his words, this colonial intelligentsia

> happily appropriated the idea of civilizational hierarchy. This also assisted them in problematizing any straightforward notion of European racial superiority. Drawing from contemporary British writings, these authors ... in the context of Asia and Africa ... reproduced various racialized discourses

about the relationship between the physical appearance of local populations and their level of civilizational progress. They portrayed Europe as a continent of nations, Asia and Africa as continents inhabited by tribes and inferior races, except for the Aryan Hindus. This position attributed to Indians actually reflected their concerns about their own position in the hierarchy of nations and races. As they became involved in constructing such a hierarchy, these writers selectively adopted and redeployed scientific notions of ethnography and colonial geography in order to establish the claim of modern Hindus as primary citizens of the land and inheritors of an ancient Aryan civilization … .

(Basu 2010, 79)

It was precisely this modernist desire to acquire a classical history (see Dirks 1990), and simultaneously to speak for all that lived in that territory, that the young Gandhi reflected in his early years in England. His early interlocutors into that antiquity and the content of his own religious and national past were idiosyncratic, New-Agey and overwhelmingly white (Edwin Arnold, Madam Blavatsky and the Theosophists, Americans enthused by eastern spiritualism such as Thoreau, and others believing in vegetarianism, élan vital, raw foods, odd forms of spirituality, etc.). Both in England and South Africa, Gandhi's self-fashioning made him heir to this great Indic tradition and positioned him between whites and his countrymen as interpreter, translator, spokesman, and later, a proponent of self-rule.[5]

Gandhi returned to India in 1891 and two years into a frustrating and unsuccessful period there came an invitation to serve as a lawyer for a rich Muslim Gujarati merchant in Durban. His facility in English and Gujarati, alongside his legal training, made him an ideal candidate. He arrived in Durban in late May of 1893 for what he thought would be a few months: he ended up staying for over two decades, returning to India only in 1914. The merchant community in South Africa was overwhelmingly Muslim, styled themselves as 'Arab' and dressed distinctively in an effort to distance themselves from the vast number of Indian 'coolies' – indentured laborers of lower caste working in plantations and mines.

Gandhi's initial activism was aimed at petitioning white governments in South Africa and Britain for redress against discrimination (usually on issues of franchise, extent of immigration, mobility between various provinces, and forms of surveillance such as finger-printing or identity cards) visited upon the prosperous Muslim merchants and the few educated, middle-class Indian professionals. Gandhi made it clear that similar measures targeting indentured laborers were probably justifiable and at any rate not his concern.

Central to his politics was distinguishing upper-class Indians from indentured laborers. The material and ideational context was one that militated against the emergence of a unified category called Indian and instead provoked the construction of a social fragment or synecdoche he called 'British Indians' who stood in for the whole and were hierarchized as superior because of their proximity to whiteness. While Benedict Anderson (1991) has reminded us that the first imaginations of the modern nation occurred not in Europe but among the creole communities of the New World, it is important that the very act of imagining India in South Africa was simultaneously also unraveling or diffracting: some were more Indian than others.

In her careful work on Gandhi in this period, Kathryn Tidrick (2007, 54) writes:

> The campaign focused on the political rights of the merchant class. The documents drafted by Gandhi put forward the merchants' view that they deserved to be treated better than those with whom the law would lump them – the indentured, or recently indentured, laborer and the African native. The … petition deplored a law that sought to put 'all Indians, indentured, and freed, and free … in the same scale'. In another document the race feeling which meant the Indian was treated like a "raw Kaffir" was condemned … . The glories of Indian civilization were cited in the merchants' favor … . He sought both to appeal to the British sense of fair play and to reassure the whites that if they let the Indians keep the vote (subject to the prevailing £50 property franchise) they need never fear the consequences. Relatively few Indians would qualify, and those who did would be "too much taken up with their spiritual well being" to claim a role in politics.

A number of themes resonate here that are worth spelling out. First, educated, propertied Indians are the only ones deserving of political rights, and precisely because they are not inclined to use such rights for political purposes but rather to engage in spiritual pursuits. Second, while the 'coolie' was not the right sort of Indian, it was an insult to equate him with the 'African native' or the 'raw Kaffir.' Third, what makes the upper-class Indian worthy is that he is heir to a great civilization. That the Indians whose cause he was espousing here were largely Muslim and that many of the ideas of Indian civilization by this time were heavily freighted with a Hindu cosmology seems not to have detained him at this point.

Till 1910, when the (Dutch) Boers and English buried their differences to form the Union of South Africa, Gandhi's politics depended on appealing to Whitehall in London over the provincial regimes. Joseph Lelyveld details the process with clarity:

> Gandhi had based his case on his own idealistic reading of an 1858 Proclamation by Queen Victoria that formally extended British sovereignty over India, promising its inhabitants the same protections and privileges as all her subjects. He called it the 'Magna Charta of the Indians,' quoting a passage in which her distant majesty had proclaimed her wish that her Indian subjects, of "whatever race and creed be freely and impartially admitted to offices in our service." It was Gandhi's argument that those rights should attach themselves to 'British Indians' who traveled from their homelands to outposts of the empire such as the British-ruled portions of South Africa … .
>
> *(Lelyveld 2011, 11)*

The queen's proclamation, with its usual rhetorical excess, was not intended to secure political or economic rights for diasporic Indians. It is significant that Gandhi immediately sensed and tried to leverage the prevailing imperial international system in favor of his constituency. Yet, as we see later, when Dalits would try something similar – either with the colonial government during the national movement for independence or at the Durban conference – it would be regarded as treasonous to the national/religious 'family.'

In all this the native African often did not even register on Gandhi's imaginary. Lelyveld (2011, 12–13) observes,

> it was as if none of this larger South African context and all it portended – the blatant attempt to postpone indefinitely any thought, any possibility, of an eventual settlement with the country's black majority – had the slightest relevance to his cause, had been allowed to impinge on his consciousness. In the many thousands of words he wrote and uttered in South Africa, only a few hundred reflect awareness of an impending racial conflict or concern about its outcome.

As he also drily notes, this was not because Gandhi was some ethnocentric narrowly obsessed with the concerns of his fellow countrymen: in fact, nearly all his close friends were white, as were many of the correspondents with whom he exchanged letters on a range of topics, and he wrote voluminously on matters western and European.

One cannot make the case that Gandhi was unexceptional in being trapped within a narrow national imaginary at this time. These decades were rich with internationalist movements, not the least of which was communism (with an Indian, M. N. Roy, making his presence felt at this time within the Comintern,) movements of black solidarity across North America and Africa, suffragette struggles, anarchism, and others. Gandhi's provincialism in this regard is in striking contrast to contemporaries like Lala Lajpat Rai, and those younger than him such as Jawaharlal Nehru, not to mention the likes of Du Bois, Frederick Douglass, and various others (see Roy 2007; Prashad 2007; Young 2001; Abraham forthcoming; D'Souza 2014).

Gandhi twice served as head of a volunteer all-Indian stretcher corps that he himself proposed and mobilized: on the first occasion on the side of the British against the Afrikaners in the Boer War, and the second occasion on the side of the white regime against the Zulus in the war that broke out after the Union of South Africa's 1913 forced alienation of Africans from their own lands. On both occasions, Gandhi sought favors for his constituency by proving his loyalty to white empire – literally over native black bodies. On both occasions, as well, the stretcher corps was seen by him as a consolation prize for being denied the opportunity to serve actively as an armed combatant and thereby prove the worthiness (manliness) of Indians and their parity with the colonizer.

In later years, Gandhi would make much of the impact the slaughter of the Zulus had upon his conscience (something Lelyveld (2011, 71) bluntly describes as a "retrospective tidying up" of the historical record). Yet during and in the aftermath of the wars themselves, he pressured the regime in South Africa for more opportunities for Indians in combat and for more concessions to them in return for their service. He admired the bloodlust of the English soldiers – something he saw as explaining their rule over much of the world and even justifying their colonizing of India.[6]

Analyzing the paucity of Gandhi's writings on native Africans, Lelvyeld shows he was unaware that 'kaffir' was the equivalent of 'nigger' and it took him a very long time to stop using the term – even as he repeatedly expressed outrage at being called a 'coolie lawyer.' As late as 1908, fifteen years after arriving in South Africa, he described Africans as uncivilized, troublesome, dirty and living like animals. He was outraged when put in a prison with native Africans, and protested vehemently when the regime sought to construct public housing after a plague that integrated Africans with the indentured laborers. He talked of the purity of races and the need to maintain the same. He referred to the plight of indentured laborers as something of a punishment that may have accrued to them for sins committed in past lifetimes.

There was a transcoding of caste and race – Gandhi's descriptions of blacks in Africa and of lower castes and untouchables in India seem cut from the same cloth. His obsession with their cleanliness, his haste to attribute their problems to their lack of sanitation, propensity to drink, sexual promiscuity, and other 'moral' failings (as distinct from arising from exploitation and conditions barely distinguishable from slavery) never ceases to both grate and outrage a reader for their sheer obtuse-ness – even at the distance of more than a century.[7] Significantly, Lelyveld (2011, 58) notes that many of Gandhi's explicitly racist comments about Africans seemed directed to the whites:

> If we want to give him any benefit of the doubt, we might say that the eager-to-please advocate was maybe playing to his audience, seeking to advance his argument that so-called British Indians could safely be acknowl-edged as cultural and political equals of the whites, worthy citizens bound to them by their common imperial ties – that equality of sorts for Indians would not, in the near or far future, undermine the dominance of whites.

In positioning "British Indians" such as himself above blacks and thereby closer to whites, Gandhi was acting in a way that has a long pedigree in settler societies. Such affiliation among migrants that desire whiteness is a constitutive element in the consolidation and reproduction of the overall racist order, with the new immigrant lauded for his quiescent work ethic and held up as a model for the more intransigent native or indigenous inhabitant. In every such instance, the hierarchy is anchored on the backs of indigenous peoples and slaves, with more recent colored immigrants positioned, and positioning themselves, as upwardly mobile buffers in between (see Fanon 1967; Ignatiev 2008; Wolfe 1998; Prashad 2000; Prashad 2007).

My purpose here is not to launch an anachronistic critique of Gandhi's views on caste and race, though there is nothing to apologize for subjecting them to robust scrutiny. It is to show the emergence of a certain racial-spatial order in which educated, upper-caste Indians bolstered by their claims to an ancient and gloried civilization position themselves as authoritative interlocutors between their societies and the white international system thereby racially mapping the world. It is not the exceptionalism of Gandhi that I am targeting here, but rather the degree to which he was representative of his stratum of an Indian intelligentsia. The self and nation that emerged in this process was one that was already splitting and fractionating even as it was coalescing for the first time historically (see Krishna 2012).

Gandhi's last campaign in South Africa would also be the first and only that tapped into the energy and militancy of the indentured laborers. The immediate provocations for the strikes that began in 1913 were a £3 tax levied on all ex-indentured laborers; changes in legislation that de-recognized a large number of their marriages; and restrictions on immigration from India. From around October of 1913, mass protests and strikes spread across plantations and mines as indentured laborers, first in dozens, then hundreds, and eventually over ten thousand, struck work, peacefully broke the law, courted arrest in huge numbers, and engaged in civil disobedience. Gandhi blew an uncertain trumpet and was outflanked (and constantly professed to be amazed) by the militancy and discipline of the largely Tamil workforce. The strength and durability of the strikes were enough to force the regime into making significant (if temporary) concessions to indentured laborers. Gandhi himself was imprisoned for over five weeks and emerged as their hero.

Gandhi wrote of this movement at the height of its militancy that "they struck not as indentured laborers but as servants of India. They were taking part in a religious war." Many of the common slogans raised during the protests were in the vein of "Victory to Ramachandra," "Victory to Dwarakanath," and "Vande Mataram" – all heavily laden with Hindu symbology. Gandhi's equation of these "servants of India" with "religious warriors" and his explicit disavowal of any notion of class identity in their politics added up to a vexing brew. At minimum, it indexed an understanding of the nation as one inextricable from a Hindu ethos and a strange distaste for the political actions of the poor if motivated by economic plight or exploitation. His politics also revealed a highly top-down and pedagogical approach to leadership even as those he claimed to represent frequently outflanked him. Lelyveld (2011, 128) notes in an emblematic phrase that captured the chasm between Gandhi and the indentured laborers: "he could speak of them and for them, but mostly, he wasn't speaking to them."

This final campaign allowed Gandhi – whose stature had been in free-fall since the establishment of the Union of South Africa in 1910 and who was in danger of becoming a forgotten footnote in the history of the Indian diaspora – to return to India in 1914 in triumph. He had gained a reputation as one of very few political activists who could command the allegiance of masses of Indians, and was more-over the proponent of a new form of struggle – nonviolent Satyagraha. Lelyveld for one is very clear that had it not been for this final struggle in South Africa, Mohandas Gandhi might never have become the Mahatma.

South Africa was a moment in the consecration of a postcolonial racial/social order by which middle-class, upper-caste Indians like Gandhi stood in for the nation, positioned themselves as interpreters of that space to a (largely) white global audience, and regarded the lower-class/caste Indians and Africans as bringing up the rear of this hierarchy. Gandhi's distinctive idiom of politics has drawn our eyes to his uniqueness – what I would like to do in the rest of this essay is to instead argue that he was not so much unique as exemplary of the postcolonial racial/ spatial world he was inscribing at this time.

Gandhi, Dalits, and the impossible nation

Hailing from the 'untouchable' Mahar community in western India, Bhim Rao Ambedkar (1891–1956) emerged as a leader of the Dalits, the architect of independent India's constitution, and foremost intellectual adversary of Gandhi. In elementary school, Ambedkar was made to sit on the floor in a corner of his classroom away from the other students and not allowed to drink water from the same fountain as them. He completed his BA from Elphinstone College in Bombay and his academic excellence earned him a scholarship from the Maharajas of Baroda and Kolhapur. Ambedkar obtained a PhD from Columbia University in New York (his years there coinciding with the Harlem Renaissance), where he studied with, among others, the pragmatist philosopher John Dewey whose work would leave a deep imprint on his ideas about democracy and fraternity. This was followed by another doctorate, this time from the London School of Economics, besides being called to the Bar in England.

By the 1920s, Ambedkar was a leading spokesman for Dalits and attended both the first and second Round Table Conference (RTC) (held in 1930 and 1931) to discuss political devolution in British India. These were part of a gradual and halting process of expansion of both franchise and responsibilities accorded to 'natives' in their own governance. It was clear that numbers affiliated to various socio-religious categories (Hindu, Muslim, Sikh, 'Untouchable', etc.) were becoming salient in an unprecedented manner, and their impact on politics would prove to be both profound and enduring.[8]

The Second Round Table Conference, held in London in late 1930, became the site for the definitive encounter between Gandhi and Ambedkar on the issue of the Dalits' political rights. By then Gandhi was the foremost leader of the Congress party. On the issue of caste and untouchability, he was contradictory and far more equivocal than he might have been. For example, faced with an intransigent Brahmin clergy in the southern town of Vaikom in (today's) Kerala who refused temple entry for Dalits, he backed down in a most pusillanimous manner. He justified the refusal of upper castes to inter-dine with lower castes on the bizarre *non sequitur* that eating, like defecating, was something best done in private in any case. He was at this time resolutely against intercaste and interreligious marriage. At various points he justi-fied the four-fold order of the caste system (the 'varnashrama dharma') and argued a person born into a particular caste should follow the profession deemed appropriate.

Gandhi strenuously argued that caste and untouchability were best addressed by social reform and changing the minds and hearts of upper-caste Hindus – and not through political action or legislation passed by the colonial state. Social change ought not to come from the organized militancy of lower castes and Dalits; that would be a spurious and superficial change, according to him. In order for change to be genuine, it had to come from the changed hearts and magnanimity of those higher up the caste ladder.

In London, Ambedkar proposed India's 50 million Dalits (per the census of 1931 – the last one in which caste was explicitly enumerated) be awarded a separate electorate to determine their representatives in all legislative bodies. This would ensure that the elected representatives of the Dalits not become the stooges of the larger parties, especially Congress, as well as recognize the Dalits as a separate category, on a par with the Muslims, Sikhs, and others. Gandhi, who did not seem to have a problem with separate electorates for Muslims at the RTC, refused to accept Dalits having one and threatened to embark on a fast unto death if this was awarded.

Gandhi's arguments at and after the RTC in London hinged on the following: (a) Dalits were an indivisible part of the Hindu family; (b) he, Gandhi, was a truer representative of theirs than Ambedkar, and this could be handily demonstrated by the fact that he could defeat the latter even given an electorate exclusively of Dalits; (c) the Congress party represented all Indians and the presence of 56 other invited representatives at the conference was the usual divide-and-rule tactics of the colonial government; and (d) the awarding of a separate electorate to the Dalits would freeze their identity into perpetuity and prevent the removal of the institution of untouchability over time.

Ambedkar's refutation of each of these points was both robust and immediate. The claim that Dalits were a part of the Hindu family was belied at every turn and in every corner of India where their oppression and exclusion by caste Hindus continued apace. Gandhi, Congress and upper-caste Hindus acknowledged Dalits as Hindu only when their numbers could be used to inflate those whom they professed to represent – never when it came to their full rights as economic, political, religious, and social participants in the life of the nation. If separate electorates were permissible for Sikhs and Muslims, why not for Dalits? That Gandhi had a greater visibility amongst all Indians including Dalits was not because of what he had done for them. Rather as a member of the majority community bankrolled by India's wealthiest capitalist and continually lionized by the upper-caste media, he began with a far greater advantage than someone like Ambedkar. Any devolution without a prior settling of the issues of caste hierarchy, Ambedkar argued, would amount to replacing white rule with the rule of Brahmin and Bania (a merchant caste – Gandhi himself was one). And finally the argument that the creation of a separate electorate would freeze Dalit identity into perpetuity was specious. A full-scale legal and economic assault on untouchability, along with political representation by, of, and for them through separate electorates, would ensure development and equalize access to opportunities for education, farming, modern professions, and other means of advancement.[9]

When the 'Communal Award' granting Dalits a separate electorate was finally announced in August, 1932, Gandhi delivered on his threat and commenced a fast unto death. That his fast deviated from avowed principles of Satyagraha is shown by Lelyveld (2011, 184), who notes: "He … was opposed to using fasting as a weapon to force the pace. Fasts were to be used not coercively against those who opposed you politically but … only against allies and loved ones when they backslid on pledges … ."

Ambedkar saw the fast for exactly what it was: blackmail of the worst sort. In a move he would bitterly regret till his dying day, he was forced to give in and accept a compromise that came to be called the "Poona pact."[10] By this pact the Dalits gave up separate electorates for "reserved constituencies," that is, general constituencies from which only Dalit representatives could be elected. Dalits would select, through primaries, their candidates who could run for office – but Ambedkar's fear that such representatives would turn out to be lackeys of the larger parties turned out to be well founded.

A separate electorate was the sort of bargaining chip (as Jinnah would soon prove) that might have enabled Dalits to negotiate with Congress from a stronger position. It was the denial of this principle of parity and the unfairly lumping of Dalits back into the fold of those whom Ambedkar held to be uniquely oppressive – caste Hindu society – that caused him such bitterness then and in later years. As Ambedkar noted during his parleys with Gandhi over the Poona Pact, "Gandhiji, I have no nation." That sentence expressed and contained all the frustration of someone habituated to being constantly 'included out' of the fold: Dalits were neither permitted to exit India/Hinduism nor accorded any respect or recognition within it. And this frustration would lead him to Buddhism in the last years of his life.

This confrontation needs to be examined from a slightly different tangent for my arguments regarding a postcolonial racial/spatial order. First, Gandhi couched his opposition to the idea of a separate electorate on the grounds that Dalits were an indispensable and constitutive element of Hindu society. At the same time, his narrow notion of their 'uplift' emphasized personal piety and transformation of the conscience of upper castes. As ever with Gandhi, the Dalit was not important in and of himself: he was important merely as the occasion or opportunity for the upper-caste Hindu to test his morality or ethics.

Second, the distinction between the political, on the one hand, and the social/religious on the other, besides mystifying the issue of caste-based oppression, denied Dalits any agency while ceding their liberation to the very class that was oppressing them. It was a crucial step in confining caste to an idiom regarded as uniquely Hindu/Indian – something best left to 'Indians' to understand and interpret. This provincializing of caste militated against expanding it to a comparative framework in which Dalit oppression might be likened to that of other minorities within India, or racial groups such as blacks in the United States or South Africa or elsewhere in the world. That same provincializing, as distinct from universalizing, of caste was the government's strategy in the UN Conference against Racism in Durban, 2001.

And finally, the colonial regime and the British government in London played along in mystifying caste and undergirding Indian exceptionalism, as they essentially said the "Poona pact" was fine with them as long as it was fine with Ambedkar. For one thing, it hung the latter out to dry as Gandhi's life came to depend entirely on Ambedkar backing down. More importantly, by conceding the issue not on principle but on personality (Gandhi's) it both underlined the non-comparative and unique character of the caste question in their eyes, and contributed to the deification of Gandhi. "This is not something we understand or can legislate about and we are happy to defer to you on this," seems to be the subtext of the British government here.

Academia and racial/spatial order at Durban

I am increasingly coming around to the view (to mangle Walter Benjamin) that every document about Indian or Indic civilization is also testament to its barbarity, especially when viewed from the perspective of the Dalit. That it has taken me three decades in academia to arrive at this point is a sign of my own myopia as well as the blinding light of what Perry Anderson (2013) has called "Indian ideology" in his recent excoriation of this celebratory, upper-caste, middle-class, self-construction of Indian exceptionalism.[11] While many postcolonial intellectuals of Indian provenance would unhesitatingly agree that one cannot understand the United States without foregrounding slavery and genocide, we find it impossible to submit our constructions of India and ourselves to the Dalit eye.

It was not always thus when it came to race and caste. In the late nineteenth century, one of the pioneers of the struggle against casteism, Jyotirao Phule, had already made comparisons to, and sought inspiration in, the condition of black slaves in the United States and their militant resistance to it. W. E. B. Du Bois and Frederick Douglass had written about the analogous nature of casteism and racism, and the former had corresponded with (though not met) Ambedkar. In the 1930s one could speak of a caste school of race studies in the US. From the late 1950s onwards, the work of the American anthropologist Gerald Berreman had made a strong case for comparing race in the United States and untouchability in India, and had exploded the myth that either lower castes in India or southern blacks were quiescent or blinded by tradition in their understanding of hierarchy. Berreman argued as well that American lynching found its counterpart in Indian upper-caste violence against Dalits. In the 1970s, as Dalit youth adopted a more militant idiom of resistance, they chose to call themselves the Dalit Panthers after the Black Panther party in the United States (see, for example, Berreman 1960; Berreman 1972; Berreman and Cox 1961; Berreman 2009).

In a recent essay, Kamala Visweswaran (2009) adumbrates the sociology of knowledge that produced a discourse about the distinctiveness of caste and the alleged non-utility of comparing it with race or other forms of discrimination. She points out that, irrespective of the various schisms and traditions of inquiry among Indian sociologists and anthropologists, what was common to all of them were far more significant. Most important among these were: (a) a tendency to view caste as something distinctively Indian whose essence might be misunderstood by comparison or generalization; (b) the overwhelmingly upper-caste background of most Indian social anthropologists; (c) accounts of caste and untouchability that were rarely, if ever, based on the material histories and lived experiences of Dalits and lower castes but were rather theorizations *about* them relying on a Sanskritic notion of India; (d) an incredible paucity of actual data on the extent of caste discrimination and untouchability in contemporary society; and (e) a rigid demarcation between race seen as a biological fact and caste seen as something embedded in social and religious practices and reproduced through endogamy and economic structures.

In a variety of different ways, both Indian exceptionalism on the matter of caste, and its supposedly lessened salience in the post-independence period (except in the nasty matter of reservations for lower castes and Dalits, and during elections when they were ostensibly 'vote banks' for political parties), were threads that ran through all these various positions within Indian sociology and anthropology.

The convergence between aspects of this deeply conservative academic tradition and the Indian government's position at Durban can be illustrated by looking at the work of one of India's leading sociologists, Andre Beteille (2001), who vehemently opposed efforts to equate racism with casteism. He begins by demolishing the case for any biological basis for race. He then argues that since 'race' is itself illusory or dubious, for the United Nations to equate 'race' with 'caste' would be to compound this folly. Further, those arguing for the inclusion of caste within the category of race must be doing so out of ulterior or base motives. And finally, though racism and casteism are to be opposed, to do so by talking as if race were real was contradictory and unsustainable.

First, Beteille's argument that since the biological validity of 'race' as a category is suspect racism as a reality must be suspect as well is simplistic. As scholars such as Howard Winant, Anthony Appiah, David Theo Goldberg, and a number of others have shown, irrespective of the simulacral nature of the biological concept of race, the consequences of acts of discrimination and violence done in its name are all too real. As social constructions, both race and caste are similar and comparable in their effects – peoples' beliefs in their reality lead them to act in ways that are discriminatory and violently oppressive to others.

Second, Beteille's conviction that a scientific consensus on the non-existence of race means it is not relevant in the real world precisely exemplifies what Kancha Ilaiah (1996) and others describe as abstractly theoretical and non-material histories of caste oppression written by upper-caste academics. A theoretical disproof of a category is sufficient for them – as the lived realities of damage inflicted by those categories are not part of their lives or their research.

Third, remember Gandhi's distaste for the indentured laborers' economic demands couched in economic terms, and his preference for regarding their struggles as a moral or religious crusade. It's precisely this aesthetic distaste that Beteille exemplifies when he avers that those seeking to equate race with caste must be "interested parties" acting in "politically mischievous" ways under forms of "pressure" that "one can only guess" (all his terms). Each of these phrases drips with suspicion and delegitimizes those who equate racism and casteism on grounds that they must be acting out of self-interest. There is in Beteille's prose a distaste for the instrumental, and an *a priori* judgment that "interested parties" must also be unethical. As always, privilege prefers to clothe itself in aesthetic form and regards any overt, political, and material attack on its own foundations as vulgar, crude, and instrumental.

Finally, Beteille's point that one cannot throw race out through the front door because it oppresses people and let it in by the back door as a category to favor the oppressed is an exact analogue to Gandhi's view that separate electorates for Dalits would perpetuate them as a category and deny them the possibility of assimilation into the larger community of Hindus/Indians. What is striking about both positions is their desire to escape history and seek refuge in the static 'truth' of an ideal that has not been reached. The succinct rejoinder to such a position came from US Supreme Court justice Blackmun in the context of debates over affirmative action: "To get beyond racism, we must first take account of race" (quoted in Berreman 2009, 75).[12]

The discipline of international relations, especially in its Indian variant, reveals the interlocking character of academia and its reinforcing of the government's stance at Durban. First, with its overweening emphasis on state sovereignty and the injunction against external interference in the domestic realm, IR is the discipline par excellence when it comes to resisting arguments premised on supranational norms. Yet, such prizing of sovereignty is not so much a matter of principle as it is of selectively undergirding upper-caste privilege. Gandhi in South Africa had no qualms about appealing to an imperial international system (over the heads of local and provincial regimes) to seek redress for 'his' Indians. And from the very inception of the UN, India used that stage to condemn racial discrimination inside South Africa and the dispossession of Palestinians inside Israel. However, as Gandhi's fast against Ambedkar and the Indian stance at Durban in 2001 reveal, sovereignty is asserted against the subaltern and for the dominant castes.

Second, in the early decades of what one might call Indian IR, a reigning theme was Gandhi and India's uniquely nonviolent struggle for independence standing at odds with the world of realpolitik. India's leadership of the non-aligned and global south was routinely ascribed to this legacy, with Nehru serving as the westernized, rational, developmental amanuensis of the same. This legacy has positioned India, with some success, as a moral force against discrimination in all forms and has deflected attention away from its deeply hierarchical domestic order (see Krishna 1999).

Third, it is through questions not asked and ideas not imagined that hegemony works. Ambedkar, despite being the architect of India's constitution, is invisible in the discourse of Indian IR, and there is simply no discussion of caste and its role in the definition of the nation that this discipline is premised upon. Ambedkar's plaint, "Gandhiji, I have no nation," is underscored by IR's obliviousness to that statement, its author, and his import. Contemporary versions of Indian IR are only too willing to trace our strategic culture, our ideas of realism and idealism, and sundry other concepts, to the same corpus of traditional, scriptural upper-caste Hindu India that I problematized in the first part of this chapter.

Perhaps the main difference in the Indian context between disciplines such as history and anthropology on the one hand and IR on the other has been that the former have developed an auto-critique that has examined the conditions, limitations, and myopias of their own formation. While I have detailed the limits of such an exercise, at least they have looked critically at what constitutes 'tradition,' how it emerged during and after the colonial encounter, and are reflexive about the race, caste, and class character of those who came to represent 'India' and its outside. Indian IR, despite being the discipline charged with understanding the world it inhabits, still awaits such an auto-critique. In its amnesia, Indian IR remains a true and junior partner of the more worldwide discipline of mainstream international relations with its similar neglect of issues of race, caste and hierarchy. The postcolonial racial-spatial order that Gandhi entered speaking and creatively reproduced reigns hegemonic over a discipline that should serve as a locus for its critique and transformation.

Conclusion

Gyan Pandey's (2013) recent book comparing Dalit and black middle classes notes that our times are characterized as the era of "the universal declaration of human rights; and of the "universal" condemnation of continuing European imperialism, apartheid in South Africa, segregation in the United States, and *untouchability in India*" (italics mine). Pandey goes on a bit later in the book to list what he considers some "uncomfortable facets of modern existence – slavery, *untouchability,* drug-trafficking and genocide" (italics mine). As I ponder these sentences, I have to ask, does untouchability really have the same visibility worldwide that segregation (in the US) and apartheid (in South Africa) had/have? Does it really register on a world conscience in ways that genocide or slavery has done?

I think not: caste and untouchability simply do not draw the same global opprobrium or attention associated with slavery or apartheid. Why is this? I have argued that at least part of the answer lies in the mystification of caste and untouchability as something uniquely Indian/Hindu. I have also argued that a certain postcolonial racial-spatial worldview as exemplified and articulated by someone such as Gandhi had much to do with this. And that India's post-independence leadership of the global south from a position of moral opposition to racism and colonialism externally has further distracted the international eye away from such practices that continue to be salient and violent internally.

The postcolonial racial-spatial order that emerged in nineteenth century India, and was thereafter reproduced both in the diaspora and within India during the decades of the independence struggle, and is now reinscribed through events such as the Durban conference, should give us pause. There is no easy category called "non-western" when it comes to our understanding of global politics. The leaders of anti-colonial resistance are themselves from societies with deep and troubling imbrications of caste, race, hierarchy, and inequalities that are still ongoing. Even, or perhaps especially, those such as Gandhi who have become iconic as alternatives to the idioms of power, privilege, and domination that run through mainstream international relations discourses have to be subject to critical scrutiny to understand how hegemony works. The positioning of leaders and societies from the postcolony as a distinctive third voice during the heyday of the Cold War, and their leadership of the global south in matters of development, sustainability and a host of other issues since, have to be weighed against the racial-spatial orders they both benefit from and have been instrumental in constructing. Du Bois' expectation that the problem of the twentieth century would be the problem of the color line remains as true today as when it was written. Except that we need to remember that color may reveal as much as it may hide.

Notes

1 I thank Itty Abraham, Kanti Bajpai, Uday Chandra, Jonathan Goldberg-Hiller, Jairus Grove, Akta Kaushal, Srirupa Roy, and Nate Roberts for helpful comments on an earlier draft. A special thank you to Robbie Shilliam for sound advice and much patience. The usual disclaimers apply.

2 An exemplary instance is Martin Wight (1991) who places Gandhi outside his threefold typology of IR traditions (realist, idealist and rationalist) as an unelaborated fourth category typifying pacifism and figuring the 'east' as a harmonious and therapeutic space preserving values that may yet rescue the west.

3 The word 'Dalit' literally means 'broken' or 'shattered' in the western Indian language of Marathi and was adopted by India's erstwhile 'untouchables' – those considered so low as to be even beyond the pale of the caste hierarchy of Hinduism and usually in professions such as scavenging, leather-work, and cremation, deemed to be polluting. Dalits prefer this name over patronizing terms such as 'harijan' (children of God) coined by Gandhi to refer to them.

4 See also the special issue of the Indian journal *Seminar* titled "Exclusion" on the Durban conference" (www.india-seminar.com/2001/508.htm) for more on the conference.

5 I have relied primarily upon three recent histories of Gandhi: Tidrick (2007), Swan (1985) and Lelyveld (2011). What is common to all three is that they continually focus on Gandhi's actions and counterpoise contemporary accounts, recollections, and reports of those actions against his own later recollections. In other words, they refuse Gandhi the monopoly of authoring his own life – something most other writing on Gandhi seems too willing to do.

6 Violence was an indispensable, even constitutive element of Gandhian nonviolence. Nonviolence was a virtue if and only if its practitioners had a credible ability to inflict violence. Absent that, it was no more than making a virtue of necessity, or worse, disguised cowardice. Violence had to be *overcome* in order for nonviolence to achieve the status of satyagraha. This centrality of violence to Gandhi's is examined in Devji (2012), Mantena (2012), Nandy (1980), and Krishna (2010).

7 Gandhi's and more generally upper-caste Hindus' attitudes towards caste/race is strikingly similar to late Victorian English and Christian missionary attitudes toward the poor which blamed their poverty on their penchant for drink, debt, promiscuity, and an inability to defer gratification (see Viswanath 2014).

8 While the advent of number was of tremendous import for the consolidation of religious, caste, and linguistic identities, I can do no more than signal them here. For more refer to Pandey (2012), Appadurai (1996), and Krishna (2002).

9 Per the Award itself, separate electorates would be phased out in 20 years, thus countering Gandhi's view that it would "freeze" untouchability into perpetuity. In any event, only a single election (following the Government of India Act of 1935) would ever be held

with a separate electorate for the Dalits and the issue would be moot thereafter. Reserved seats for Dalits, however, continue to this day in India.

10 In an interview with the BBC towards the end of his life, in 1955, Ambedkar expressed himself with characteristic bluntness about Gandhi's typically passive-aggressive blackmail during this and other encounters. It makes for fascinating viewing: www.youtube.com/watch?v=TNAdYLbGLKY.

11 Others who have helped include Ilaiah (1996) and especially the works of Bhim Rao Ambedkar. For the latter, see among others, Rodrigues (2002).

12 Beteille's position is not so much race- or caste-blind as it is blind *to* race or caste.

Bibliography

Abraham, Itty (forthcoming) *How India Became Territorial: Foreign Policy, Diaspora, Geopolitics.* Stanford: Stanford University Press.

Anderson, Benedict (1991) *Imagined Communities: Reflections on the Origins and Spread of Nationalism.* London: Verso.

Anderson, Perry (2013), *The Indian Ideology.* London: Verso.

Appadurai, Arjun (1996) Number in the Colonial Imagination. In *Modernity at Large: Cultural Dimensions of Globalization.* Minneapolis: University of Minnesota Press, 114–38.

Basu, Subho (2010) The Dialectics of Resistance: Colonial Geography, Bengali Literati and the Racial Mapping of Indian Identity. *Modern Asian Studies* 44 (1), 53–79.

Berreman, Gerald D. (1960) Caste in India and the United States. *American Journal of Sociology* 66 (2), 120–7.

——(1972) Race, Caste and Other Invidious Distinctions in Social Stratification. *Race: A Journal of Race and Group Relations* 13 (4), 385–414.

——(2009) Caste and Race: Reservations and Affirmations. In Natarajan, B. and Greenough, P. (eds) *Against Stigma.* New Delhi: Orient Blackswan, 47–77.

Berreman, Gerald D. and Cox, Cromwell Oliver (1961) Letters. *American Journal of Sociology* 66 (5), 510–12.

Beteille, Andre (2001) Race and Caste. *The Hindu,* March 10.

Buchanan, Rachel (2011) Why Gandhi Doesn't Belong at Wellington Railway Station. *Journal of Social History* 44 (4), 1077–93.

Devji, Faisal (2012) *The Impossible Indian: Gandhi and the Temptation of Violence.* Cambridge, MA: Harvard University Press.

Dirks, Nicholas B. (1990). History as a Sign of the Modern. *Public Culture* 2 (2), 25–32.

D'Souza, Radha (2014) Revolt and Reform in South Asia: Ghadar Movement to 9/11 and After. *Economic and Political Weekly* 49 (8), 59–73.

Fanon, Frantz (1967) *Black Skin, White Masks.* New York: Grove Press.

Ignatiev, Noel (2008) *How the Irish Became White.* New York: Routledge.

Ilaiah, Kancha (1996) *Why I am Not a Hindu: A Sudra Critique of Hindutva Philosophy, Culture and Political Economy.* Calcutta: Samya.

Krishna, Sankaran (1999) *Postcolonial Insecurities: India, Sri Lanka, and the Question of Eelam.* Minneapolis: University of Minnesota Press.

——(2002) Methodical Worlds: Partition, Secularism and Communalism in India. *Alternatives* 27 (2), 193–218.

——(2010) Comparative Assassinations: The Changing Moral Economy of Political Killing in South Asia. In Abraham, I., Newman, E. and Weiss, M. L. (eds) *Political Violence in South and Southeast Asia: Critical Perspectives.* London: United Nations Press, 27–46.

——(2012) IR and the Postcolonial Novel: Nation and Subjectivity in India. In Seth, S. (ed.) *Postcolonial Theory and International Relations: A Critical Reader.* London: Routledge, 124–43.

Lelyveld, Joseph (2011) *Great Soul: Mahatma Gandhi and his Struggle with India.* New York: Alfred Knopf.

Louis, Prakash (2003) *The Political Sociology of Dalit Assertion*. New Delhi: Gyan Publishing.

Mantena, Karuna (2012) Another Realism: the Politics of Gandhian Nonviolence. *American Political Science Review* 106 (2), 455–70.

Nandy, Ashis (1980) Final Encounter: the Politics of the Assassination of Gandhi. In *At the Edge of Psychology: Essays in Politics and Culture*. Delhi: Oxford, 70–98.

Natarajan, Balmurli and Greenough, Paul (eds) (2009) *Against Stigma: Studies in Caste, Race and Justice Since Durban*. New Delhi: Orient Blackswan.

Pandey, Gyanendra (2012) *The Construction of Communalism in Colonial North India*. Delhi: Oxford.

——(2013) *A History of Prejudice: Race, Caste, and Difference in India and the United States*. Cambridge, MA: Cambridge University Press.

Prashad, Vijay (2000) *The Karma of Brown Folk*. Minneapolis: University of Minnesota Press.

——(2007) *The Darker Nations: A People's History of the Third World*. New York: The New Press.

Robb, Peter (2003) *The Concept of Race in South Asia*. Delhi: Oxford.

Rodrigues, Valerian (ed.) 2002 *The Essential Writings of B. R. Ambedkar*. Delhi: Oxford University Press

Roy, Srirupa (2007) *Beyond Belief: India and the Politics of Postcolonial Nationalism*. Durham, NC: Duke University Press.

Swan, Maureen (1985) *Gandhi: the South African Experience*. Ravan Press.

Tidrick, Kathryn (2007) *Gandhi: a Political and Spiritual Life*. London: I. B. Tauris.

Trautmann, Thomas R. (1997) *Aryans and British India*. University of California Press.

Viswanath, Rupa (2014) Rethinking Caste and Class: 'Labour', the 'Depressed Classes', and the Politics of Distinctions, Madras 1918–1924. *International Review of Social History* 59 (1), 1–37.

Visweswaran, Kamala (2009) India in South Africa. In Natarajan, B. and Greenough, P. (eds) *Against Stigma*. New Delhi: Orient Blackswan, 326–74.

Wolfe, Patrick (1998) *Settler Colonialism and the Transformation of Anthropology: the Politics and Poetics of an Ethnographic Event*. London: Bloomsbury.

Wight, Martin (1991) *International Theory: The Three Traditions*. Leicester: Leicester University Press.

Young, Robert (2001) *Postcolonialism: an Historical Introduction*. London: Blackwell.

9

THE COLD WAR, AMERICAN ANTICOMMUNISM AND THE GLOBAL 'COLOUR LINE'

Richard Seymour

Introduction

Race has been expunged from the history of international relations and yet, as the introduction to this book points out, "race and racism continue to subliminally structure world politics, in both material and ideological ways". Du Bois had argued that despite its absence from dominant explanations, the racial order, as manifested in colonialism and other forms of expansionism, was the infrastructure of the world system behind the crisis of the European state system culminating in World War I. In a similar fashion, the world system after 1945 must be interpreted in view of the tectonic shifts in its racial order. The absence of race from explanations of the Cold War must therefore be rectified. This chapter will argue that one of the ways in which race has been simultaneously repressed and its effects sustained in the international order is through the deployment of anticommunism in the Cold War.

The history of anticommunism is enfolded within a history of race. In two great waves of US anticommunism, the first immediately following the Russian Revolution, and the second following the defeat of the Third Reich, race figured centrally in the understanding of communism and in the organisation of its suppression. The rise and breakdown of the anticommunist consensus was, when it came, intricated with the overthrow of the colonial world system and the concomitant upsurge of civil rights activism. The modes of repression and the techniques of ascriptive denigration deployed in each case were contiguous. As Heonik Kwon put it,

> [b]eing a white person or person of color was a major determining factor for an individual's life career for a significant part of the past century, but so was the relatively novel color classification of being 'Red' or 'not Red' in many corners of the world, including the United States and South Africa.
>
> *(Kwon 2010, 37)*

Anticommunism did not, however, abut white supremacy in an uncomplicated manner. White supremacy was essential to organising class dominance within the US. Racism formed a crucial component of the dominant ideology, its assumptions shared by governing elites under successive administrations. Brewing conflicts over race were effectively suppressed by Cold War anticommunism for a period of approximately a decade following World War II (WWII). However, in the global conflicts over communism, the US needed to project a beneficent liberal and egalitarian image in order to secure a multi-racial alliance in favour of US-led liberal capitalism. As a result of these pressures, increased as national liberation movements acquired momentum, US administrations felt compelled to adopt racial reforms, however gradually ("with all deliberate speed") (Dudziak 2000; Borstelmann 2001; Marable 2007).

To make full sense of this question, however, it is necessary to query the integrity of the concept of anticommunism, as revisionist historians of the Cold War have done. While most Cold War histories focus on the contest over Europe, a growing number of scholars challenge this emphasis, drawing attention to the hot wars around colonialism and race. They unpick the spurious unity of the category of "the Cold War", and in doing so draw attention to the diverse logics unfolding in Indonesia, Vietnam, the Congo, Italy and Greece, and so on (see, for example, Horne 2007; Horne 1985; Von Eschen 1996; Westad 2007; Kwon 2010). There are a variety of distinct processes subsumed under "anticommunism", even when the focus is limited to the American variety of anticommunism: the geopolitical contest with the USSR; the organisation of a coalition of anti-socialist states under an American-led alliance; the engagement with, and often war against, emerging popular and anticolonial forces in the "Third World"; and the suppression of domestic radicalism.

Hegemony and uneven and combined development

To interpret these various manifestations, this chapter will at points deploy the Gramscian concept of hegemony. This must be applied with care. The concept of hegemony is arguably one specifically crafted for the *national* terrain, where a particular relationship between "state" and "civil society" obtains. Nonetheless, there is sufficient philological evidence to suggest that Gramsci himself envisioned hegemony having *some* international applications. And the internationalisation of production, commerce, "civil society" and states themselves, strongly suggests that it can have relevance beyond the level of the national. Indeed, international relations are necessarily intricated with the national. They, as Gramsci put it,

> intertwine with these internal relations of nation-states, creating new, unique and historically concrete combinations. A particular ideology, for instance, born in a highly developed country, is disseminated in less developed countries, impinging on the local interplay of combinations. This relation between international forces and national forces is further complicated by the

existence within every State of several structurally diverse territorial sectors, with diverse relations of force at all levels.

(Gramsci 1971, 182)

Gramsci goes on to make the point that the relationship between a dominant nation and an oppressed nation cannot be purely military in character, since it relies on "the state of social disintegration of the oppressed people, and the passivity of the majority of them".

The consolidation of hegemony in one state, particularly the leading imperialist state, could not but produce certain effects not only in the international order but in the internal organisation of other states. The practices – ideologies, apparatuses, production methods – through which hegemony is achieved in dominant states can be swiftly disseminated within other states, albeit producing different effects. This insight can be grounded in Leon Trotsky's concept of "uneven and combined development". Insofar as the existence of many states is grounded in a tendency toward uneven development (of ecological systems, social forms and productive resources), they also exhibit the pattern of combined development, wherein distinct social formations interpenetrate – a tendency sharpened once the capitalist mode of production, with its universalising tendencies, takes root. Imperialist states have indeed actively taken up the mission of spreading and developing capitalist property relations in the regions they dominate, a mission that during the Cold War went under the rubric of liberal internationalism buttressed by "modernisation theory". This is precisely the "geopolitical management" of uneven and combined development of which Justin Rosenberg speaks (Ives and Short 2013; Allinson and Anievas 2009; Gilman 2003; Schmitz 2006, 12–13; Rosenberg 1996 as quoted in Anievas 2014).

It is important, however, to distinguish between hegemony as a *state of affairs,* and hegemony as a *strategy.* As Stuart Hall points out, hegemony in the former sense is "a very particular, historically specific, and temporary 'moment' in the life of a society. It is rare for this degree of unity to be achieved" (Hall 1986, 15). Nonetheless, hegemonic strategies are constantly deployed and are arguably the "normal" mode of political domination in capitalist democracies (Poulantzas 1978). Further, hegemonic practices should not be reduced to those which secure ideological consensus. Consent and coercion are usually different moments in a unitary hegemonic project, such that consent is permanently structured by violence (Thomas 2009; Poulantzas 2000, 80–1).

Conceiving of hegemony in this way permits us to understand that hegemonic practices can – within limits determined by the conjuncture – be organised across borders so that, for example, a dominant imperialist power can seek to organise popular consent for its "historic mission" across a range of allied states by means of ideology, material incentives and strategic repression. And such was the position of the United States of America as it assumed global dominance. US planners, informed by the work of the geographer Isaiah Bowman, sought to organise US power on the basis of a hierarchy of national states open to capitalist investment, gradually displacing direct colonial authority as the mode of domination (Smith 2004). However, the risk of a too-rapid displacement was either that national development of postcolonial states would take a form that was directly hostile to US capitalist penetration, or – more ominously for the US – that the very class systems through which they would be able to organise their imperialist dominance would be overthrown.

Managing this dilemma required hegemonic struggle in the following ways: 1) US state planners had to secure a consensus among elites for significant military and other imperialist investments in order to contain anticolonial independence movements and expand US strategic power into former colonial territories; 2) this power bloc then needed to organise the consent of diverse class strata within the US for this same strategy, while simultaneously disorganising and repressing opposition; 3) internationally, the American state had to penetrate the national states of allied ruling classes and to win the support of particularly European ruling classes but also subaltern populations for the same agenda; 4) the violent suppression of anticolonial rebellions was usually accompanied by attempts, to varying degrees, to achieve consent from certain constituencies.

The dominant idiom through which hegemonic practices were secured at key points in the twentieth century was anticommunism. Anticommunism acted as a quilting point linking American ideas of race and nationality in a single set of articulations. It was able to unify "contradictory subject-positions" because, in anticommunist discourse, "common nuclei of meaning" were "connotatively linked to diverse ideological-articulatory domains". Domestically, this enabled a process of "transformism": the "partial absorption and neutralisation of those ideological contents" through which resistance to class domination was expressed (Hall 1985, 122; Laclau 1977, 160–161). It provided a language in which the defence of racial hierarchy was commensurable with the legal norm of national self-determination. It undergirded a missionary American nationalism which connotatively linked Americanism to democracy, against what Mary Dudziak calls the "negative ideograph" of "totalitarianism". The opponents of white supremacy were belaboured as bearers of the "totalitarian bacillus", both in the United States itself, and in its imperial zones of intervention (Fousek 2000; Foglesong 2007; Dudziak 2000; Borstelmann 2001; Lewis 2004; Woods 2004).

Anticommunism in its repressive capacity involved what can be called "counter-subversive" practices, a form of activity that enabled the disorganisation of popular classes as an essential correlate of achieving consent. Ellen Schrecker foregrounds the centrality of the "anticommunist network" in this respect, an alliance of forces situated in capital, the state and civil society. In each case, Schrecker points out, the state is essential: it is what gives the network teeth, puts weapons in the hands of vigilantes, and empowers employers. It is also the element of the network which is capable of actualising on an international level a strategic response to communism as a global problem (Schrecker 2002, 12–14 and 25).

First wave: anticommunism as an American racial practice

The first wave of anticommunism in the US, in the period 1917–19, was integral to the development of Wilsonian "liberal internationalism", which had as one of its central aims the containment of the Russian revolution and its destabilising effect on the global states system. Indeed, the central ideological claims of Wilsonian doctrine – the "self-determination of nations" above all – were purloined from Bolshevik discourse in an attempt to neutralise the latter's appeal. Race framed the understanding of "the communist threat" on the part of US state personnel, prosecutors and organic intellectuals. And just as the communist threat was global, so the racial order in whose fortunes the US was implicated did "not stop at the water's edge". For Wilson had no intention of permitting "self-determination" to apply to non-white nations, and his team had pointedly rejected Japan's "racial equality" resolution at Versailles. It was therefore essential that the US should attempt to manage the gap between its propaganda and its practical ideology. The simplest way to manage this gap was to uphold white supremacy as a norm, and to assert – as Wilson did – that self-government was a privilege of whiteness (Manela 2007). In this sense, communism could be seen as a threat to democracy precisely insofar as it threatened white supremacy.

Domestically, Wilson-era anticommunism was weighted toward repression far more than ideological consensus. In its repressive register, anticommunism belongs to a family of "countersubversive" practices. Countersubversion has a particular historical role in the formation of American nation, as the presumed conspiracies of Freemasons, Catholics, Mormons, African Americans, the "yellow peril", and of course "Reds", have serially aroused movements in defence of "Americanism". Inoculating a racial-national space, countersubversion is historically also a patriarchal practice linked to the masculinist "regeneration through violence" (Melley 2002; Slotkin 1973; Davis 1960). It is communism as a *subversive conspiracy*, then, that this form of anticommunism takes as its object. To this extent, there is no mystery about the affinity – one might say "elective affinity" – between anticommunism and the defence of racial hierarchy.

Anticommunism has a particular role to play in racial states. Three such states in the twentieth century manifested a particular concern with anticommunism: the United States, Australia and South Africa. Despite significant differences in land mass, demographics and global reach, these states shared some similar historical experiences. In all three cases, a colonial pattern of capitalist development predominated, with the "frontier" being the chief metaphor through which primitive accumulation was organised, while white supremacy formed the basis of state formation (Marx 1999; Kwon 2010, 37–8; Fischer 2005). In these states, anticommunism was peculiarly intense and was imbricated with the defence of racial systems in remarkably similar ways. For example, Southern US politicians held that US civil rights organisations were damned as representing the cuspate end of a communist conspiracy intent on global dominion. South African leaders similarly argued that the ANC was deemed the local auxiliary of a Moscow design to take over the region's South African mineral treasures (Lewis 2004). Anticommunism, enforced through "physical violence, civil ordinance laws, incarceration, sackings and injunctions against strike action", took aim at a "vague conglomerate of hostile causes" (Fischer 2005). To be depicted as a "Red" was to be externalised and "Othered"; while the rebellion of the racially oppressed was construed as an outcome of "Red" plotting. Finally, anticommunism was entangled with an imperialist "civilising mission", particularly in the Cold War era (Clark 2008; Kiernan 2002).

In the US, furthermore, anticommunism had always drawn on the practices of countersubversion established through previous waves of racial terror. Just as radical reconstruction was resisted and segregation imposed in the Deep South by Klans allied to the dominant planter class and linked to the formerly dominant Democratic Party, so America's first bout of anticommunist repression in the period 1917–19 involved the deployment of parapolitical "civil society" organisations in alliance with business groups organised around the nexus of state power. In the latter case, the rise of militant imperialist sentiment in the US under Woodrow Wilson was linked first to hysteria about treacherous African Americans in sympathy with Germans, then subsequently about "Reds" stirring up domestic disorder (Ellis 2001).

The dominant key of the ensuing countersubversion offensive was nativist and racist. American race theorist Lothrop Stoddard saw in Bolshevism the death of "white-world supremacy". Robert Lansing, George Simons and military intelligence credited the fraudulent thesis of the *Protocols of the Elders of Zion* to explain the success of the Bolsheviks. The Sedition Act (1918) was used pointedly against "aliens", while J. Edgar Hoover used his position in the Bureau of Investigation to raise alarm over the alleged propensity of African American leaders toward communism. Communists had "done a vast amount of evil damage by carrying doctrines of race revolt and the poison of Bolshevism to the Negroes". The Lusk Commission established in 1919 to look into radicalism "argued that there was 'not a single system of Anglo-Saxon socialism, nor a single system of Latin race socialism'. The only scientific system of socialism was 'of German-Jewish origin'". This was a particularly portentous accusation after the feverish anti-German propaganda that shadowed US entry into the First World War. Civil society and vigilante organisations such as the American League, the Daughters of the American Revolution, war veterans groups, and bodies of Minute Men, often funded by business blocs led by local Chambers of Commerce, were organised around nativist thematics (Woods 2004, 86; Gaughan 1999; Foglesong 2007, 58; Heale 1990, 60–96; Kovel 1997, 14–22).

Importantly, this was closely linked to an attempt by the administration to preserve a global racial hierarchy in which "Anglo-Saxon" civilisation was seen as the best safeguard of democracy. This was the essential ideological correlate of the American attempt to manage the "contradictions" arising from the uneven and combined development of capitalist relations, which had manifested themselves in the "ruptural unity" of the Russian revolution (Althusser 2005, 99). The traditional means of such geopolitical management was imperialist, and racist. Thus, the encircling of revolutionary Russia at Versailles, the intervention on behalf of the counter-revolutionary White Army in Siberia, and the policy of non-recognition, were all embedded in racist and imperialist discourses.

One of the key Wilson administration anticommunist intellectuals was John Spargo, a former Marxist from Britain who took a pro-war position once the US decided to intervene in WWI. Spargo's neoconservatism *avant la lettre* led him to join the American Alliance for Labor and Democracy, a pro-war labour organisation affiliated with the government. He was sent on speaking tours by the administration's Committee for Public Information, authored much of the administration's propaganda, and drafted its policy of non-recognition. He was if anything utterly disappointed by what he saw as the government's lack of commitment in its military engagements in Siberia.

Spargo's chief argument about the Bolshevik revolution was that Russia was a backward civilisation, unable to handle the problems of radical self-government. The result was that a weakened "Slavonic" race, otherwise a natural ally of "the West", would find itself in a global racial nexus between "Teutons" and the "semi-Oriental" Japanese monarchy – an orientation "full of peril" for democracy. Spargo was far from seeing communism as being a simple racial conspiracy, in the sense imagined by Lothrop Stoddard, but as one of the most progressive Wilsonian intellectuals he could not help but interpret its effects in the context of a global racial order in which white domination was co-extensive with the development of democracy (Ruotsila 2006; Seymour 2008, 105–6; Seymour 2009). In effect, then, this phase of anticommunism worked to code the American defence of its own racial order and of a global racial hierarchy in whose fortunes it was increasingly invested.

Second wave: the Cold War, American nationalism and the Deep South

After 1945, the relationship between anticommunism and the racial order became more complex. The US assumed a dominant position among an alliance of capitalist classes opposed to socialism in this period. The rise of anticolonial struggles, often influenced or led by communist parties, demanded that the US engage in a complex series of operations. While its global interventions were often in defence of racial hierarchies that were perceived to be efficiently anticommunist (Borstelmann 2001; Schmitz 2006), the logic of defending worldwide "freedom" against its negative "totalitarian" ideograph placed limits on this and also penetrated the domestic sphere. The issue of segregation "became international in scope", a fact that its opponents made use of (Woodward 1966, 131–2).

Dudziak (2000) summarises the thrust of this logic: the world in which America wished to operate was in some senses like a panopticon. Egregious abuses would be witnessed by world opinion, which would in turn apply pressure. If the US wished to assemble a multiracial alliance against communism, as it plainly did and struggled to do, this pressure could matter. Dudziak maintains the US government was deeply reluctant to implement changes to the racial order and did so largely on the basis of global hegemonic considerations, fortifying the American model as an attractive one for decolonising populations. As Richard Nixon put it, following a visit to the newly independent state of Ghana in 1957, "We cannot talk equality to the peoples of Africa and Asia and practice inequality in the United States" (Borstelmann 2001, 109).

Thus, while Southern industry and politicians were by far the most committed and militarily aggressive component of the Cold War anticommunist bloc, they clashed with policies designed to win the Cold War with "soft power" by ameliorating the Southern racial system. The uses of anticommunism by Southern politicians and businessmen in the defence of Jim Crow were not merely opportunistic. For Southern conservatives, the racial caste system was a local cultural ecology protected by Jeffersonian "states' rights" republicanism, a meritocratic system expressing the real innate differences between the "races", and an important component of Americanism. The Federal imposition of racial equality in any capacity constituted, for them, a statist abridgment of free enterprise alien to American traditions. In toto, legislation for racial equality constituted a "blueprint for totalitarianism" (Smith 2010, 33–9; Sensing 1964).

Even so, the Deep South was central to the anticommunist coalition, with Southern politicians in local and federal state bodies taking the lead in promulgating securitarian and ideological responses to leftist and anti-racist movements, and providing a template of 'Americanism' that was dominant in the classical phase of Cold War anticommunism. This was logical. Anticommunism provided Southern state leaders such as Senator James Eastland and Governor Orval Faubus with the ideologies and above all the political apparatuses (mini-HUACs abounded) to deal with opponents of segregation. It also provided a language for mobilising "Massive Resistance" when it came (Lewis 2004, 10–29; Braden 1980). Marable (2007, 17) estimates that the Cold War delayed the Civil Rights movement by approximately a decade, in part because the anticommunist offensives deterred many potential supporters from participating in a movement tarnished with the label of communism and threatened with legal repression.

The extraordinary breadth of the classical anticommunist front, in which were linked labour unions, leftists such as Norman Thomas and Dwight MacDonald, anti-racist organisations such as the NAACP, the "Vital Center" liberals convoked in the ADA, business lobbies and the white despotisms in Southern states, reflects the success of the anticommunist idea as a hegemonic "quilting point" capable of articulating diverse class and political discourses. It helped produce a new popular "common sense" favourable to "free enterprise" and American "leadership", while also legitimising the repressive, "counter-subversive" practices necessary to disorganise the minority excluded from the Cold War "historic bloc". Cold War anticommunism had to plausibly incorporate within it elements of popular aspirations, and anxieties. In one mode, it offered material measures to secure popular consent (rising wages in exchange for productivity was at the heart of the Fordist production model), and in another it operated on fears of global communist expansionism and domestic subversion that, though significantly exaggerated and ideologically distorted, were not simply invented (Rupert 1995; Schrecker 1999, 161).

It was this "historic bloc" which materially underpinned the missionary American nationalism that went under the rubric of "liberal internationalism". It was because such diverse constituencies could be cohered around a shared mission, because the repressive teeth of the state needed only to be applied to a select minority of opponents, that the US ruling class could successfully project such power overseas. By using anticommunism to defend white supremacy inside US borders, it could also use anticommunism to seize control of white supremacy abroad.

Second wave: anticommunism and decolonisation

The post-WWII world system was one overwhelmingly dominated by the United States. The US pioneered a global architecture of international legal institutions and trade institutions informed by New Deal thinking (Rupert 1995; Gowan 2003a). The US was in a position to extend a new system of dominance based on a "protectorate system" in the capitalist core extending to Western Europe and an arc of power in Southeast Asia, while gradually attaining strategic control of the colonial territories. Within the protectorate system, consent to US domination was achieved partially on the basis of its demonstrated military supremacy, above all its occupations of West Germany and Japan, and partially on the basis of material incentives (Marshall Plan) and anticommunist ideology. American war planners, with the assistance of the geographer Isaiah Bowman, elaborated a strategy of carefully shaking loose some of the colonial possessions of Old Europe and opening them to US capital. Control of productive resources, Bowman suggested, was far more important than territorial control (Gowan 2003b; Smith 2004).

However, the handling of colonial breakdown was necessarily delicate so far as US planners were concerned. Initially, the US had hoped that the United Nations, which it had played such a crucial role in organising, would be able to take control of the "dependencies". However, citing the exigencies of the anticommunist struggle, the US increasingly sought to conserve the colonial authorities. Here, it was the ruling class intellectual George Kennan who crystallised the emerging strategic thinking. Just as Spargo had supplied much of the rational for Wilson's anticommunist stance some decades before, so George Kennan's "Long Telegram" provided the crucial ideological lynchpin for America's anticommunist foreign policy. Kennan's intransigent hostility to the USSR was inescapably bound up with his sense of the global racial hierarchy, and the US role in it. He distrusted African Americans and Jews, and was repelled by "most Third World Peoples – Asians, Arabs, Latinos and Africans – whom he tended to lump together as impulsive, fanatical, ignorant, lazy, unhappy, and prone to mental disorders and other biological deficiencies", and had written in 1938 that the US should be turned into a "benevolent despotism" of upper-class white males, excluding women, immigrants and blacks from the franchise (Kovel 1997, 53; Borstelmann 1993, 40).

In his early Cold War writings, particularly his "Long Telegram" and his more famous article "The Sources of Soviet Conduct", Kennan argued that the Russian Revolution had overthrown "the Westernized upper crust" of the Tsarist elite, and revealed a population Orientalised by a century of contact with "Asiatic hordes". Russia had thus became "a typical Oriental despotism", engaged in a remarkable conspiracy against "Western civilization" and the colonial system. He anticipated that Russia's strategy would be to violently weaken or overthrow or subvert Western influence "over colonial, backward, or dependent peoples". The only answer was for Americans to accept the "moral and political leadership" that, at any rate, history had plainly intended for them (Kovel 1997, 39–63; Roark 1971; Borstelmann 2001, 50).

Were Kennan's mandarin musings merely indicative of his own prejudices, they might be unremarkable. However, what they in fact demonstrate is that the anticommunist discourse of American elites was already connotatively linked to the preservation of white-world supremacy. As David F. Schmitz (2006) has shown, the underlying assumptions of white superiority were an important component of policymaking in the Cold War, even under the much-admired liberal Kennedy administration. Their most urgent fear regarding the colonial world was "premature independence". This was linked to the belief that those insufficiently tutored in the art of self-government by their white masters – those "immature and unsophisticated" people, as the National Security Council described Africans in 1957 – would be easy meat for communist takeover. Thus, the vital strategic concepts for US planners were "eventual self-determination", "evolutionary development" and so on. In practice, this turned out to be a rationale for supporting the colonial powers (Schmitz 2006, 13; Krenn 2006, 79–80). As a result, the US acted as a vital prop for European colonial allies, above all the British Empire. As William Roger Louis and Ronald Robinson write:

> Marshall Plan aid and eventually the Mutual Security programme met the otherwise prohibitive charge on the balance of payments of sustaining British power overseas up to 1952 and at need thereafter … . From 1949 onwards, the Pentagon joined the War Office in the traditional imperial Great Game of securing the Indian sub-continent's frontiers from Kabul and Herat to Rangoon and Singapore.
>
> *(Louis and Robinson 2004, 154)*

The strategic rationale for this was to assist allies in the struggle against communism, and to forestall its triumph in the colonial states. The intellectual framework for this approach was supplied by "modernisation theory", an attempt to rival Marxism as a theory of historical development and to demonstrate that communism was a "disease of the transition to modernity". As Schmitz writes:

> one of the leading modernization theorists, member of Kennedy's national security staff, and national security advisor to President Johnson, Walt Whitman Rostow, argued, the revolutionary process of modernization in the Third World was when these nations were most in danger of falling to communism. The 'weak transitional governments that one is likely to find

during this modernization process are highly vulnerable to subversion'. The communists were the 'scavengers of the modernization process' who knew that once the 'momentum takes hold in an underdeveloped area – and the fundamental social problems inherited from the traditional society are solved – their chances to seize power decline'. … Dictatorships, therefore, were necessary in the Third World until the modernization process had developed enough to allow 'these societies [to] choose their own version of what we would recognize as a democratic, open society'.

(Schmitz 2006, 12)

Aside from those arenas where the US chose to embark on direct, violent repression, and those where it used repression by proxy, the institutions of international civil society formed a critical terrain of anticommunist struggle for the US government. Through Marshall Plan aid and the export of Fordist production methods linked to a "productivist" ideology, the American state successfully mobilised US labour, as represented by the AFL-CIO, into helping organise its hegemony within Europe. Its illicit intervention in the affairs of European Left and labour movements is well documented, as is the wider attempt to orchestrate a cultural and ideological consensus in favour of an orientation toward "the free world" (Rupert 1995; Wilford 2003; Carew 1987, 69; Saunders 2000).

Beyond Europe, the attention of US planners to developing hegemonic strategies was limited. For example, the continent of Africa had barely featured except as an appendage of Europe in US discussions during the early years of the Cold War. "Security" interests on the part of the US were minimal, although American capital salivated over the potential market (Metz 1984). As anticolonial nationalism matured, however, the US increasingly came to the conclusion that it would have to intervene in order to forestall communist influence, and that organised labour could be a key vector for building US hegemony in the colonial world. Nixon's report following his 1957 tour of Africa urged the Eisenhower administration to focus on building trade union relations. British trade unions were drafted into the official attempts to quarantine the emerging African labour movements against a rising Pan-Africanism, giving the AFL-CIO the opportunity, working through the anticommunist International Congress of Free Trade Unions, to expand US influence. They increasingly called for a policy of national independence, partially in competition with British unions for influence, whom they felt were too soft on communists, and partially because they feared that without such a pro-active policy "communist" and Pan-African sentiment would prevent the US from assuming the dominant role (Carew 1996; Zeleza 1984).

Crisis and breakdown: the 'geopolitical management' of Southeast Asia

The region of Southeast Asia had long been a source of fascination for American race thinking and a testing bed for its imperial projects. From the annexation of

Pacific islands to the anti-immigration laws and purges to the colonisation of the Philippines, the US attempted to subordinate parts of "the East" on the basis of its extant racial ideologies and techniques, and open it up for investment. Japan's state-led "modernization", a classic instance of uneven and combined development (Allinson and Anievas 2010), was understood by Americans as simply the application of "white man methods" by people who remained "savages" and "barbarians", as WWII propaganda had it (quoted in Krenn 2006, 67). In America's post-war flush of success, it organised its domination of Southeast Asia by reconstructing the Japanese state along "American" lines in part, it seems, to bring the "martial" spirit of the Japanese "race" under control – and by supporting a network of clients and colonial allies (Jacobson 2001; Dower 1987; Seymour 2008, 80–90, 111–17 and 130–42).

The Cold War was bracketed at either end by two major anticommunist wars, both in Southeast Asia, and both "race wars" in the sense of being strategically bound up with the maintenance of white-world supremacy, and in the sense of being ideologically permeated by a racist "common sense". The first major anticommunist war, in Korea, was at least in part a race war in this tradition. For President Truman [the Koreans were] "the inheritors of Genghis Khan and Tamerlane, the greatest murderers in the history of world". General McArthur bristled with stereo-types about "the Oriental" and his natural propensity to "follow a winner". General Willoughby lamented that civilised Americans were being killed by "simple coolies", "half-men with blank faces". To another official, North Koreans were "half-crazed automatons". Such views formed part of the "common sense" of imperialist statecraft, and were integrally linked to it (Deane 1999, 29–30). However, by deploying anticommunism as the main legitimising argument for intervention, the US suc-cessfully organised a hegemonic coalition within the United States, and involved the most extensive deployment of hegemonic operations beyond. It secured a consensus among elites, broad coalition of popular support, an alliance of states, and a legal basis through the United Nations (Bell 2004; Sandler 1999; Mayers 2007; Casey 2008). The US thus intervened to divert Korea's "modernization" process away from the communist route. It was not able to entirely extirpate the revolutionary movement (Armstrong 2003) which had taken power in the north of Korea. However, in defending its southern regime, its strategy of supporting author-itarian client regimes in those states it deemed not yet ready for full self-government was consolidated (Cummings 1981; Deane 1999).

The second major anticommunist war, in Vietnam, was likewise part of a racist praxis, linked to the maintenance of white-world supremacy. The war began as a complex manoeuvre in defence of French colonialism (with the ultimate goal of supplanting it). The US sent a total of $3.6bn in aid to the French client Bao Dai until 1954. This was linked to the official perception of Vietnam as a "medieval country", which colonialism was dragging into modernity. However, as before, the racial dynamic was at an ideological level commuted through the discourse of anticommunism. Accordingly, the Vietnamese revolution was interpreted as a manifestation of a desire to be modern – essentially, to be American – expressed in a pathological form as "communism". The job of the US was to help Vietnam – by crushing its revolution – back onto the right track (Krenn 2006, 89–93).

As the French withdrew, the US reverted to its pattern of supporting an anti-communist client dictator, and shifted its weight behind Ngo Dinh Diem. Diem was encouraged to build up a repressive apparatus, killing thousands and jailing over 150,000 people. The Kennedy administration, belligerent and operating on the assumptions of still regnant Cold War orthodoxy, dedicated itself to the development of an effective counterinsurgency program. One expression of this was the "Strategic Hamlet Program", similar to the American use of concentration camps for civilians in the Philippines. In under two years, 16,000 such "hamlets" appeared across South Vietnam. This was eventually accompanied by aerial attacks and a build-up of troops eventually reaching half a million. The escalation was justified in part by racism in both the mandarin and demotic registers, with "modernisation theory" providing the former and the "mere gook rule" supplying the latter (Gettleman, Franklin, Young & Franklin 1995, 295; Kolko 1994, 80–2; Gerson 2007, 130–66).

However, the anticommunist consensus was already brittle by the time the US was seriously engaged in Vietnam, precisely because the success of the anticolonial movements and the rise of the civil rights struggle in the Southern US combined to disrupt the binary of communism vs. anticommunism. Certainly, a consensus initially held among policymaking elites and allied intellectuals regarding the nefarious reach of communism. Labour was broadly in favour of war, and such popular criticisms as did emerge were initially muted (Small 2002; Tomes 1998; Levy 1994, 47–51). Even so, the broad, integral unity of diverse classes and class sectors that had been successfully organised around anticommunism was weakened.

As ever, race did not stop at the water's edge. The civil rights movement, when it did emerge, was intimately tied to anticolonial struggles, and its radicalisation in the early 1960s would owe much to their success. The example of India's independence struggles had exerted a profound effect on African American struggles. In the case of Martin Luther King, it was Gandhi's doctrine of non-violent resistance that he adopted for the US civil rights movement. "We have found them to be effective and sustaining – they work!" (King, King Jr, Carson, Holloran, Luker and Russell 2005, 5; Horne 2008). In 1960, the same year that sit-ins and freedom rides began, a host of independent African states came into being: Congo, Benin, Togo, Cameroon, Somalia, Niger, Mauritius, Burkina Faso, Ivory Coast, Chad, the Central African Republic, Gabon, Senegal and Mali. The emerging "New Left" paid attention. The famous Port Huron declaration of Students for a Democratic Society in 1962 celebrated the "revolutionary feelings of many Asian, African and Latin American Peoples" and the "social sense of organicism characteristic of these upsurges" against which American apathy stood in "embarrassing contrast" (Westad 2007, 106). By 1963, the Organization of African Unity had been formed to represent the interests of the newly independent states, a move which would inspire Malcolm X to co-found the Organization of Afro-American Unity the following year (X 1964). The 'solid South' crumbled under this pressure. Segments of the US ruling class, including business leaders of the "New South", viewed segregation as a burden. Local state leaders such as Ben West of Nashville were persuaded to oppose segregation; others – "pragmatic segregationists" – began to adopt a strategy of implementing racially laden family, crime and welfare policies rather than open segregation (Marable 2007, 67; Woods 2004, 218–24; Eyes on the Prize 3: Ain't Scared of Your Jails (1960–1)).

The successes of the civil rights movement provided a material basis for the emerging antiwar movement in the US: a tactical repertoire (civil disobedience), a layer of leaders (many antiwar activists having been educated in the CORE or the SNCC), and a body of intellectual experience in the realities of white supremacy and its centrality to the American system. And when civil rights activists began to challenge the US war in Vietnam, they regarded it not as an anticommunist issue, but a *race* issue. The growth of the antiwar movement, linked to a wider search for racial justice, disembedded significant popular layers from the anticommunist coalition, and began to assemble them into a new, radical coalition which ultimately embraced six million participants and 25 million sympathisers. In this context, and in view of the effective military resistance of the Vietnamese National Liberation Front, even the consensus among elites and state-aligned intellectuals did not hold (Gettleman, Franklin, Young and Franklin 1995, 296–304; Zaroulis and Sullivan 1984, 27–32; Small 2002, 5–6). As social struggles escalated, anticommunism could no longer link diverse constituencies in a single bloc. The old anticommunist bloc disintegrated, some of its elements shaken loose and redistributed into new civil rights and antiwar coalitions. The Cold War 'historic bloc' was finished, consumed in the overthrow of white-world supremacy.

Conclusion

The Cold War represented a particular transitional moment in the geopolitical management of the uneven and combined development of capitalism, in which an emerging norm of national self-determination embodied in the legal superstructure of the United Nations conflicted with the established norm of white-world supremacy. The US ruling class was strategically committed in the long run to replacing formal colonial control of non-white states with a hierarchy of self-determining states with the US at its apex. Further, it was invested in hegemonic practices designed to win it global allies in the struggle against communism, including its claim to oppose empires and its insistence that Russia was the most menacing imperialist power. This also raised questions about its domestic racial system, which was a significant impediment to its ability to win allies in the Third World. However, the domestic class system relied upon the maintenance of white supremacy. Further, the US state leaders did not merely doubt the capacity of non-whites for self-government: they had an interested opposition to national self-determination if it was claimed by forces that might be hostile to American capitalist penetration. Finally, their key global allies and accomplices in power were themselves the colonial powers.

Cold War anticommunism did not resolve all of these conflicts, but it provided a framework within which they could be managed for a period of time. It ensured the hegemony of the ruling class domestically. It consolidated a "historic bloc", a broad alliances of classes and groups organised around an ideologically defining mission, that of resisting communism. This suppressed brewing domestic conflicts over segregation and provided a material basis for US geopolitical management, including the consent necessary for military investments and deployments. It further provided the bedrock upon which the US could then cultivate allies and seek to deploy hegemonic strategies within allied states. Ultimately, anticommunism supplied the narrative ballast for the deployment of outright violence where US strategists deemed it necessary.

However, the Cold War "historic bloc" had always been predicated on an unstable unity, its global reach dependent in part upon the tacit, or explicit, acceptance that white supremacy was preferable to the perceived threat of communist rule. The bargain was that apartheid, colonialism and Jim Crow would be tolerated so long as it meant defending the institutions of democracy elsewhere. The downfall of the colonial system, and the ensuing fall of the "solid South", was ruinous to this logic. It broke the chain of equivalents linking anticommunism and democracy, and that associating democracy with whiteness.

The later refulgence of anticommunism associated with the neoconservative movement and the Reagan administration proved that its racial charge was far from exhausted. Reagan had built his presidential bid on the classic "Southern strategy" of appealing to racist white voters, and would find himself allied to white supremacy abroad upon taking office. Anticommunism supplied the rationale not only for the continued maintenance of right-wing dictatorships, but particularly for the administration's defence of apartheid South Africa. As the neoconservative intellectual Jeane Kirkpatrick argued on being appointed US ambassador to the UN, "racial dictatorship is not as onerous as Marxist dictatorship" (Crespino 2007; Borstelmann 2001, 261). Insofar as communism was still understood centrally as a conspiracy against civilisation, anticommunism continued to provide a language of racial conservatism. Moreover, it still provided the idiom through which the policy of imposing "modernising" dictatorships on the Third World could be rationalised.

However, the ability of anticommunism to cement hegemonic alliances in defence of racial hierarchy had been lost. As a strategy for managing the problems of uneven and combined development, it was viable only so long as it could defend white supremacy in the United States by organising all social struggles along the axis of communism vs. anticommunism. Once this binary was disrupted by anticolonial and civil rights struggles, the result of mobilising anticommunism in defence of white supremacy was no longer the sanctification of the latter, but the clear discrediting of the former.

Bibliography

Allinson, Jamie C. and Anievas, Alexander (2009) The Uses and Misuses of Uneven and Combined Development: An Anatomy of a Concept. *Cambridge Review of International Affairs* 22 (1), 47–67.

——(2010) The Uneven and Combined Development of the Meiji Restoration: A Passive Revolutionary Road to Capitalist Modernity. *Capital & Class* 34 (3), 469–90.

Althusser, Louis (2005) *For Marx* (London: Verso).

Anievas, Alexander (2014) International Relations between War and Revolution: Wilsonian Diplomacy and the Making of the Treaty of Versailles. *International Politics*, forthcoming.

Armstrong, Charles K. (2003) *The North Korean Revolution, 1945–1950* (Ithaca, NY: Cornell University Press).

Bell, Jonathan (2004) *The Liberal State on Trial: The Cold War and American Politics in the Truman Years* (New York, NY: Columbia University Press).

Borstelmann, Thomas (1993) *Apartheid's Reluctant Uncle: The United States and Southern Africa in the Early Cold War* (Oxford: Oxford University Press).

——(2001) *The Cold War and The Color Line: American Race Relations in the Global Arena* (Cambridge, MA: Harvard University Press).

Braden, Anne (1980) The Civil Rights Movement and McCarthyism. *Guild Practitioner* 37 (Fall), 109–16.

Carew, Anthony (1987) *Labour Under the Marshall Plan: The Politics of Productivity and the Marketing of Management Science* (Manchester: Manchester University Press).

——(1996) Conflict within the ICFTU: Anti-Communism and Anti-Colonialism in the 1950s. *International Review of Social History* 41 (2), 147–80.

Casey, Steven (2008) *Selling the Korean War: Propaganda, Politics, and Public Opinion 1950–1953* (Oxford: Oxford University Press).

Clark, Jennifer (2008) *Aborigines and Activism: Race, Aborigines and the Coming of the Sixties to Australia* (Crawley: University of Western Australia Press).

Crespino, Joseph (2007) *In Search of Another Country: Mississippi and the Conservative Counterrevolution* (Princeton, NJ: Princeton University Press).

Cummings, Bruce (1981) *The Origins of the Korean War, Vol. I: Liberation and the Emergence of Separate Regimes, 1945–1947* (Princeton, NJ: Princeton University Press).

Davis, David Brian (1960) Some Themes of Counter-Subversion: An Analysis of Anti-Masonic, Anti-Catholic, and Anti-Mormon Literature. *The Mississippi Valley Historical Review* 47 (2), 205–24.

Deane, Hugh (1999) *The Korean War, 1945–1953* (San Francisco, CA: China Books).

Dower, John (1987) *War Without Mercy: Race and Power in the Pacific War* (London: Pantheon).

Dudziak, Mary L. (2000) *Cold War Civil Rights: Race and the Image of American Democracy* (Princeton, NJ: Princeton University Press).

Ellis, Mark (2001) *Race, War, and Surveillance: African Americans and States Government during World War I* (Bloomington, IN: Indiana University Press).

Eyes on the Prize 3: Ain't Scared of Your Jails (1960–61) (1990). Film directed by Henry Hampton (Boston: Blackside).

Fields, Karen E. and Fields, Barbara J. (2012) *Racecraft: The Soul of Inequality in American Life* (London: Verso).

Fischer, Nick (2005) The Australian Right, the American Right and the Threat of the Left, 1917–35. *Labour History* 89 (Nov), 17–35.

Foglesong, David (2007) *The American Mission and the 'Evil Empire': The Crusade for a 'Free Russia' Since 1881* (Cambridge: Cambridge University Press).

Fousek, John (2000) *To Lead The Free World: American Nationalism and the Cultural Roots of the Cold War* (Chapel Hill, NC: University of North Carolina Press).

Gaughan, Anthony (1999) Woodrow Wilson and the Rise of Militant Interventionism in the South. *The Journal of Southern History* 65 (4), 771–808.

Gerson, Joseph (2007) *Empire and the Bomb: How the US Uses Nuclear Weapons to Dominate the World* (London: Pluto Press).

Gettleman, Marvin, Franklin, Jane, Young, Marilyn B. and Franklin, H. Bruce (eds) (1995) *Vietnam and America: The Most Comprehensive Documented History of the Vietnam War* (New York, NY: Grove Press).

Gilman, Nils (2003) *Mandarins of the Future: Modernization Theory in Cold War America* (Baltimore, MD: Johns Hopkins University Press).

Gowan, Peter (2003a) US: UN. *New Left Review* 24 (Nov/Dec), 5–28.

——(2003b) The American Campaign for Global Sovereignty. *Socialist Register* 39, 5.

Gramsci, Antonio (1971) *Selections from the Prison Notebooks of Antonio Gramsci* (London: Lawrence & Wishart).

Hall, Stuart (1985) Authoritarian Populism: A Reply to Jessop et al. *New Left Review* 151: May/June, 115–24.

——(1986) Gramsci's Relevance for the Study of Race and Ethnicity. *Journal of Communication Inquiry* 10 (2), 5–27.

Heale, M. J. (1990) *American Anti-Communism: Combating the Enemy Within, 1830–1970* (Baltimore, M.D.: Johns Hopkins University Press).

Horne, Gerald (2007) *Cold War in a Hot Zone: Labor and Independence Struggles in the British West Indies* (Philadelphia, PA: Temple University Press).

——(1985) *Black and Red: W. E. B. Du Bois and the Afro-American Response to the Cold War, 1944–1963* (Albany, NY: State University of New York Press).

——(2008) *The End of Empires: African Americans and India* (Philadelphia, PA: Temple University Press).

Ives, Peter and Short, Nicola (2013) On Gramsci and the International: A Textual Analysis. *Review of International Studies* 39 (3), 621–42.

Jacobson, Matthew Frye (2001) *Barbarian Virtues: The United States Encounters Foreign Peoples at Home and Abroad, 1876–1917* (New York, NY: Hill & Wang).

Kiernan, Ben (2002) Cover-up and Denial of Genocide: Australia, the USA, East Timor, and the Aborigines. *Critical Asian Studies* 34 (2), 163–92.

King, Martin Luther Jr, Carson, Clayborne, Holloran, Peter, Luker, Ralph and Russell, Penny A. (2005) *The Papers of Martin Luther King, Jr., Volume V: Threshold of a New Decade, January 1959–December 1960* (Berkeley, CA: University of California Press).

Kolko, Gabriel (1994) *Anatomy of A War: Vietnam, the United States, and the Modern Historical Experience* (New York, NY: The New Press).

Kovel, Joel (1997) *Red Hunting in the Promised Land: Anticommunism and the Making of America* (London: Cassell).

Krenn, Michael L. (2006) *The Color of Empire: Race and American Foreign Relations* (Lincoln, NE: Potomac Books/University of Nebraska Press).

Kwon, Heonik (2010) *The Other Cold War* (New York: Columbia University Press).

Laclau, Ernesto (1977) *Politics and Ideology in Marxist Theory, Capitalism-Fascism-Populism* (London: Verso).

Levy, Peter B. (1994) *The New Left and Labor in the 1960s* (Champaign, IL: University of Illinois Press).

Lewis, George (2004) *The White South and the Red Menace: Segregationists, Anticommunism, and Massive Resistance, 1945–1965* (Gainesville, FL: University of Florida Press).

Louis, William Roger and Robinson, Ronald (2004) Empire Preserv'd: How the Americans Put Anti-communism before Anti-imperialism. In Duara, Prasenjit (ed.) *Decolonization: Perspectives from Now and Then* (London: Routledge).

Manela, Erez (2007) *The Wilsonian Moment: Self-Determination and the International Origins of Anticolonial Nationalism* (Oxford: Oxford University Press).

Marable, Manning (2007) *Race, Reform and Rebellion: The Second Reconstruction and Beyond in Black America, 1945–2006* (Oxford, MS: Mississippi University Press).

Marx, A. W. (1999) *Making Race and Nation: A Comparison of South Africa, the United States and Brazil* (Cambridge: Cambridge University Press).

Mayers, David. (2007) *Dissenting Voices in America's Rise to Power* (Cambridge: Cambridge University Press).

Melley, Timothy (2002) Agency, Panic and the Culture of Conspiracy. In Knight, Peter (ed.) *Conspiracy Nation: The Politics of Paranoia in postwar America* (New York, NY: New York University Press), p. 61–73.

Metz, Stephen (1984) American Attitudes Toward Decolonization in Africa. *Political Science Quarterly* 99 (3), 515–33.

Nesbitt, Francis Njubi (2004) *Race for Sanctions: African Americans against Apartheid, 1946–1994* (Bloomington, IN: Indiana University Press).

Poulantzas, Nicos (1978) *Political Power and Social Classes* (London: Verso).

——(2000) *State, Power, Socialism* (London: Verso).

Roark, James L. (1971) American Black Leaders: The Response to Colonialism and the Cold War, 1943–53. *African Historical Studies* 4 (2), 253–70.

Ruotsila, Markuu (2006) *John Spargo and American Socialism* (London: Palgrave Macmillan).

Rupert, Mark (1995) *Producing Hegemony: The Politics of Mass Production and American Global Power* (Cambridge: Cambridge University Press).

Sandler, Stephen (1999) *The Korean War: No Victors, No Vanquished* (Lexington, KY: University of Kentucky Press).

Saunders, Frances Stonor (2000) *Who Paid the Piper? The CIA and the Cultural Cold War* (London: Granta).

Schmitz, David F. (2006) *The United States and Right-Wing Dictatorships, 1965–1989* (Cambridge: Cambridge University Press).

Schrecker, Ellen (1999) *Many Are the Crimes: McCarthyism in America* (Princeton, NJ: Princeton University Press).

——(2002) *The Age of McCarthyism: A Brief History with Documents* (London: Palgrave Macmillan).

Sensing, Thurman (1964) *The Civil Rights Bill: Blueprint for Totalitarianism* (Southern States Industrial Council).

Seymour, Richard (2008) *The Liberal Defence of Murder* (London: Verso).

——(2009) John Spargo and American Socialism. *Historical Materialism* 17 (2), 272–85.

Slotkin, Richard. (1973) *Regeneration through Violence: The Mythology of the American Frontier, 1600–1860* (Middletown, CT: Wesleyan University Press).

Small, Melvin (2002) *Antiwarriors: The Vietnam War and the Battle for America's Hearts and Minds* (Wilmington, DE: Scholarly Resources Press).

Smith, Neil (2004) *American Empire: Roosevelt's Geographer and the Prelude to Globalization* (Berkeley, CA: University of California Press).

Smith, Robert C. (2010) *Conservatism and Racism: And Why in America They Are the Same* (Albany, NY: SUNY Press).

Stoddard, Lothrop (1920) *The Rising Tide of Color Against White World-Supremacy* (New York: Charles Scribner & Sons), republished at Project Gutenberg, September 2011, www.gutenberg.org/ebooks/37408.

Thomas, Peter D. (2009) *The Gramscian Moment: Philosophy, Hegemony and Marxism* (Chicago, IL: Haymarket Books).

Tomes, Robert (1998) *Apocalypse Then: American Intellectuals and the Vietnam War* (New York, NY: New York University Press).

Westad, Odd Arne (2007) *The Global Cold War* (Cambridge: Cambridge University Press).

Wilford, Hugh (2003) *The CIA, the British Left and the Cold War: Calling the Tune?* (London: Routledge).

Woods, Jeff (2004) *Black Struggle, Red Scare: Segregation and Anti-Communism in the South, 1948–1968* (Baton Rouge, LA: Louisiana State University Press).

Woodward, C. Vann (1966) *The Strange Career of Jim Crow* (Oxford: Oxford University Press).

Von Eschen, Penny (1996) *Race Against Empire: Black Americans and Anticolonialism, 1937–57* (Ithaca, NY: Cornell University Press).

X, Malcolm (1964) *Speech on the Founding of the OAAU*, 28 June. Available at: www.thinkingtogether.org/rcream/archive/Old/S2006/comp/OAAU.pdf.

Zaroulis, Nancy and Sullivan, Gerald (1984) *Who Spoke Up? American Protest Against the War in Vietnam, 1963–1975* (New York: Doubleday and Company).

Zeleza, Tiyambe (1984) Colonialism and Internationalism: The Case of the British and Kenyan Labour Movement. *Ufahamu: A Journal of African Studies* 14 (1), 9–28.

10

RACE, RACIALISATION AND RIVALRY IN THE INTERNATIONAL LEGAL ORDER

Robert Knox[1]

Introduction

As noted by Anievas, Manchanda and Shilliam in the introduction to this collection, debates about *imperialism* have been – in an oblique manner – one of the main ways in which international relations has grappled with the question of race and racism. The contemporary resurgence in IR scholarship on race is no different, part of a wider scholarly and political revival in the study of empire and imperialism. As has often been noted, this wider revival occurred in the wake of a wave of military interventions. Thus the 1999 Kosovo 'humanitarian intervention', the 2001 invasion of Afghanistan and the wider "war on terror" and the 2003 invasion of Iraq were all central to the re-emergence of debates about 'empire'.

Analysing these military interventions in terms of empire and imperialism has also brought their *racialised* nature to the fore. The justifications for all of these military interventions implied and relied upon a stark distinction between different regions of the world, with some states being entitled to intervene, and others existing to be intervened in. This points more generally to the fact that it has often been through issues of military violence that the global colour line has been understood and contested.

This is a familiar story to any student of IR. Indeed, as the introduction to this volume notes, the discourse of rogue states and new wars, and the technologies of contemporary military violence all bear the stamp of race. Yet there is something missing from this picture. While military interventions obviously involve questions of force, power and political economy, they also crucially involve questions of *law*. Military interventions are almost always accompanied by attempts to argue for their legality. Indeed, the discourse of 'rogue states' emerged as part of the broader legal architecture of the war on terror, and some of the most heated debates over drones have been conducted in juridical terms. This should draw our attention to the fact that the last wave of contemporary military interventions have been quite intensely juridical – with much of the specificity of humanitarian intervention and the war on terror lying in their juridical characterisations.

As such, one can draw important connections between the global colour line, military intervention and international law. In this respect, it is unsurprising that critical scholars of international law have attempted to map these connections. These approaches have tended to locate the use of force within a wider dynamic of a 'civilising mission', in which the role of law is to racialise peripheral territories in such a way as to justify the intervention of advanced capitalist powers. Building on a previous article (Knox 2013), this chapter will argue that the conceptions of race and imperialism that underlie such approaches cannot sufficiently account for the shifting patterns of legal argument over the past decade. Briefly examining some of the major military incursions of the 1990s and 2000s, this chapter argues that the difference between the legal justifications for the first invasion of Iraq and the later invasions cannot be accounted for by the concept of racialisation outlined above. It argues that instead it is necessary to foreground the role of *inter-imperialist rivalry* in creating particular legal forms of racialisation.

The chapter then attempts to reflect more broadly what role inter-imperialist rivalry plays in the relationship between imperialism and international law and how this can illuminate questions of racialisation more directly. In so doing it attempts to shed light on the complex and shifting nature of the global colour line.

Race, war and law

Civilising interventions?

Some of the most important contemporary scholars on the relationship between race and international law are those writing in the *soi-disant* Third World Approaches to International Law movement. Focusing particularly on the cases of humanitarian intervention and the war on terror, these scholars have argued that the law on the use of is structured by the racialising logic of a 'civilising mission' inherited from international law's colonial past.

In the case of humanitarian intervention, this logic is almost immediately apparent. As Makau wa Mutua has argued, the legal arguments around humanitarian intervention embed and invoke a number of colonial tropes (2001). In particular, he argues humanitarianism is structured by a metaphor of 'savages, victims and saviors'. Essentially, Mutua argues, discourses of humanitarian intervention are *always* aimed at the Third World, despite the repeated violations of human rights by European states (Mutua 2001, 214–16). The content of these discourses always interpellates non-European cultures as *savage* in some way (Mutua, 219–27). It is because of this savagery that these non-Europeans are said to violate the human rights of *victims*. These victims – also non-European – are portrayed as passive and powerless before their own savage culture. In order to stop this they need to be saved by an outside agency, the West (Mutua 2001, 229). Here, the West acts as a *saviour* who will transform the savage culture through human rights (Mutua 2001, 233–43). The rootedness of this discourse in racialised categories should be obvious. Humanitarian intervention essentially relies on a colonial logic in which the 'natives' are both savage and powerless and can only be saved by being transformed by Western intervention.

Antony Anghie has argued that this civilising logic is also at play in the war on terror. The war on terror has largely been conducted under the rubric of self-defence. In particular, under the 'Bush Doctrine' it was argued that an expanded right of self-defence would be needed to counter the new continuous threat of stateless terrorism. Given international law's universality, this *could* have presented a problem, since all states would have been entitled to an expanded right of pre-emption (Anghie 2005a, 49). Of course, the United States could simply have allowed this to have been a formal juridical possibility but one which was limited by the realities of the unequal distributions of power on the world stage, but it did not. Instead, pre-emption was coupled with the idea of rogue states. The need for pre-emption was not generated by *all* states, but rather caused by a small number of terrorist-supporting states or 'failed states' which could not control their populations. These states could not *possess* the right to pre-emptive self-defence and were in fact its legitimate *target*.

Anghie argues that this mirrors the nineteenth-century colonial international law in which international legal personality was linked to 'civilisation'. Only states that were civilised according to European standards could be members of the 'Family of Nations' and so possess the full right to go to war (Anghie 2005a, 51). The Bush Doctrine took this even further however. Since rogue states were the source of instability in the world, it was necessary to intervene in order to *transform them* into liberal, democratic and stable states. Hence the war on terror has always been accompanied by 'humanitarian' and regime change arguments. In this way, once again, the structure of the civilising mission is reproduced (Anghie 2005, 309).

In these accounts, then, the law on the use of force is racialised because – in the words of the introduction – its terms 'remain embedded within the same racialised logics that they claim to displace'. However, the racial logic invoked by the accounts is a particular one, whereby racialisation is both 'primary' and 'binary'. The racial logic is *primary* because they see racialisation as the *driving force* behind international legal argument. In this sense, law exists in order to reproduce the distinctions between the civilised and the uncivilised.

The logic is also binary. First because it operates with a classical notion of colonial Manicheanism, whereby the primary division is between the civilised and the uncivilised (Fanon 1963, 41). In this vision, the importance of the law lies in designating 'uncivilised' areas as outside the 'Family of Nations' and positing them as legally inferior and thus open for intervention. Second because this Manichean logic is seen as *determining* the particular way in which racialisation occurs.

What this ultimately means is that the *form* in which racialisation occurs is determined by the relationship between an advanced core and an exploited periphery. The logic of civilisation is deployed as part of a process whereby this core is enabled to exploit and oppress the periphery. Thus, both the war on terror and humanitarian intervention have been understood as doctrines whose purpose is to legitimate US military interventions into peripheral territories (Amin 2006, Bartholomew 2006, Bowring 2008 and Chimni 2004.)

Whilst there is much to recommend in these accounts, they suffer from a problematic conception of imperialism and its relationship to race. Underpinning them is a vision of imperialism in which a dominant, unified imperialist core exploits an oppressed periphery. Here, the logic of imperialism is immediately racial, and racialisation can be explained purely according to the logic of the core exploiting the periphery. Yet, such an account is incapable of explaining the shifts in the specific legal arguments that have been deployed to justify military interventions. As will be argued below, over the past twenty years one can distinguish between at least three different types of legal argument that have been deployed to justify military intervention. If the law on the use of force is directly driven by a racial logic that serves simply to legitimate expansion into the 'Third World', it seems difficult to understand why these different legal justifications have been deployed at all.

New world orders?

The law on the use of force is structured around the idea of self-defence. Article 2(4) of the UN Charter forbids the threat or use of force 'against the territorial integrity or political independence of any state'. There are two exceptions to this: Article 51, which concerns self-defence, and Chapter VII. Chapter VII, the 'collective security' aspect of the Charter, deals with Security Council (SC) authorisations of the use of force. If the SC determines that there has been a threat or breach of the peace or an act of aggression it can authorise the use of force under Article 42 (using the phrase 'all necessary means'). Since these authorisations are decided by the SC, they can be prevented by a veto from any of its permanent members. Throughout the Cold War the collective security regime was 'paralysed' owing to the geopolitical rivalries between the 'Western' countries and the Soviet bloc (de Cuéllar 1989). This was to change.

In 1990, the Iraqi military invaded Kuwait. The Kuwaiti government immediately invoked a claim of 'collective self-defence'. However, the main legal justification for the invasion of Iraq was authorisation by the SC under Chapter VII. Resolution 660 declared that there had been a breach of international peace and security and under Resolution 678 the SC authorised member states to use 'all necessary means' to enforce Resolution 660.

The political discourse that accompanied this event depicted Saddam Hussein and the Iraqi state as essentially uncivilised barbarians (Said 1994, 353–5). This was reflected in the international *legal* logic of the argument. The SC essentially declared Iraq to be a pariah state and source of instability that had to be attacked and contained. The reason that it had to be stopped was that it had attacked 'powerless' Kuwait. In other words, this was a racialised form of legal argument, relying on tropes associated with the civilising mission. However, the particular *form* that the legal argument took was a Chapter VII authorisation.

This is important because a Chapter VII authorisation is one of the most uncontroversial ways in which a military intervention can occur. It does not incur the problems of 'thresholds' which have to be reached in the case of self-defence, such as whether an 'armed attack' has occurred or how 'imminent' an attack needs to be. Equally, acting under Chapter VII means that one is not limited to respond in a proportionate way to any armed attack but can take *all* measures 'necessary' to restore international 'peace and security' (Schachter 1991, 460). Despite the manifest advantages that were gained in adopting this particular form of legal argument, its usage has not been common.

Terror and humanitarianism

The next important part of this story occurs with NATO's 'humanitarian intervention' in Kosovo. Here, although the SC characterised the situation as a threat to international peace and security (Resolution 1199), it did *not* call for the use of 'all necessary measures'. Consequently, when the US-led NATO coalition declared it might intervene, it could not directly reference Chapter VII. Instead, it was forced to make different legal arguments. The first was that that although the SC had not explicitly called for intervention, this was *implicit* in its determination that the situation in Kosovo was a threat to international peace and security (Lobel and Ratner 1999, 152). This was reinforced by the fact that in this instance the SC was once again 'paralysed' by the geopolitical wrangling of the permanent members.

This was taken much further by those who advocated 'unilateral humanitarian intervention'. (Henkin 1999, Wedgwood 1999, Reisman 1999). They argued that the international legal order had changed and states were no longer the possessors of an untrammelled 'sovereign' right (International Commission on Intervention and State Sovereignty 2001, 11–19). States now had a duty, or responsibility, to protect their nationals. When states failed in this duty, it was necessary for the international community to intervene, ideally through the UN, but otherwise through the action of regional organisations of responsible law-abiding states (International Commission on Intervention and State Sovereignty 2001, 51–5).

The war on terror has largely been justified in terms of self-defence. The pattern for this was set by the NATO-led military intervention in Afghanistan following the September 11 attacks. Following these attacks the SC passed Resolution 1368, which reaffirmed the inherent right of self-defence against terrorism. This was important because traditionally the UN had dealt with terrorism as a criminal activity (Frederking 2007, 160). This left the door open for military incursions against terrorists justified under Article 51 of the Charter *independently of SC authorisation*. This was the main justification deployed by the US in its occupation and transformation of Afghanistan. This necessarily involved transformations in the 'traditional' account of self-defence. Traditionally, self-defence is not conceived of as an armed reprisal. Military force can be deployed to repel an attack that has occurred, or prevent one which is *imminent*. Under the customary rules derived from the *Caroline* affair, imminence was defined as a situation where although the threat had not yet materialised the 'necessity of that self-defence is instant, overwhelming, and leaving no choice of means, and no moment for deliberation'.

In respect to Afghanistan, it was argued that terrorism represented a continuous and continuing threat to the US. Of course, since there was no immediate threat, this also necessarily involved a changed understanding of what imminence was to mean. Here, the Bush administration argued that in the changed conditions of the post-9/11 age, where terrorists and terrorist-supporting states could acquire weapons of great destructive power and might attack at any time, such an approach could not work. Whereas a conventional military attack could be predicted by a build-up of troops or intelligence, attacks under the new conditions simply could not be anticipated. As such, the US could not let the 'smoking bomb turn into a mushroom cloud' (Blitzer 2003) and would have to intervene pre-emptively.

The doctrine also ran into the problem that in the traditional understanding of self-defence there also needed to be a connection between the armed attack suffered and the state against which force was used. This was negotiated in various ways – through the idea that there was a right of self-defence directly against non-state actors (Trapp 2007) or that rogue or failed states were incapable of controlling terrorism and hence needed to be intervened in (Murphy 2002, 50). The net result of this was the legal framework for the war on terror, whereby the US essentially asserted its right to spatially and temporally unlimited military intervention. Although this is known as the 'Bush Doctrine', it has in fact been the primary legal justification that the Obama government has deployed in its continuing military interventions (Koh 2010).

One intervention not mentioned in the above accounts but which animated a great deal of political and legal debate was the second invasion of Iraq in 2003. Some – although none in the governments of the invading coalition – made an argument for pre-emptive self-defence (Sofaer 2003). Others made a humanitarian argument. This did find itself expressed by some government officials but was not the 'official' legal position. Instead the argument was that – even without a SC Resolution explicitly authorising the use of force – the SC had implicitly authorised this. Thus it was argued that because of Resolution 1441, which declared Iraq was in 'material breach' of its international obligations under Resolution 687, which revived the earlier Resolution 678, there was no need for a second resolution to authorise the use of force (Gray 2008, 358–66).

Of vetoes and rivalries

This brief excursion into the ways in which law has been used to frame military interventions is important because it allows us to pose an important question. While all of the interventions described above operate according to a racialised imperial logic, the particular legal form that this racialisation takes has varied. Crucially, given the uncontroversial nature and broad scope of Chapter VII authorisations, why has *this* been a relatively rare form of legal argument?

The importance of this question is that it undermines any notion of racialization as primary and binary. While the war on terror and humanitarian intervention *are* racialised forms of legal argument, this racialization could have been carried out through other, less controversial, legal arguments, so some other factor must be in play. One obvious point about the interventions described above is that they all legally authorise action outside of the SC, and so away from the possibility of a veto.

The significance of this can be illuminated by examining debates on the form and nature of imperialism. As previously noted, many contemporary accounts rely on an understanding of imperialism which foregrounds almost exclusively the relationship between a 'core' and a 'periphery'. While most accounts of imperialism do accept this division to some degree, there have been disagreements about the degree to which one can say that there is a unified 'core' of imperialist powers, or whether there is rivalry between them (Brewer 1990, 89).

In the 'classical' accounts of imperialism, this was incredibly important. For Kautsky the tendency of imperialism was towards creating a single world trust, in which the imperialist powers would collectively exploit the rest of the world (1970). Against this, Lenin and Bukharin insisted that the tendency of imperialism was towards creating intensified military and political competition between rival imperialist powers (Bukharin 1972, 133–43). In present times the debate about rivalry has resurfaced sharply, although the question now concerns the development of the United States into the world's 'sole superpower'. Here the issue has been whether the strength of US imperialism is such that it has no 'rivals' to speak of, but is instead able to dominate the globe through its overwhelming military and economic power. In such accounts, the use of the legal doctrines of humanitarian intervention and the war on terror is seen as a sign of the unopposed dominance of US hegemonic ambition (Amin 2006, 112–13).

However, the above examination suggests the contrary. While there was a period in which the particular imperialist coalition led by the US was able to act through international institutions in a relatively uncontroversial way, this was short-lived. Hence, in the brief period around the end of the Cold War, when Russia and China were at their weakest, it was possible to rely on arguments through the Security Council (Brenner 1991, 132). Yet as the position of these states in the international order was strengthened, they were able to plausibly threaten the power of wielding their veto within the SC.

In all of the interventions described above, the resort to legal justifications outside of the SC was driven by the knowledge that a veto was forthcoming. In the case of Kosovo, it was widely understood that given Russia's traditional closeness with Serbia, and political interests in the region, it would veto any attempt at authorising the use of force (Chinkin 1999, 842). Indeed, both Russia and China attempted to pass a resolution condemning the NATO bombing (Gray 2008, 42). The war on terror is more complicated. Initially, there was a great deal of international sympathy for the US, and Russia and China both had an interest in seeing an end to the Taliban (Frederking 2007, 168). However, even at the time, the Chinese government was sufficiently assertive that it attempted to impose a series of conditions on any military mission, and it was likely for this reason that the United States instead sought to rely on self-defence (Frederking 2007, 165). By the time of further interventions under the rubric of the war on terror, Russia and China had grown sufficiently combative as to render any SC Resolutions unlikely. Here, therefore, it seems that the particular *form* of legal argument adopted, was driven by the need to circumvent *imperialist rivals*.

Viewed from this perspective, we can begin to see further commonalities. Essentially, in the cases surveyed above a similar pattern of argument has occurred. When the US (and its allies) were blocked by the threat of a veto by the SC, it was necessary to articulate a legal doctrine that would give them freedom of action. When such a legal doctrine was articulated it always began by positing that an event, or series of events, represented a threat to the international system *as a whole*. Following this, it was then asserted that owing to the actions of the certain states – typically Russia and China – who were acting *against* the interests of the world order, the 'normal' channels of international law were blocked. As such, the argument proceeded, it was necessary for a select group of states to act as *guardians* of the system, moving outside of its 'normal' channels in order to protect it. Crucially, the rival states are *not* part of this select group and so are not able to rely on these special legal privileges.

This structure of legal argument bears a great deal of similarity to what Gerry Simpson has called 'legalised hegemony'. Simpson argues that the international legal order has been structured by the presence of elite states with special legal 'privileges, rights and duties' (Simpson 2004, 68). In this system, elite states are able to entrench their status *through* international law, by claiming to uphold the system as a whole. In Simpson's account, one can only find the presence of Great Powers when they act *collectively* to guard the system as a whole. Consequently, for him, during the Cold War there were no Great Powers, just 'superpowers' vying for dominance (2004, 75). Here, then, Simpson also reflects a 'binary' understanding of imperialism. Yet this seems unwise. Taking the last 100 years, it can hardly be said that 'harmony' between the major powers has characterised their interactions or their position in the international legal system. Instead there have been two world wars, and a Cold War that Simpson explicitly argues was not one of Great Powers. Thus, on Simpson's own reading, what he describes as the 'normal' situation of the international legal order would in fact be aberrant.

If, on the other hand, we understand the linkage between attempts to articulate legalised hegemony and inter-imperialist *rivalry* a different picture emerges. Rather than seeing legalised hegemony as a sign of unified imperialist strength we can now see it as a sign of fragmented imperial weakness. Imperialist states attempt to legally entrench their hegemonic position when their rivals are able to act through the 'normal' channels of international law and so block their ability to act.

On this reading, the doctrines of humanitarian intervention and the war on terror are a response to the increasing power of China and Russia internationally, which is reflected in their willingness to use the 'normal' mechanism of the SC to thwart their imperial rival. In response to this, the United States has attempted to create legal doctrines that entrench its ability to intervene in the peripheries without running the risk of a veto. A necessary component of this is also that these other states *cannot* use these doctrines and intervene in such a way.

The racialised nature of these doctrines needs to be seen in this light. Most obviously, we can no longer see race as the 'primary' issue here. The drive to create 'Others' is not able to explain the particular legal forms that racialisation takes. It is more conjunctural issues that condition this form, with inter-imperialist rivalry being a key aspect of these conjunctural issues. This also sheds light on the flaws of the 'binary' account. The issue is not simply who is intervening and who is being intervened in, but also, who is permitted to intervene and who is not. Imperial rivals *themselves* are cast in racialised roles: usually in terms of being irrational or selfish, which is said to be deeply rooted in their internal, non-liberal regimes. This – in a more mild form – mirrors the colonial language of civilisation. The purpose of this characterisation is both to justify acting outside of the SC *and* to prevent these rival states from relying on these doctrines. Crucially, however, such doctrines are not designed to justify direct military intervention against the rival states. In this way a rigid civilised/uncivilised dichotomy is problematised because there is a more fragile attempt to articulate a hierarchy within the advanced capitalist countries.

Here, one particularly pertinent example would be the attempt to divide between 'Old Europe' and 'New Europe' in the run-up to the 2003 Iraq war. However, the most important examples in this respect are Russia and China. Hence in the 2002 National Security Strategy speech, alongside the idea of rogue states there were heavy references to 'Russia's uneven commitment to the basic values of free-market democracy' and China 'following an outdated path' of 'threaten[ing] its neighbors' (National Security Strategy 2002). Even with Obama's 'liberal' 2010 National Security Strategy one can find similar references. Indeed, in November of 2011 Obama demanded that China 'act like a grownup', whilst outlining his plans to expand and consolidate US influence in the Asia-Pacific region (The Guardian 2011).

Inter-imperialist rivalry has therefore been central in two respects. First, the particular *legal form* that the racialisation of the peripheries takes is driven by the need to undercut imperial rivals. Second because these rivals are themselves directly racialised, so to prevent them from utilising these doctrines and undermine their position in the world order.

Materialist race theory

History, rivalry, territory

Although the above account has been limited primarily to considerations of the law on the use of force, it has much broader implications. This chapter has argued that while the law on the use of force clearly is racialised, one cannot simply understand this racialisation as a process of creating a group of 'Others', who are outside of the normal protections of international law and can be intervened in with impunity. Instead, it has argued that one of the crucial dimensions of racialisation is to carve out a space for imperialist states and their allies to act in the face of rival interests, while at the same time attempting to racialise those rivals in such as way as to prevent them from utilising these doctrines.

This dynamic does not simply occur at the level of the law on the use of force. For instance, James Gathii (2002) has argued that inter-imperialist rivalry was a central part of the law on the acquisition and maintenance of title to territory. While it is clear that these rules initially served to posit non-European (and perhaps more importantly, non-capitalist) territories as mere 'objects', thus rendering them open to European acquisition and colonialism, the rules that concerned this acquisition of territory were concerned with regulating the relative claims of different European powers (Gathii 2002, 599). The particular modes in which territory could be acquired and the relationship between them was always rooted in the European competition to exploit the non-European peripheries.

One ought not to forget, for instance, that while the Berlin Conference did impose European territorial organisation on non-European societies, this was largely in response to inter-imperialist rivalries. The scramble for Africa was seen as generating intense rivalry between European powers, which needed to be managed. The aim of the Conference was to clarify how Africa was to be divided and according to what rules, so as to mediate between different European claims.

Thus, in the same moment international law was both subordinating non-European societies and mediating between the various European states that were claiming these territories. Thus, as Matt Craven notes, one cannot simply view treaties between colonial powers and tribal chiefs as being purely concerned with the relationship between colonial powers and tribal chiefs:

> It is perfectly plausible to argue that, so far as the colonial powers were concerned, such treaties were not concluded with the local 'sovereigns' in mind at all, but functioned rather as a means of demonstrating a relationship of authority or control to other European powers.
>
> *(Craven 2007, 21)*

If one was to deal with these questions purely in terms of the 'primary/binary' understanding – in which the international law on territory was simply about the creation of racialised 'Others' whose land could be appropriated – then the question arises as to why law was needed at all? One might, perhaps, argue that it served a justificatory or ideological role. But justification for whom? Surely not for those who were subject to imperial and colonial domination and whose resistance occurred irrespective of what international law decreed. Equally, it seems unlikely that it is designed to assuage any doubts of the populaces of imperial metropoles, who had very little access to international legal expertise.

Even if one were able to construct such an argument, it could not account for why this racial ideology would take the specific form of law. The most distinctive feature of law is that it resolves disputes between abstract, formally equal actors, whilst maintaining their equality (Miéville 2005). Internationally, the disputes between abstract, formally equal actors can be nothing other than inter-imperialist rivalry: with the historical actors in the Family of Nations, treating each other as formal equals whose disputes arose over the 'property' represented by the 'unciv-ilised world'. As such, we might conclude with Pashukanis that the 'real historical content of international law, therefore, is the struggle between capitalist states' with the remainder 'a simple object of their completed transactions' (Pashukanis 1980, 172).

Anghie (2005, 6) argues that simply focusing on the question of 'order among sovereign states' – which has been a central concern of the international legal dis-cipline – is incorrect because it cannot 'illuminate the prior question of how certain states were excluded from the realm of sovereignty in the first place'. On one level this is absolutely correct. However, he further argues that the real generating force of international law is its confrontation with and management of cultural difference (Anghie 2005, 37). The problem with this account is that it falsely assumes there is a duality between these two approaches. What the above suggests is that the management of cultural difference and the question of 'order among sovereign states' are part of the *same process of imperialism*. Here we can say that law articulates both in the same moment.

Thus, in their rivalries, imperialist states need to assert their interests as against other imperialist states, and this is achieved through the form of law, which acknowledges their status as formally equal. In the absence of this dynamic it is difficult to know why it is that a need for law would have arisen in the first place. Territory could have been appropriated through direct force, and any number of justifications could have been deployed to defend this.

Race and rivalry

The consequence of all this is that it is necessary to go beyond seeing 'race' as the primary driving force of legal argument. It is only in this way that the particular legal *forms* that racism takes can be adequately accounted for. Interestingly, the question of the changing forms of racialisation was also one that dominated Franz Fanon's attempts to theorise a materialist concept of race. Fanon was clear that racism can in no sense be seen as the primary driving force of imperialist processes (2008, 100), and instead argued that it must be traced to the material structures of those societies which exhibit racism (2008, 87 and 202).

As such, he viewed it as his task to trace the material conditions that produce race as a specific *social relation*. Like many authors, Fanon began with the idea that racism arises from the phenomenon of exploitation. In basic terms, he argued, racism is generated by the 'shameless exploitation of one group of men by another which has reached a higher stage of technical development' (1967, 38). In his account racism is the 'most visible' and 'day-to-day' element of the 'systematised hierarchisa-tion' that results from imperialist exploitation (1967, 32). For Fanon the material basis of imperialism – that of capitalist exploitation – necessitates the oppression and transformation of subject populations, as well as the justification for this exploita-tion. This gives rise to forms of racial difference, which posit subject populations as inferior and compel practices aimed at erasing their distinctive cultural identities

(Fanon 1967, 41). At the same time race is not *reducible* to this basic relationship. The material conditions of imperialism mean that 'race' is not simply a 'super-structural' phenomenon, but rather takes on a key role in organising the distribution of the material benefits of imperialism (Fanon 1963, 40).

While arguing that this basic logic is what gives rise to the general phenomenon of racism, Fanon was also keen to understand the way in which specific material configurations gave rise to distinctive forms of racism. For Fanon, if racism was part of a broader system of imperialist exploitation, then changes in this system would also result in changing forms of racism (1967, 32). In his account, with the development of more complex forms of capitalist exploitation, racism moved from a crude, biological determinism, to a more subtle form of cultural racism, since the exploitation of which racism is an articulation becomes increasingly covert:

> Progressively, however, the evolution of techniques of production, the industrialization, limited though it is, of the subjugated countries, impose a new attitude upon the occupant. The complexity of the means of production, the evolution of economic relations inevitably involving the evolution of ideologies, unbalance the system. Vulgar racism in its biological form corresponds to the period of crude exploitation of man's arms and legs. The perfecting of the means of production inevitably brings about the camouflage of the techniques by which man is exploited, hence the forms of racism.
>
> *(Fanon 1967, 35)*

Thus, while Fanon did – to some degree – subscribe to a 'binary' understanding of racism, he nonetheless attempted to explain its changing forms by reference to the transformations in material conditions. While this does provide the foundation of what a materialist account of race's role in international law might be, it does not yet provide a sufficient explanation for how we might understand the role of inter-imperialist rivalry.

The particular understanding evinced by Fanon is obviously one which has undergirded a number of materialist accounts of race. Indeed the very idea of a 'global colour line' is premised upon such an account, since it concerns 'how far differences of race, which show themselves chiefly in the color of the skin and the texture of the hair, are … the basis of denying to over half the world the right of sharing [in] … the opportunities and privileges of modern civilization' (Du Bois 1970, 258–9). However, such accounts fail to deal both with the explicit racialisation of imperial rivals that takes place in legal terms and with how the racialisation of the exploited is *driven* by this rivalry.

Despite some rhetorical declarations to the contrary, one ought not to overstate the degree to which these authors actually hold to a 'Manichean' or binary vision of racialisation, in which the only division is between 'White' and 'not-White'. Fanon, for example also argued that racialisation also involves stratification. In a process that Fanon dubs the 'racial distribution of guilt', he argued that a key move of imperial powers is to differentiate between the various oppressed and exploited minorities, so as to co-opt them and set them against one another. Hence, the Arab is told the Jew exploits him, the Jew is told he is better than the Arabs, the Negro is told he is the best soldier in the Empire, and so on (Fanon 2008, 103). In this way racial 'inferiors' are subject to further 'sub-divisions' and hierarchies, with relative levels of privilege and entitlement flowing according to these sub-divisions. This enables oppressed populations to be better managed and for their resistance and antagonism to the existing order to be diverted and channelled.

This understanding of the role of race as stratifying the oppressed and exploited is one which has also driven a number of materialist explanations of the domestic role of racism. Materialist scholars of labour and race, such as David Roediger, have stressed the role that racial discourse has played as a 'strategy of rule' through constituting a certain part of the working class as racially privileged – attracting a series of economic, political and ideological benefits – and therefore enabling them to divide and manage labour (Roediger 2008; Roediger and Esch 2012).

What these analyses point to is that on top of a fundamental division thrown up by imperialist exploitation, processes of racialisation are shaped by a number of 'tactical' and 'conjunctural' imperatives. While managing particular antagonisms is one important aspect of these, it is not difficult to see how rivalries with other powers also enter into the picture. Roediger, for instance, notes that in seventeenth-century America '[m]ercantile goals combined with security concerns to encourage continued distinctions between Indian tribes and individuals … not as an undifferentiated race' (2008, 21). Here, a vital element determining the racialisation of 'Indians', was the desire to secure exclusive trading rights and undercut rival powers. This, then, explains how inter-imperialist rivalry might be able to enter into a materialist account of racialisation. Equally, once this concern with rivalry is brought into the issue of stratification more broadly, we can ask why racialisation might not function directly to stratify potential *rivals*?

One can imagine explanations for why this was not taken up by 'Third World' Marxist theorists of race. At the time in which they were writing, the 'Third World' was in the midst of a generalised uprising against the colonial and neo-colonial powers. In this struggle they were frequently aided by the USSR and the other Soviet bloc countries, which they understood to be in some sense non-capitalist. In these conditions, it is unsurprising that inter-imperialist rivalry does not feature heavily, although there was some acknowledgment of the differences between various imperial powers (Fanon 1963, 79) because much of the imperialist world *was* unified against them, and so not warring amongst itself.

Yet in the period that followed, the changing material conditions gave rise to a new configuration in which the 'Third World' became an entirely different political actor – either disempowered or de-radicalised. At the same time, importance has shifted to the actions of the United States and its contestation by European states, Russia and China. Thus if, with Fanon, we expect racial forms to change in line with material conditions, we can argue the following: racialisation is *directly generated* – in part – by imperialist exploitation, positing a Manichean division in which the oppressed and exploited are seen – and treated as – inferior to their oppressors and exploiters. Yet within this Manichean division there are also further 'sub-divisions' in which the racially 'inferior' are themselves sub-divided into degrees of greater on lesser inferiority. It is in this way that race becomes linked to the management of social antagonism.

At the same time, the material structure of imperialism also creates intense rivalries. The dual tendencies within capitalist imperialism of territorialisation (Anievas 2008, 201) and the intensification of international competition serve as an important material condition for the generation of racial discourses. This basic material drive is fundamental in conditioning the *forms* that the racialisation of the peripheries takes, with imperial powers attempting to assert different forms of racialisation so as to tactically undercut their rivals in addition to tactically stratifying the oppressed.

At the same time, this international competition directly throws up discourses of racialisation against rival imperialist states. Such discourses have been – in one way or another – a relatively common feature of life under capitalism, particularly in periods of increased economic and military competition or periods of crisis. However, these are much weaker forms than those generated through exploitation, liable to shift at a given moment and are much more amenable to tactical deployment. Given international law's close connection to processes of imperialism, this is reflected in the racial patterns that international law embodies and articulates.

Conclusion

The ultimate conclusion of this chapter is that we must understand the 'global colour line' in more complex ways. It is not simply a 'line' which divides black from white, or civilised from uncivilised. While there is a basic, fundamental racialised division, founded on the differentiation between the advanced imperialist powers and the peripheral formations, this itself shifts according to a whole series of con-junctural and tactical imperatives. At the same time, there are a number of other lines which intersect with it, as imperial powers attempt to stratify their rivals, without ever putting them on the other side of the more foundational colour line. Understanding this complex picture is key to understanding how to navigate contemporary imperialism. Failing to take this into account can lead to an overly simplified picture in which opposition to the US is seen as always and automatically 'anti-imperialist'.

This becomes even more important in the context of international law's intimate relationship with these racialised processes. This chapter has attempted to show that international law plays an absolutely key role in instantiating the racialised relations of imperialism, with rivalry being a key part of this process. A corollary of this is that one must be extremely suspicious of those claiming to uphold the UN as against US unilateralism. This has been a very strong tendency among the left, widely considered. As this article has argued, even the most 'normal' and 'uncontroversial' multilateral interventions remain racialised and imperialist (Miéville 2008).

Thus, as Akbar Rasulov has argued, one should understand much of the oppo-sition to the US 'unilateralism' as the equivalent of a kind of feudal socialism.

Other powers attempt to re-assert their own position in the imperial order through clinging to international law in a manner analogous to the feudal aristocracy rebuking the bourgeoisie (Rasulov 2010, 466). In these circumstances one cannot simply counterpose the imperialist, unilateral and racialised uses of force by the US to the UN Charter regime. To do so is to miss the way in which these oppositions are playing out a contested process of inter-imperialist rivalry. Any anti-imperialist project must instead take aim at the material relations of imperialism and their complex racial articulation, a project that must go beyond the mere assertion of legality.

Note

1 My thanks to the organisers and the peer-reviewers of the original CRIA symposium where a rather different version of this article was debuted. For this particular article, I would like to extend my thanks to the usual Hive-mind subjects (you know who you are) for providing me with a sounding board for these kind of ideas (and frequently for the Port which generated them); putting themselves through the horror of reading my drafts, and enduring my neurotic responses. Most of my thanks have to go to Alex Anievas, for commissioning this, reading it, and then relentlessly prodding me for a draft until I felt ready to strangle him. As usual, I am not allowed to blame any errors on anyone else, so all errors of style and substance remain mine alone.

Bibliography

Anghie, Antony (2005) *Imperialism, Sovereignty and the Making of International Law* (Cambridge: Cambridge University Press)
——(2005a) 'The War on Terror and Iraq in Historical Perspective', *Osgoode Hall Law Journal*, 43:1, 45–66
Amin, Samir (2006) *Beyond US Hegemony? Assessing the Prospects for a Multipolar Road* (London: Zed Books)
Anievas, Alexander (2008) 'Theories of a Global State: A Critique', *Historical Materialism*, 16:2, 190–206
Bartholomew, Amy (ed) (2006) *Empire's Law: The American Imperial Project and the 'War to Remake the World'* (London: Pluto Press)
Blitzer, Wolf (2003) 'Search for the "Smoking Gun"', available at: http://articles.cnn.com/2003-01-10/us/wbr.smoking.gun_1_smoking-gun-nuclear-weapons-hans-blix
Bowring, Bill (2008) *The Degradation of the International Legal Order? The Rehabilitation of Law and the Possibility of Politics* (Oxford: Routledge-Cavendish)
Brenner, Robert (1991) 'Why is the United States at War with Iraq?' *New Left Review*, 185: Jan/Feb, 122–37
Brewer, Anthony (1990) *Marxist Theories of Imperialism: A Critical Survey* (London: Routledge)
Bukharin, Nikolai (1972) *Imperialism and World Economy* (London: The Merlin Press)
Callinicos, Alex (2009) *Imperialism and Global Political Economy* (Cambridge: Polity Press)
Chimni, Bhupinder S. (2004) 'International Institutions Today: An Imperial Global State in the Making', *European Journal of International Law*, 15:1, 1–37
Chinkin, Christine (1999) 'Kosovo: a "Good" or "Bad" War?', *American Journal of International Law*, 93:4, 841–47
Craven, Matt (2007) 'Introduction', in Matt Craven, Malgosia Fitzmaurice and Maria Vogiatzi (eds) *Time History and International Law* (Leiden, Netherlands: Martinus Nijhoff Publishers), 1–27

de Cuéllar, Javier Pérez (1989) 'Nobel Lecture', available at www.nobelprize.org/nobel _prizes/peace/laureates/1988/un-lecture.html

Du Bois, W. E. B. (1970) 'Address to the Nations of the World', in Philip S. Foner (ed) *W.E.B. Du Bois Speaks: Speeches and Addresses 1890–1919* (New York, US: Pathfinder Press), 124–28

Fanon, Frantz (2008) *Black Skin, White Masks* (New York, US: Grove Press)

——(1963) *The Wretched of the Earth* (New York, US: Grove Press)

——(1967) *Toward the African Revolution* (New York, US: Grove Press)

Frederking, Brian (2007) *The United States and the Security Council: Collective Security Since the Cold War*, (London: Routledge)

Gathii, James Thuo (2002) 'Geographical Hegelianism in Territorial Disputes Involving Non-European Land Relations', *Leiden Journal of International Law*, 15:3, 581–622

Gray, Christine (2008) *International Law and the Use of Force* (Oxford: Oxford University Press)

Henkin, Louis (1999) 'Kosovo and the Law of "Humanitarian Intervention"', *American Journal of International Law*, 93:4, 824–8

International Commission on Intervention and State Sovereignty (2001) 'The Responsibility to Protect', available at http://responsibilitytoprotect.org/ICISS%20Report.pdf

Kautsky, Karl (1970) 'Ultra-Imperialism', *New Left Review*, 59: Jan/Feb, 41–6

Knox, Robert (2013) 'Civilizing Interventions? Race, War and International Law', *Cambridge Review of International Affairs*, 26:1, 111–32

Koh, Harold Hongju (2010) 'The Obama Administration and International Law', available at www.state.gov/s/l/releases/remarks/139119.htm

Lobel, Jules and Ratner, Michael (1999) 'Bypassing the Security Council: Ambiguous Authorizations to Use Force, Cease-Fires and the Iraqi Inspection Regime', *American Journal of International Law*, 93:1, 124–54

Marks, Susan (2003) 'Empire's Law', *Indiana Journal of Global Legal Studies*, 10:1, 449–65

Miéville, China (2005) *Between Equal Rights: A Marxist Theory of International Law* (Leiden, Netherlands: Historical Materialism Books, Brill)

——(2008) 'Multilateralism as Terror', *Finnish Yearbook of International Law*, 19, 63–95

Mutua, Makau Wa (2001) 'Savages, Victims and Saviors: The Metaphor of Human Rights', *Harvard International Law Journal*, 42:1, 201–45

Murphy, Sean D. (2002) 'Terrorism and the Concept of Armed Attack in Article 51 of the UN Charter', *Harvard International Law Journal*, 43:1, 43–51

National Security Strategy (2002), available at *http://georgewbush-whitehouse.archives.gov/nsc/ nss/2002/*

——(2010), available at *www.whitehouse.gov/sites/default/files/rss_viewer/national_security_strategy.pdf*

Pashukanis, Evgeny (1980) 'International Law', in Piers Beirne and Robert Sharlet (eds) *Pashukanis: Selected Writings on Marxism and Law* (London: Academic Press), 168–83

Rasulov, Akbar (2010) 'Writing about Empire: Remarks on the Logic of a Discourse', *Leiden Journal of International Law*, 23:2, 449–71

Reisman, W. Michael (1999) 'Kosovo's Antinomies', *American Journal of International Law*, 93:4, 860–62

Roediger, David R. (2008) *How Race Survived US History: From the American Revolution to the Present* (London: Verso)

Roediger, David R. and Esch, Elizabeth D. (2012) *The Production of Difference: Race and the Management of Labor in US History* (Oxford: Oxford University Press)

Said, Edward W. (1994) *Culture and imperialism* (London: Vintage Books)

Schachter, Oscar (1991) 'United Nations Law in the Gulf Conflict', *American Journal of International Law*, 85:3, 452–73

Seymour, Richard (2011) 'War on Terror as Political Violence', available at http://lse.aca demia.edu/RichardSeymour/Papers/386719/The_war_on_terror_as_political_violence

Simpson, Gerry (2004) *Great Powers and Outlaw States: Unequal Sovereigns in the International Legal Order* (Cambridge: Cambridge University Press)

Sofaer, Abraham (2003) 'On the Necessity of Pre-emption', *European Journal of International Law*, 14:2, 209–26

The *Guardian* (2011) 'Obama's Pacific tour: South China Sea change', 17 November, available at www.guardian.co.uk/commentisfree/2011/nov/17/obama-pacific-tour-south-china-sea

Trapp, Kimberley N. (2007) 'Back to Basics: Necessity, Proportionality, and the Right of Self-Defence Against Non-State Terrorist Actors', *International and Comparative Law Quarterly*, 56:1, 141–56

Wedgwood, Ruth (1999) 'NATO's Campaign in Yugoslavia' *American Journal of International Law*, 93:4, 828–34

PART III

Reflections on the global colour line

11

WHAT WOULD IT MEAN TO TRANSFORM INTERNATIONAL RELATIONS?

David Roediger

In the middle 1970s I was carrying around an early issue of *Dialectical Anthropology* and ran into a very distinguished, very senior radical historian of Africa. He glanced at the title and offered, 'At last anthropology has a journal to preside over its own demise.' I was at the time preoccupied with getting next week's seminar readings done, not the fate of disciplines, but I have often since thought of that remark when trying to change a discipline, sub-discipline, or inter-discipline—or more often when rooting for others trying to do so – in ways that run up against the history, logic, and limits of the enterprise being challenged. What is it to champion a critical legal theory? To forward critical management studies? To queer imperial history? Before considering the tremendous possibilities raised by this volume, it is apposite to think briefly about the project of bringing IR into confrontation with both the loudly proclaimed theories of racial hierarchy at its origins and the stealthy racialization of its recent past and present.

My own meager experience in this regard is all outside of IR but may be instructive. As a partisan of the 'new labor history' in the 1970s, I saw a sub-discipline transformed to the point that virtually every study proclaimed its distance from the 'old labor history.' Old Left Marxism and the moderate union-centered studies growing out of labor economics and industrial relations programs were even-handedly denounced in favor of social history, study of working-class everyday life, and emphasis on movements from below. Nevertheless, today labor history has, with the collapse of trade unions and above all of strikes, become a more marginal sub-field. It is, with noteworthy exceptions, also too often a mainstream enterprise dedicated in large measure to defense of the historical record of dwindling bureaucratized unions. The episodic but flattering attention paid by the disastrous John Sweeney leadership of the American Federation of Labor to labor historians quickened this transition. In some cases spectacular rightward political motion of leading figures of the 'new history' as they positioned themselves as mainstream pundits and even politicians of the center-right was involved. In the cases of Sean Wilentz (2014) in the United States and Michael Ignatieff (2003) in Britain and Canada, inventions in international relations highlighted the repositioning away from history 'from below.' But most of the drift of the field followed from changed political circumstances. What seemed possible in the glow of the freedom movements and wildcat strikes of the 1960s and 1970s proved difficult to sustain.

Thus, if building a 'Critical IR' – aware of race and empire – is a goal, close attention to the political terrain that makes such an initiative possible or not would seem imperative. Such would apply with special force in IR in that, unlike labor history, the field has traditionally included and lionized those who are active players in imperial policy debates. They are bound with the best intentions to be pulled toward a 'left wing of the possible' set of positions and assumptions (and sadly often then to move further towards and beyond the center than that) that can only contest epistemological groundings of the discipline within sharp limits. Part of me thinks that to transform International Relations it would be necessary to transform international relations.

Then too there is the peril of transforming a discipline in ways that makes further transformations more difficult. As Srdjan Vucetic's fascinating essay in this volume points out, Charles Mills has recently written of his own discipline, philosophy, as 'one of the very "whitest" of the humanities.' Many of the essays – perhaps we always best see, once we see them, the limits of our own endeavors – make an eloquent case that IR fits that 'whitest' bill as well. I would also want to throw labor history into that mix. The 'from below' emphasis that I hoped would open the study of workers up to the full consideration of race has often and disappointingly left consideration of the decisive role of workers of color, and the disoriented position of white workers, inadequately examined. I make this point in connection with my one reservation regarding the present volume. While the editorial introduction makes a strong call for transformative work on gender, as well as on racialization and empire, only one essay – the powerful contribution of Randolph Persaud – fully delivers an analysis of gender. Not coincidentally it also offers the fullest treatment of labor in the collection. Remarking on this point comes not out of any criticism of the other essays but out of a sense of the possibilities that might open up with the consideration of sexuality and gender. In the case of Richard Seymour's superb piece in the volume, for example, it is true that 'red' and 'black' were the colors that excited Cold War concern. But, as David Johnson details in his important 2003 study *The Lavender Scare: Cold War Persecution of Gays and Lesbians in the Federal Government*, the pink or lavender color of homosexuality also structured anxieties in ways deeply imbricated with discourses on race and radicalism. The Cold War state paired homophobia and security insistently. I also offer this point as a caution. It is easy to imagine that the breath of fresh air this volume represents will automatically open up all manner of other discussions. In my experience this is not necessarily the case.

The one other attempt to intervene in the workings of knowledge production that I have been a part of bears more directly on this volume and on the invitation extended to me to help to conclude it. That arena is the critical study of whiteness, as it has anarchically developed in the last two decades (for an overview, see Roediger, 2011). In many ways, those of us writing in this area faced the same problems that those bringing race and empire consciously (back) into IR confront. That is, both seek to lay bare the extent to which an open identification with white supremacy and white advantage structured much of the world before 1945 and that a less-announced commitment to whiteness has continued to shape the more recent past. (For IR, John Hobson's reference in this volume to the 'subliminal strategy' within which race-thinking operates is especially deft.) But institutionally the settings differ greatly. While IR exists as a distinct and weighty specialization to be transformed, there happily were and are no 'whiteness studies' to be remade – unless we think of the university itself as embodying such an agenda. Nor, with the important exception of the Australian Critical Race and Whiteness Studies Association, have scholars studying whiteness critically sought to create institutions. In my case and that of many others the idea of critical whiteness studies as an intervention within ethnic studies has cut against any desire for, say, centers for the study of whiteness. I suspect that this lack of desire for a disciplinary presence has had some advantages in terms of keeping ambitions realistic and foregrounding an emphasis on productive working networks of co-thinkers. A similar set of sensibilities toward what is possible and desirable in changing academia is found in the development of queer of color critique in the recent past, mainly in the United States.[1]

None of this is to say that the transformation of IR along the lines laid out in the stimulating essays in this collection is less than important or even less than possible. Actually, *Dialectical Anthropology* has managed to produce wonderful scholarship in the face of a burdensome past and an often miserable present. It is to say that the collective effort of producing a volume like this is as important as the immediate and measurable impact that it makes.

From its title forward, *Confronting the Global Colour Line* pays apt tribute to the work of W. E. B. Du Bois. His insights directly structure the introduction as well as several of the essays. However, whether Du Bois establishes even a small foothold in the history of IR for critical race theory is a complex question. Especially welcome is Errol Henderson's important evocation of Du Bois' 1915 essay 'The African Roots of the War,' published in *Atlantic Monthly*. In redirecting attention to the article's brilliance in anticipating Lenin's later writings on imperialism and the war, Henderson permits entry into the question of how Du Bois was able to make such searing arguments within the context of a popular US magazine. Later he would likewise do so within what were at the time venues announcing the maturation of IR as a discipline. Certainly personal genius matters much here, but so too did the fact that the United States was not a competitor in the scramble for a formal African empire that Du Bois connected to the war. Nor was it yet officially on a side in the alliances organizing inter-imperial rivalry during the war.

When the United States did enter the war, Du Bois' 'Close Ranks' charted a course very different from Lenin's. Much criticized from the left, Du Bois' not very critical support for the war was tied to promises of postwar civil rights gains at home and the possibility of appeals to Wilsonian internationalism on behalf of the colonized world. Being at once a 'socialist of the path,' a US 'race man,' and an anticolonial internationalist – being both an outsider and an outsider sometimes invited onto the margins of policy debates – made Du Bois a fount of complex ideas but also a contradictory figure. Alberto Toscano's forthcoming '"America's Belgium": W. E. B. Du Bois on Race, Class, and the Origins of World War' (2014) is perhaps the most surefooted and balanced elucidation of these matters (see also Allen, Jr. 1979). Nor is Du Bois alone in these complexities. In some ways the radical African American intellectual and later diplomat Ralph Bunche, author of the important 1936 volume *A World View of Race*, represents an even more vivid example of IR accommodating and incorporating anti-racist critique.

Toscano's work is also useful to this project for its extremely sophisticated appreciation of Du Bois as internationalist and nevertheless a thinker highly shaped by specifically combatting binary Jim Crow color lines in the United States. The editors' introduction, and in a different way Robert Knox's essay, well remind us that there was not a singular color transnationally and that simple binaries ought to be interrogated. Indeed Du Bois' famous identification of the color line as the 'problem of the twentieth century' occurs not once but twice in his 1903 collection *Souls of Black Folk*. The book's second sentence reads: 'the problem of the Twentieth Century is the problem of the color-line.' This comes in the context of an appeal to the 'Gentle Reader' to care about 'the strange meaning of being black here in the dawning of the Twentieth Century.' The reader is presumably white and American and 'here' is clearly the United States. It is in returning to his prediction about the twentieth century at the outset of the second chapter of *Souls* that Du Bois defines the color line globally: 'the relation of the darker to the lighter races of men in Asia and Africa, in America and the islands of the sea.'

Confronting the color line is thus, as several of the essays make clear, about confronting extraordinarily diverse and changing sets of relations. Nevertheless, by the end of the twentieth century, though not at the end of the nineteenth, the power of US discourses regarding a black-white color to overwhelm the sprawling ways white supremacy is expressed in the world. It is regrettable that perhaps the best-known attempt to address this problem, Pierre Bourdieu and Loïc Wacquant's 1999 article in *Theory, Culture, and Society*, 'On the Cunning of Imperialist Reason,' set matters out so tendentiously, as the problem is real and nuanced (see Amado 1971, Shohat and Stam 2012). More generally, in considering the limits of United States' imperial domination and sorting out the varying ways *hegemony* is used by Gramscian scholars and by world systems theorists influencing IR – an important matter in Richard Seymour's fine essay – I highly recommend Thomas McCormick's wry and wise 1995 history *America's Half-Century*.

Balancing Du Bois' exemplary framing of matters with the fact that the history he lived let him see some things with remarkable clarity and others with less facility introduces also the question of race and international relations where European and American realities were not at the center. As some of the best of recent scholarship shows, Du Bois joined many other people of color in the United States and in the colonized world in hoping that the presence of Japan as a world power might puncture white supremacy symbolically and even aid anticolonialism materially. For Du Bois, this led for a time to profound illusions about Japanese imperialism – particularly Japanese interests and actions in Korea and China (Onishi 2013; see also Horne 2005). Again, the point here is not to diminish Du Bois' contributions but to contextualize them and to encourage work on empire and racialization outside Europe as central to transforming IR. Sankaran Krishna's bracing and astringent contribution to *Confronting the Global Colour Line* exemplifies the rich possibilities of such work.

Inevitably many of my concrete suggestions for future research agendas reflect training in history and working class studies. One area often slighted when we proceed from the United States Jim Crow color line that Du Bois sometimes invoked is that of settler colonialism. While the work of Patrick Wolfe (2001) and of Marilyn Lake and Henry Reynolds (2008) on settler colonialism is alluded to in some of the essays it ought to be underlined that this work, along with essays by the indigenous Australian scholar Aileen Moreton-Robinson (forthcoming), represents perhaps the most successful writing on white supremacy beyond national boundaries. Moreover, even as the scramble for Africa anticipated the brutalities of World War 1, the dispossession of native peoples was a proving ground for all manner of transnational genocide and incarceration. Reservation policy in the United States interested South Africa mightily and much that we see as colonial violence was also an attack on the indigenous, as in the American occupation of the Philippines. Indeed the 'doctrine of discovery' codified from various imperial experience by the United States Supreme Court in the Johnson *v.* McIntosh case on indigenous land sales in 1823 became the basis for international law on the division of spoils to a considerable extent. The relative absence of Palestine in the wide-ranging essays on offer here is perhaps suggestive of the necessity to foreground questions of settler colonialism (Cheyfitz 1993).

Likewise deserving of more attention within transformative writing on IR and racialization are questions of immigration. Within Europe, the United States, and the world the questions of who can live and work where and of who has rights are both IR matters and domestic racial issues. When the British comic Stewart Lee recalls Tory campaigns in Birmingham with leaflets headed 'If you want a nigger for a neighbour, vote Liberal or Labour,' the Conservative appeal nods toward defending white neighborhoods but also articulates immigration policy and an international hierarchy of races. When Labour's home secretary Jack Straw portrayed gypsies as immigrants who defecate in the doorways of good British citizens in 1999, or when Tories make the same pitch in 2014, the line between national and international policy is similarly breached (Seymour 2014). Indeed, immigration policy historically functioned in ways that defined transnational racial hierarchies, causing significant inter-state bitterness as they did so (Chang 2009). When migration is conditioned by willingness to serve in an imperial army, as is so well-explored in Vron Ware's 2012 study *Military Migrants: Fighting for YOUR Country*, state-making, war-making, and migration are joined.

Finally, in the United States, IR about as often abbreviates industrial relations as it does international relations. One task in future work ought to be bringing questions of race and the management of workers in (as well as from) the Global South and relatively undeveloped parts of Europe and the United States to the fore. Persaud's contribution raises this issue well around the questions of accumulation and immigration policy, using in part Walter Rodney's penetrating work on race and the control of labor in Guyana. In thinking through questions of race and production, IR scholars will again not so much be importing a new set of concerns to the field as reminding its practitioners that those concerns were present at the foundation. In 1913, writing in the third volume of the *Journal of Race Development*, which evolved into *Foreign Affairs*, Major John Finley reflected on how the United States occupation had transformed the 'Moros and pagans of the Southern Philippines.' He credited 'race development by industrial means' for the miracle that had supposedly occurred. Five years later in the same journal the anthropologist of Latin America, Philip Ainsworth Means, named the uplift of those peoples whom history had left behind as 'race appreciation.' Means' phrasing evokes both the process of accumulation and the hubris with which empire-builders ranked peoples as candidates for productivity and development. The editor of the *Journal of Race Development* urged identifying the 'best primitive races' and working on them (Finley 1913; Means 1918; Hall 1910; see also Vitalis 2010).

Transnational and comparative study of what Elizabeth Esch and I have called 'race management,' alongside what she has more recently defined as 'race development,' is difficult. It ideally demands local grounding in specific and changing relations of production and apprehension of the often fanciful nature of the imperial claims made regarding being able to understand and control racialized labor. But when done well, as in Bruce Cumings' recent accounts of transnational management and workers in gold production in Korean history, it is a key node in the story of IR and race. Moreover, production is critical to the accounts of civilizationist racism, on which so many of the best chapters in *Confronting the Global Colour Line* converge. (Branwen Gruffydd Jones' tracing of the trajectory from 'modernisation to failure' as a lens for looking at the Global South is especially noteworthy in this regard). As Esch shows in her forthcoming transnational account of Fordism in the United States, Brazil, and South Africa, *The Assembly Line and the Color Line*, the realm of production is vital to understanding IR within a world in which combined and uneven development was racialized. It also helps us to penetrate what was peculiar about United States hegemony, which was premised on claims to export management of racialized workers to the world as well as on an uneven commitment to free trade and unmatched military expenditure (Cumings 1990; Esch and Roediger 2012; Esch forthcoming).

Note

1 For a wonderful recent collection charting some of the directions of scholarship reflecting queer of color critique, see Hong and Ferguson (2011).

Bibliography

Allen, Jr. Ernest (1979) '"Close Ranks": Major Joel E. Springarn and the Two Souls of W. E. B. Du Bois,' *Contributions in Black Studies* 3, 25–38

Amado, Jorge (1971) *Tent of Miracles* (New York: Knopf)

Anievas, Alexander (ed.) (2014) *Cataclysm 1914: The First World War and the Making of Modern World Politics* (Leiden, NL: Brill Press)

Chang, Kornel (2009) 'Enforcing Transnational White Solidarity: Asian Migration and the Formation of the US-Canadian Boundary,' *American Quarterly*, 60 (3), 671–88

Cheyfitz, Eric (1993) 'Savage Law: The Plot Against American Indians in Johnson and Graham's Lessee v. M'Intosh and The Pioneers.' In Donald Pease and Amy Kaplan (eds) The Cultures of United States Imperialism (Durham: Duke University Press), 109–28

Cumings, Bruce (1990), *The Origins of the Korean War*, vol. 2, *The Roaring of the Cataract, 1947–1950* (Princeton, NJ: Princeton University Press)

Esch, Elizabeth and Roediger, David (2012) *The Production of Difference: Race and the Management of Labor in the United States* (New York: Oxford University Press)

Esch, Elizabeth (forthcoming) *The Color Line and the Assembly Line: The Ford Motor Company and the Transnational Management of Race in Brazil, South Africa, and the United States.*

Finley, John (1913) 'Race Development by Industrial Means among the Moros and Pagans in the Southern Philippines,' *Journal of Race Development*, 3 (Jan), 343–68

Hall, G. Stanley (1910) 'The Point of View toward Primitive Races,' *Journal of Race Development*, 1 (July), 5–12

Horne, Gerald (2005) *Race War! White Supremacy and Japanese Attack on the British Empire* (New York: New York University Press)

Hong, Grace Kyungwon and Ferguson, Roderick A. (eds) (2011) *Strange Affinities: The Gender and Sexual Politics of Comparative Racialization* (Durham, NC: Duke University Press)

Ignatieff, Michael (2003) *Empire Lite: Nation-Building in Bosnia, Kosovo, and Afghanistan* (London: Minerva)

Lake, Marilyn and Reynolds, Henry (2008) *Drawing the Global Colour Line: White Men's Countries and the International Challenge of Racial Equality* (Cambridge: Cambridge University Press)

Means, Philip Ainsworth (1918) 'Race Appreciation and Democracy,' *Journal of Race Development*, 9 (2), 180–84

Moreton-Robinson, Aileen (forthcoming) *White Possession and Indigenous Sovereignty Matter: Essays in Social and Cultural Criticisms*

Onishi, Yuichiro (2013) *Transpacific Antiracism: Afro-Asian Solidarity in 20th-Century Black America, Japan, and Okinawa* (New York University Press)

Roediger, David (2011) 'Accounting for the Wages of Whiteness: US Marxism and the Critical History of Race,' in Wulf Hund, David Roediger, and Jeremy Krikler (eds) *The Wages of Whiteness and Racist Symbolic Capital* (Berlin: LIT), 9–36.

Seymour, Richard (2014) 'They Shit in Doorways, Don't They?' *Lenin's Tomb* (available at: www.leninology.com/2014/01/they-shit-in-doorways-dont-they.html)

Shohat, Ella and Stam, Robert (2012) *Race in Translation: Culture Wars Around the Postcolonial Atlantic* (New York: New York University Press)

Vitalis, Robert (2010) 'The Noble American Science of Imperial Relations and its Laws of Race Development,' *Comparative Studies in Society and History*, 52 (4), 909–38

Wilentz, Sean (2014) 'Would You Feel Differently about Snowden, Assange, and Greenwald if You Knew What They Really Thought?' *New Republic*, January 19 (available at: www.newrepublic.com/article/116253/edward-snowden-glenn-greenwald-julian-assange-what-they-believe)

Wolfe, Patrick (2001) 'Land, Labor, Difference: Elementary Structures of Race' *The American Historical Review* 106 (3), 866–905

12

UNWRITING AND UNWHITENING THE WORLD

Charles W. Mills

My fellow commentator David Roediger begins on a note both personal and disciplinary, so let me follow suit. When Robbie Shilliam first e-mailed me in December 2012 with the request to do an afterword for this planned volume, I was simultaneously honored and delighted by the coincidence. For I had recently "discovered" that a revisionist body of literature was challenging the orthodoxies of mainstream international relations (IR) theory, and was eagerly devouring it: Shilliam's (2011) edited collection, *International Relations and Non-Western Thought*; Branwen Gruffydd Jones's (2006) edited collection, *Decolonizing International Relations*; John Hobson's (2012) authored *The Eurocentric Conception of World Politics*.[1] Reading this material, I felt that I was emerging into the sunlight from a Cave of Darkness – though a cave less classically Platonic than Rawlsian.

The late John Rawls is usually judged to be the most important Anglo-American political philosopher of the twentieth century (his fans would drop the qualifying "Anglo-American"), and the exclusive theme of his work is social justice (1999b). Rawls asserted in his *A Theory of Justice* – an assertion generally accepted by other mainstream political philosophers – that the best strategy for theorizing about social justice was to begin with a concept of society as "a cooperative venture for mutual advantage," regulated by rules "designed to advance the good of those taking part in it," and conceived of "as a closed system isolated from other societies" (ibid. 4, 7). In a later work on international relations, *The Law of Peoples*, this last stipulation was relaxed, but Rawls's implicitly autarkic assumptions remained: the "causes of the wealth of a people," he declared, were basically their political culture, traditions, and degree of industriousness (Rawls 1999a). So if some nations were rich while others were poor, the explanation lay in national factors.

But what – you ask – about imperialism, colonialism, genocidal white settlement, structures of global Euro-domination? Not a word. How can you even get to the coercive Euro-shaping of the world if your theoretical starting point is society as a closed system? Good question. And given the centrality of exploitation and social hierarchy to all modern societies, whether through exclusions of class, gender, race, or all of the above, how can it make sense to frame society as a cooperative venture? It can't.

So that was my introduction to political philosophy when, way back in the 1970s, I naively embarked on graduate work in the discipline which advertised itself as asking and answering the "deep" questions about humanity and the human condition. I was a citizen of a small Third World country, Jamaica, which owed its very existence to these (denied and disavowed) oppressive international forces. The Spanish under Columbus had invaded the island in 1494 (characterized to us in high school as "discovery"), and eventually been driven out by the British in 1655, ushering in three hundred years of British colonialism. The indigenous Taino people had been completely wiped out by the invaders, and the population replaced by the mass importation of enslaved Africans to work in the sugar plantations. I had been politically molded by the ferment of Michael Manley's 1970s' "democratic socialist" attempt to remedy the resulting deep class, gender, and racial inequities of neo-colonial Jamaica, and also his activism on the global stage for a more just international order (Manley 1991). And here I was in North America having to negotiate a profession 98 percent white demographically, whose leading political philosopher's conceptual apparatus seemed to offer no entrée at all for dealing theoretically with the real world I had come from.

You will understand, then, why I might have begun to think that (just possibly) I had made a wrong turn somewhere. No wonder that so much of my reading was done *outside* of philosophy – in history, sociology, political science, radical geography, black studies, Third World development, and other related fields. Nor is it surprising that my first book (Mills 1997), *The Racial Contract*, written long after my graduation (as I struggled to free myself from the bondage of orthodox frameworks) should have drawn so heavily on such material, rather than the philosophical texts which provided more darkness than enlightenment on these questions. For decades, a handful of us have been trying to force the discipline to rethink itself, but I am sorry to report that the transformation Roediger describes for labor history has yet to happen in philosophy, though admittedly – thanks to our efforts – the volume of work on race, white supremacy, "whiteness," post-colonialism, and so forth, is at least far greater than when I first entered the field.[2]

So here I am as a philosopher many years later – gratified to be invited to comment on the very kind of work that helped me to liberate myself theoretically in the first place – and seeking not merely to provide some useful "philosophical" insight in my afterword to this valuable collection of essays, but intent, again, on learning what I can draw from it to take back into *my* home discipline.

What fruitful connections could be made between philosophy and IR? Well, remember the pretensions of philosophy as a discipline that I just mentioned: the quest for deep truths. In the idealist strain of philosophy – which has of course historically been the dominant strain – the assumption has been that these truths are to be found by abstracting away from the particularities of embodied humans embedded in specific social groups and social relations with one another. One leaves the vulgar material world behind for the realm of the ideal, whether in Plato or in Rawls. But there is, of course, also the oppositional materialist tradition, which develops out of nineteenth-century Marxism to become twentieth- and twenty-first-century "critical theory." And the claim here is, on the contrary, that it is through the plunge *into* the social depths that one is more likely to come up with the concrete abstractions useful for generating the relevant ideals and for understanding the material obstacles to their realization. The human condition is less illuminated by the situation of privileged humans than by the situation of its oppressed majority, and it is there that we must begin our quest. Contra Plato and Rawls, the "Cave" – the classic metaphor for the site of cognitive imprisonment – is actually the blinding world of the (putatively) trans-social Ideal and its associated conceptual Forms. *That* is the realm from which we need to exit.

From this revisionist perspective, then, class, gender, and race are legitimately "philosophical" subjects. Class and class society have, of course, long been philosophically analyzed by the Marxist and critical theory traditions, even if the global shift to the right of recent decades has somewhat diminished the appeal of this worldview (though with the planetary trend towards plutocracy, this may be changing) (see Piketty 2014). Gender theory in its different incarnations has been thriving in the academy since its "second-wave" rebirth. But before the advent of critical race theory and critical white studies, race was seriously under-discussed and under-theorized in many disciplines, certainly in philosophy, but also in IR. I would contend that despite the seemingly broad disciplinary gap between them, a "critical" IR and a "critical" philosophy of race[3] can indeed have useful things to say to each other, initiating a conversation that could be mutually beneficial. To illustrate these possibilities, I am going to use traditional philosophical sub-fields – metaphysics, social and political philosophy, and epistemology – to show how, once materialistically and critically reoriented in a *non*-traditional way, they can, in a reciprocal relationship, illuminate and be illuminated by both IR and other real-world disciplines. If philosophy is about understanding the world and its inhabitants and trying to make both morally better, then a recognition of the way that world has been whitened in both fact and representation is crucial, and IR as history and theory has been at the heart of both processes. So the unwriting and unwhitening of this unjustly racialized world should be done by philosophy and IR working in tandem.

The obvious starting point is, of course, race itself, which in one way or another (given the titular theme) figured in all of the chapters and was central to several. As Debra Thompson points out in her essay, we need to understand race as "a transnational phenomenon," a reality brought into existence by global forces. A metaphysics is then created – not of the timeless Aristotelian sort – but of the temporally bound and historically contingent variety recognized in critical theory's famous concept of a *social* ontology, a shaping of Being and of human beings no less significant and thorough because it is rooted in socio-historical events which could have happened otherwise.

Over the past two decades, the metaphysics of race has in fact been a central focus for many of us working in the field, and I was happy to see that Srdjan Vucetic has an entire chapter on this literature. (Such engagements are particularly welcome if, because of your discipline's too frequent hermeticism, or just lack of relevance, you are unused to seeing any outsiders finding it useful enough to draw on.) Faced at the time with a choice between two unsatisfactory alternatives, traditional racial biologism/racial essentialism and a facile "color-blind" racial eliminativism, most scholars in the field sought to develop a variety of anti-eliminativist constructionism, by virtue of which race could be seen as a social construct that was nonetheless real. Such a framing is obviously important for any discipline using "race" as a critical category, since it opens the door for the term to serve in social-science explanations without any dubious biologistic underpinnings. A problematic "post-raciality" in sociopolitical theory can thus be resisted, and the continuing relevance of "race" as a variable (albeit now conceptually transformed) insisted upon.

Directions for future research are manifold. Recognizing that the ontology of race is both real and social is of course a crucial initial step, but it immediately raises the question of what social dynamic is being presupposed, thereby taking us into social and political theory. Theorists can agree on race's sociality while offering sharply divergent accounts of the processes of "construction" at work, and how they manifest themselves in imperial expansionism, colonization, slavery, discrimination, and so forth. Robert Knox calls for a materialist race theory that would draw on Fanon and be sensitive to "conjunctural imperatives," while Vucetic maps the conflicts between Marxists and poststructuralists in IR, and the tensions between materialist and discursive perspectives on how "deep" the ontology of race goes.

Moreover, apart from such familiar disputes between rival holistic sociopolitical perspectives, a renascent psychological individualism that would once have been aprioristically dismissed by the left as "psychologism" has recently gained new credibility. Research in cognitive psychology has documented the extent to which we are all prone to racializing attributions and implicit bias. But how crucial is the "social" really, then? Are we back (even if in a different way) to a naturalistic ontology of race after all? If innate psychological tendencies do in fact incline us towards racialized cognition, does this mean that socio-political explanations simply become otiose? Or can they still play a role in accounting for the reinforcement and embedding of doxastic and categorizing tendencies which might otherwise be easily resisted and overcome – and of course in explaining how "race" as concept becomes "race" as social structure? Relatedly, what is the relation between race and adjacent, or at least neighboring, categories such as ethnicity, class (a question perennially pressing for Marxists), and caste? Sankaran Krishna, for example, points out the imbricated "racial/spatial order" in India and the ongoing controversy over how the situation of the Dalits should be theoretically conceived. And what about gender? Only Randolph Persaud of all the contributors, in his chapter on colonial violence in British Guiana, raises the "intersectional" issue of race and gender. But obviously the global color line will be intersecting and interacting with a global gender line also.

Questions of periodization also inevitably arise in conjunction with these contested genealogies. Are race and racism a product of modernity (or at the earliest late medievalism), as was long contended, or do they go back to the ancient world? And are they distinctively Western, as Benjamin Isaac and others have suggested, or can they be found broadly disseminated in other civilizations from antiquity onwards (Isaac 2004, Eliav-Feldon, Isaac, and Ziegler 2009)? After all, if racial categorization comes "naturally" to us, then why wouldn't we expect to find race everywhere across the planet at all times and all places? How much of a causal contribution would exploitative international relations actually then be making to this pattern? Obviously an answer to this question is crucial, requiring both empirical research and the conceptual teasing apart of "race" as a category from different possible alternatives.

But apart from these important macro-periodizations of race (origins, emergences, lines of demarcation – if they exist – between pre-racial and racial epochs), we also need internal fine-grained differentiations, both temporal and conceptual, among divergent *kinds* of racism. Biological racism, which is the variety of racism most usually recognized as such by the layperson, has been claimed by some theorists to be actually an outlier in the history of racism (assuming the long periodization), with cultural racism being the dominant variety over human history. On this analysis, medieval Islamophobia should be categorized as racism, grounded in Christendom's conflict with the East and Islam. Accordingly, Branwen Gruffydd Jones urges us to be sensitive to "a more expanded notion of racialised thought," one not limited to the "scientific" racism usually seen as originating in the late eighteenth century, but recognizing the significance of the Iberian Catholic debates on the humanity of the Amerindians that long precede it, as well as the later "stadial view[s] of history" of the Enlightenment that construct a "vertical hierarchy of civilization" on a temporally evolutionary axis. A more recent watershed historical moment is highlighted by John Hobson: the post-World War II "replacement of racial hierarchy with an equally distorted conception of 'cultural hierarchy,'" a "Eurocentric culturalism" displacing "the racial biology of the pre-1945 world." For Hobson, it is this "subliminal Eurocentric-institutional intolerance … that came to underpin IR theory during the era of decolonization."

These judgments underline the need for historical research into the comparative saliences of different types of racism in different periods – their rise and fall – as well as raising conceptual questions of definition and clarification. From the perspective of developing a perspicuous taxonomy, races (conceived of in biological terms) and biological racism do at least have the great categorical advantage of offering a clear-cut contrast with ethnic groups (conceived of in cultural terms) and ethnocentrism. But cultural racism as a concept muddies things. At what point does ethnocentrism against other ethnic groups turn into cultural racism against "races"? Can an ethnocentric but non-racist Eurocentrism be clearly distinguished from a culturally racist Eurocentrism? Can a principled "bright line" of demarcation be found, or is it arbitrary? Obviously for critical race theory to prosper as a research orientation and be forearmed against its critics (in whatever discipline) these questions need to be answered, since it is the most basic of concepts of the research program that are at stake.

Moreover, issues of genealogy have obvious implications for recognitions of the existence of racial hierarchies and racism among populations of color themselves. Discussions of racism globally have usually focused on the West versus the Rest, whites versus nonwhites. But while "nonwhite" is a convenient umbrella category in macro-contexts, it needs to be broken down for any detailed investigation. Racism against people of color was not homogeneous, because within the category of the racially inferior, some were more inferior than others – a partitioning that Knox suggests continues to obtain into the present period, even if the lines are not always drawn in the same way. Historically, in constructing their racially hierarchical pictures of the world, Europeans generally ranked Asians above Africans and Native Americans. China, India, and Persia may have suffered "Orientalist" framings, but they were usually acknowledged by Europeans *as* civilizations, even barbaric ones, as against the savagery of "tribal" Africa and Amerindia (though one would need to demarcate the European view of the great Meso-American empires). These hierarchies affected not merely ideational representation but public policy, as manifest in the divergent character of British rule over India as against its African colonies, or, as Persaud points out, conceptions of the "racial suitability" of Indians versus blacks for labor on the sugar plantations of British Guiana. Going back much further, Jones reminds us that Las Casas and other Dominican clerics suggested that Africans be imported to replace Native Americans as enslaved labor in the New World, since they had no souls, claims traceable back at least as far as Africans' depiction in Papal Bulls as "Saracens and Moors, enemies of Christianity." So there is a long history of the internal moral stratification of different nonwhite populations.

Nor was it just a matter of external Euro-perception and Euro-categorization; different communities of people of color often endorsed these distinctions and hierarchies themselves, and a deromanticized look at nominally united anti-racist struggle would need to explore the extent to which different strata of the oppressed sought to maintain or establish class, racial, and color privilege for their own group. Both nationally and internationally, the affirmation of such status distinctions compromised and hindered the development of a movement truly committed to the elimination of all forms of discrimination. Krishna cites Du Bois's 1938 observation that in the global anti-colonial battle, Indians tended to self-identify as "Aryans," "racially and culturally closer to the West, and as different from and superior to niggers, coolies, chinks, and others" (quote from Krishna). Upper-class Hindu outrage that *they* should be treated as inferiors by no means translated into any revolutionary commitment to overturn the Indian caste system itself, or to establish a global polity of racial equals. During Gandhi's years in South Africa, Krishna points out, he shared the conventional racist views of the time of black South Africans. Similarly, Fanon's native elite were all too often really incensed that they – the *évolués*, with their degrees from the Sorbonne – were not being distinguished by whites from the unreconstructed *nègres*.

Elsewhere, in Latin America, national nineteenth-century liberation from Spanish rule did not at all imply racial liberation for Indo- and Afro-Latins, whose systemic racial disadvantaging under the illusory banner of "racial democracies" continues to this day. But it is not simply white oppression that is at work, but subordinated Latin populations vying with each other for shade advantage within what has famously been termed a system of "pigmentocracy." Moving north, African American demands for racial justice in the United States have too often translated into an insistence that they get their "fair" share of the spoils of the white settler project, ignoring the crimes of Native American genocide and expropriation on which these spoils rest. President Barack Obama's 2008 statement that slavery was the "original sin" of the United States testifies to the persistence of this narrow normative racial vision. The color line is not merely global in the sense of dividing countries but global in the sense of running through and dividing all of us, encouraging us to climb higher on the racial/color/shade ladder and leave behind some other stigmatized "darker" group (whether literally or metaphorically) with whom we do not identify.

More also needs to be done on the global transmission and circulation of racist ideologies, in line with the numerous studies on the intercontinental dissemination of the officially recognized political ideologies, such as liberalism, conservatism, and socialism. As George Mosse (1985, 231) underlined decades ago, in opposition to any conceptualization of racism as unthinking "prejudice," racism was in fact "the most widespread ideology of the time." It is well known, for example, that Gobineau was translated into numerous languages. But what was the actual reception of his work in different countries? How did key aspects of his thought transmute as they crossed national boundaries? Which other European racist theorists' writings achieved widespread dissemination? That is not to say, of course, that local sites were simply dependent on metropolitan sources; rather, the circumstances of white settlement, sojourner colonies, and slave societies themselves generated justificatory complexes of racial ideas. Nonetheless, insofar as ideologies are standardly conceptualized as involving a reciprocal interaction between elite discourse and demotic ideation, both levels need to be studied. And questions of racial governance arise also, not just theory but practice: to what extent did racial powers in different nations learn from each other in matters of public policy, for example on slavery, on the reservation system for indigenes, on colonial rule? Or consider the different ways in which the eugenics movement played itself out in Latin America as against in Europe and the United States.

The *anti-racist* tradition also needs more extensive documentation. In the same way that the European heroes of modernist liberal and radical political thought (anti-absolutist, anti-capitalist) constitute a pantheon familiar to most of us, we need a wing (or maybe a new building altogether, considering that these same "heroes" were themselves usually the problem (see Losurdo 2011)) for anti-racist theorization as political and likewise central to the creation of modernity. Pioneering theorists of color like the Haitian Anténor Firmin (whose 1885 *The Equality of the Human Races* (2002) was the most thorough nineteenth-century refutation of Gobineau) need to get the recognition they deserve, as well as (Errol Henderson reminds us) the African American philosopher Alain Locke, instead of the credit going largely to white thinkers like Franz Boas. And as indicated, it would also be necessary to explore the extent to which even self-conceivedly "oppositional" anti-colonial and anti-imperialist thought sometimes appropriated and recapitulated in different guise elements from dominant white racist ideology, or produced novel variants of its own.

But social and political theory, especially in its philosophical version, also has a second-level "meta" aspect to it: the self-conscious interrogation and rethinking of the subject's inherited categories and conceptual apparatus. Drawing on my own work, Henderson shows how the terms of seventeenth- and eighteenth-century philosophical social contract theory – which have long become a lingua franca spoken broadly across other disciplines – are tainted by racialized conceptions of who the appropriate inhabitants of the real-life state of nature are, and how these representations survive today in discourses of primitive tropical anarchy. Somewhat similarly, Jones looks at the contemporary vocabulary of "failed states," and traces its origins to a long history of earlier stadial rankings which – though they may have moved "from humanity through races, civilisations and tribes to the institutional form of the state" – still "continue to position the European at the top and the African at the bottom."

The reconceptualization of hegemonic categories calls not merely for their demystified recognition as (often) racialized, but for subversive remappings of the terrain more broadly. If the nation-state is the common orthodox conceptual frame-work across various different disciplinary boundaries, a "critical" IR and a "critical" philosophy of race will ask how viewing it and associated categories through a racial prism transforms the discursive field. Apart from the obvious recognition of the state as a racial state, with all that that implies for the juridical system and public policy, radicals in the discipline have long suggested transnational categories track-ing larger political entities: colonialism, imperialism, the Anglosphere, global white supremacy. They have asked how the time and space of modernity would be rescripted by a revisionist racial history: what insurgent chronologies and geographies would be revealed by attention to the alternate clocks and maps of global racial resis-tance. In his *The Theft of History*, Jack Goody (2006) brings to our attention how deeply the temporal categories of the West – from the overarching religious sweep of the dichotomization into before and into the Christian epoch to the three-stage transition from Antiquity through Medievalism to Modernity – have colonized our temporal consciousness, and Eviatar Zerubavel (2003) posits "time maps" that hegemonic mnemonic communities agree upon amongst themselves and then impose upon others, highlighting certain events as definitive and marginalizing others as insignificant. The Haitian scholar Michel-Rolph Trouillot (1995) has famously described the whiting-out from European history of the Haitian Revolution, because of its incompatibility with the Euro-periodization of the Age of Revolution. In geography, the challenge of the Gall-Peters projection to the Mercator projection is not only, literally, to the depicted sizes of the continents but, metaphorically, to the presumed objectivity of their mapping, making clear how political this cartography was in the first place, even for a subject so seemingly solid and natural as the ground beneath our feet.

Imagine how a different narrative, centered on the gradual establishment of and resistance to global white supremacy, would recalibrate our clocks and maps, producing different metrics for the most illuminating measurements of time and space. What would it do – this is really addressed to philosophers, not IR radicals who have already thought themselves out of the conventional optics – to our conceptualizations of the polity and to the appropriate boundaries of political units if we were to recognize the White Atlantic as a macro-unit of slave power, to be resisted by Paul Gilroy's (1993) Black Atlantic? Or to seriously take up Native American perspectives? From the Amerindian point of view, Anglo and Iberian expansionism on the Northern and Southern continents meant not "settlement" but conquest by a foreign power. Could we expand IR to include relations between the United States, gradually moving westward in accordance with its manifest destiny, and the indigenous nations it was conquering, so that we could speak of IR on the continental land mass of North America? Or, more generally, to memorialize in a common time epochal events that sent shock waves through the system as a whole: Amerindian Resistance, the Haitian Revolution, the Japanese defeat of Russia?

And how would our story of modernity, our periodizations of normativity and recognized personhood, have to be revised if we were to think of anti-colonialism as a global civil rights movement – confronting a white supremacy equally global – to attain the equality supposedly already granted in the so-called Age of (Recognized White) Revolutions, but strangely still being withheld at the 1919 post-World War I Versailles Conference (Borstelmann 2001; Lake and Reynolds 2008)? Nor must we forget tensions and divisions within the imperial bloc. Knox emphasizes that white no less than nonwhite is a non-monolithic category, and that inter-imperialist rivalries may generate intra-white racialization also. Vucetic identifies the Anglosphere as the most important of the imperial systems. To what extent did national/ imperial conflicts between, say, the Anglosphere and the Gallisphere (?) override a common "whiteness"? To what extent does whiteness remain a useful overarching category at the transnational level and to what extent does it need to be nationally inflected by particular spheres of domination and influence? And what about their relation to that element of the North which claimed to be in solidarity with the South? The socialist international in its various incarnations from the nineteenth century onwards is a familiar story, but how many of us are acquainted with the long history of internationals of people of color, Pan-African and other (if admittedly often more aspirational than realized)? What about the connections between them, between red and black, or red and nonwhite more generally? Richard Seymour argues that the link is closer than normally realized and that "The history of anticommunism is enfolded within a history of race." The Bolshevik Revolution was a tectonic challenge not merely to the world capitalist system but to the world racial system, so that the preservation of one was tied to the preservation of the other. Somewhat similarly, Hobson points out the one-dimensional domination of East–West Cold War struggle categories as the structuring architectonic of the historiography of most of the twentieth century, when a supplementary North–South decolonial struggle architectonic would provide insights far more revealing of the true global dynamics of the period.

That brings us naturally to moral questions, which are supposed to be the distinctive expertise of philosophers. IR is famously associated with Hobbesian *realpolitik*, but some theorists have argued for the importance of global ethical norms not merely as normative targets but as actually constraining behavior. Jennifer Pitts (2005) cites Edmund Burke's deprecation of a "geographical morality" that limits moral concerns to one's neighbors. What sustains such a morality is a set of moralized international categories that explicitly or tacitly undermine the global South's claim to equal respect. How has it been possible – when it has been possible – to overcome this coded and codified Othering? To what extent would it be illuminating to gather under a general rubric historic patterns of white conscientization, the dawning realization that the system – whether as Euro-conquest, slavery, formal imperial and colonial rule, later neo-colonial domination – was morally wrong and needed to be opposed? Adam Hochschild's *King Leopold's Ghost* (1999) brought back to Western remembrance the movement to expose atrocities in the Congo. How many other such movements were there? Could one demarcate a specifically moral dimension to IR, and track under a single category a moral history of disinterested and principled[4] white attempts to expose and condemn atrocity, from Las Casas onwards, whether in the form of abolitionism, anti-imperialism, aborigine protection organizations, or some other vehicle, and investigate, transnationally and comparatively, their respective successes and failures?

Or more pressingly – returning to the present and my frustrations with Rawls and Rawlsianism – consider the implications of this past for current debates on global justice. Periodizations have normative implications; by centering narratives around certain dates rather than others, particular time maps (Zerubavel) are ratified at the expense of their challengers. The Rawlsian story is predicated on the importance of the 1648 Peace of Westphalia, as against, say, the conquests initiated in 1492. Unsurprisingly, then, neither in his own nor his disciples' work is much or any attention given to the imperial history and its moral implications for the present. Yet as Thompson observes, racial injustice is "built into the very fabric of the international economic order." The global justice demands put forward at the various UN conferences against racism over the past decade-plus are predicated on radically different assumptions from those in the philosophical global justice literature. The praiseworthy exception is one of Rawls's ex-students, Thomas Pogge (2008), who has been very active in advocating for a global justice that recognizes North/South domination. But apart from brief mentions, Pogge does not say much about the central role of racism and white racial rule to this process. A collaboration between critical philosophy of race and critical IR that makes clear the interconnectedness of Northern wealth and Southern poverty, its link with ideologies and practices of racialization, the establishment of global white domination, and transcontinental racial exploitation, would be far better equipped to combat the willed Western amnesia on this subject, and advance the cause accordingly.

Finally, I turn to epistemology. Historically, the epistemological literature in Anglo-American analytic philosophy (hegemonic in the "Anglosphere," and spreading globally) has been dominated by Cartesian individualism. It is to the subordinate "Continental" tradition (Hegel, Marx, Mannheim, Scheler, more recently Foucault and post-structuralism) that one has had to look for sensitivity to the shaping of cognition by the social. But in recent decades, "social" epistemology has been formally recognized in analytic circles as a legitimate development in the field, even if – that propensity for idealization again – oppressive social systems have not been the primary focus. Nonetheless, the door has been opened to the exploration of the patterns and dynamics of group miscognition. (Obviously, in other idioms – whether through classic Marxist treatments in terms of "ideology" or more recent Foucauldian "discourses" – this will be a completely familiar topic to many of us. But the point is that by contrast with these approaches analytic epistemology has the great virtue of respectability.)

A common theme running through most of the chapters has been the cognitive phenomenon of non-knowing – I phrase it this way to capture its active character, as against an ignorance that is innocent (Sullivan and Tuana 2007). The problems of white racial cognition manifest themselves far more broadly than in mere racial categorization. Both in everyday group perception and conceptualization and in formal disciplinary methodology, racial epistemologies shape what counts as knowing and non-knowing. Thompson speaks of the "calculated forgetting" of racial aphasia, Henderson and Vucetic of the silence on race of the professional journals in the field, Hobson of the whitewashing of Europe's imperial past out of world history. A set of interlocking cognitive processes is at work, operating at the multiple levels of overt and tacit background and foreground belief, Eurocentric norming, development of specific conceptual repertoires, and the formulation of theories, whose combined outcome is the erasure of the actual history. So what would be desirable is a meta-investigation into how a "white" community both global and nationally differentiated develops disciplines that generate and reproduce this ignorance. Race continually changes color, so to speak. Moreover, issues not just of epistemology but of linguistics and philosophy of language are involved. One could speak of a racial coding, a racial cryptography, by virtue of which a racial content metamorphoses through different semantic incarnations in deference to the changing norms of the time, while always remaining legible to its target audience. Hobson cites Nicolas Guilhot's notion of "conceptual proxies," avatars of earlier, now tabooed representations that essentially carry on the same work in facially acceptable guise. An epistemology oriented by the realities of social oppression on a global scale and informed by the IR history of racially tainted categories could be very useful in assisting the cognitive liberation which classically – to return to where I began, with Caves both Platonic and Rawlsian – philosophy promises to humanity.

Let me say again how honored and delighted I am to have been asked to write such an afterword. I hope it presages many future collaborations between philosophy and the progressive caucuses in the various real-world disciplines who have – embarrassingly for us – been leaving philosophy behind in their contribution to (in the words of the pioneering critical theorist who disavowed his own philosophical identity) both understanding and ultimately changing the world.

Notes

1 Hobson – whom I did not know – had been kind enough to send me an unsolicited copy of his book, which I might never have encountered otherwise.
2 For recent critical reflections on the discipline by 17 black and Latino philosophers, see Yancy (2012).
3 "Critical philosophy of race" is the term that has recently been coined for critical race theory in philosophy specifically: see the new journal (founded 2013), *Critical Philosophy of Race*, housed at the Penn State Philosophy Department.
4 The qualification is necessary because some exposés were motivated far more by national/imperial rivalries than by genuine moral principle, just as much opposition to slavery, imperial expansion, etc. was straightforwardly based on cost/benefit calculations.

Bibliography

Borstelmann, Thomas (2001) *The Cold War and the Color Line: American Race Relations in the Global Arena* (Cambridge, MA: Harvard University Press)

Eliav-Feldon, Miriam, Isaac, Benjamin and Ziegler, Joseph (eds.) (2009) *The Origins of Racism in the West* (New York: Cambridge University Press)

Firmin, Anténor (2002) *The Equality of the Human Races*, trans. Asselin Charles (Urbana and Chicago: University of Illinois Press)

Goody, Jack (2006) *The Theft of History* (New York: Cambridge University Press)

Gilroy, Paul (1993) The Black Atlantic: Modernity and Double Consciousness (Cambridge, MA: Harvard University Press)

Jones, Branwen Gruffydd (ed.) (2006) *Decolonizing International Relations* (Lanham, MD: Rowman & Littlefield

Hobson, John M. (2012) *The Eurocentric Conception of World Politics: Western International Theory, 1760–2010* (New York: Cambridge University Press)

Hochschild, Adam (1999) *King Leopold's Ghost: A Story of Greed, Terror, and Heroism in Colonial Africa* (New York: Houghton Mifflin)

Isaac, Benjamin (2004) *The Invention of Racism in Classical Antiquity* (Princeton, NJ: Princeton University Press)

Lake, Marilyn and Reynolds, Henry (2009) *Drawing the Global Colour Line: White Men's Countries and the International Challenge of Racial Equality* (New York: Cambridge University Press)

Losurdo, Domenico (2011) *Liberalism: A Counter-History*, trans. Gregory Elliott (New York: Verso)

Manley, Michael (1991) *The Poverty of Nations: Reflections on Underdevelopment and the World Economy* (London: Pluto Press)

Mills, Charles W. (1997) *The Racial Contract* (Ithaca, NY: Cornell University Press)

Mosse, George L. (1985) *Toward the Final Solution: A History of European Racism* (Madison, WI: University of Wisconsin Press)

Piketty, Thomas (2014) *Capital in the Twenty-First Century*, trans. Arthur Goldhammer (Cambridge, MA: Harvard University Press)

Pitts, Jennifer (2005) *A Turn to Empire: The Rise of Imperial Liberalism in Britain and France* (Princeton, NJ: Princeton University Press)

Pogge, Thomas W. (2009) *World Poverty and Human Rights: Cosmopolitan Responsibilities and Reforms*, 2nd edn (Malden, MA: Polity)

Rawls, John (1999a) *A Theory of Justice*, rev. ed. (Cambridge, MA: Harvard University Press, 1999)

——(1999b) *The Law of Peoples and "The Idea of Public Reason Revisited"* (Cambridge, MA: Harvard University Press)

Shilliam, Robbie (ed.) (2011) *International Relations and Non-Western Thought: Imperialism, Colonialism and Investigations of Global Modernity* (New York: Routledge).

Sullivan, Shannon and Tuana, Nancy (eds) (2007) *Race and Epistemologies of Ignorance* (Albany, NY: SUNY Press)

Trouillot, Michel-Rolph (1995) *Silencing the Past: Power and the Production of History* (Boston: Beacon Press)

Yancy, George (ed.) (2012) *Reframing the Practice of Philosophy: Bodies of Color, Bodies of Knowledge* (Albany, NY: SUNY Press)

Zerubavel, Eviatar (2003) *Time Maps: Collective Memory and the Social Shape of the Past* (Chicago: University of Chicago Press)

INDEX